MARTIN EISENSTADT

## I Am Martin Eisenstadt

The political strategist and conservative analyst Martin Eisenstadt is a senior fellow at the Harding Institute for Freedom and Democracy and founder and president of the influential Eisenstadt Group. An expert on Near Eastern military and political affairs, Mr. Eisenstadt worked alongside Senator John McCain's presidential campaign, offering advice and liaising with the Jewish community in particular. Prior to that, he consulted on the Rudolph Giuliani campaign, as well as for numerous corporate and multinational organizations on issues of security and policy development. Mr. Eisenstadt has been an influential voice in public policy debate for over a decade. By the time you read this, he will have his own place and will not be living in his mother's basement.

## Also by Martin Eisenstadt

*Near, Far, Wherever They Are: U.S. Foreign Policy Toward the Mid, Near, and Far East*, Harding Institute Press, 2007 (Out of print)

*From Willie Horton to the Swift Boaters: Collected Essays on Effective American Political Campaign Ads*, Harding Institute Press, 2006 (Out of print)

*Punditocracy! A Musical Guidebook to the Washington Media Elites*, Harding Insitute Press, 2006 (Out of print)

*A Watergate Cookbook: All the President's Recipes*, Georgetown Day School mimeograph, 1975 (Out of print)

**I Am**
**Martin**
**Eisenstadt**

# I Am
# Martin
# Eisenstadt

Wildly
Inappropriate
v
## ONE MAN'S ADVENTURES WITH
## THE LAST REPUBLICANS

**Martin Eisenstadt**

**FABER AND FABER, INC.**
An affiliate of Farrar, Straus and Giroux
New York

Faber and Faber, Inc.
An affiliate of Farrar, Straus and Giroux
18 West 18th Street, New York 10011

Copyright © 2009 by Dan Mirvish and Eitan Gorlin
Distributed in Canada by D&M Publishers, Inc.
Printed in the United States of America
First edition, 2009

Library of Congress Cataloging-in-Publication Data
Eisenstadt, Martin.
    I am Martin Eisenstadt : one man's (wildly inappropriate) adventures with
the last Republicans / Martin Eisenstadt.— 1st ed.
        p.   cm.
    Includes index.
    ISBN 978-0-86547-914-2 (pbk. : alk. paper)
    1. Political consultants—United States—Fiction. 2. Presidents—
United States—Election—2008—Fiction. 3. Satire.   I. Title.

PS3605.I8445I3 2009
813'.6—dc22

                                                          2009015215

Designed by Ralph Fowler / rlfdesign

www.fsgbooks.com

10  9  8  7  6  5  4  3  2  1

Lollotte and Miriam

# Contents

## Contents

# Preface

A funny thing happened to me this election cycle. An anonymous source accused me of not existing, going so far as to flood my Google page with postings warning people that I was a fake. And before I could set the record straight, the major media outlets (from CNN to *The New York Times* to the *Omaha World-Herald*) had jumped on the bandwagon, reporting that I, Martin Eisenstadt, was a hoax, the virtual creation of two obscure filmmakers.

Now I enjoy a joke as much as the next guy, but politics is my life. And, therefore, this is a score I must settle. As my mentor, the great political operative Lee Atwater, once instructed me, "If someone you slighted hangs from a cliff, push him off, because if you save him, he won't remember that you saved him. He'll only remember that once you slighted him." So "push him off," Lee repeated. "You got to. Otherwise, you will lose the game."

And I have no intention of losing this game. Marty Eisenstadt is a fighter, a winner. I've worked on seven political campaigns. I have a drink named after me at the Dubai Hilton. I am a sought-after strategist and consultant. So don't think I won't recover from this slander. I will.

# Foreword

Trust me. I exist.

How do I know that for sure? Because I am a senior fellow at the Harding Institute for Freedom and Democracy, a neoconservative think tank based in Washington, D.C. I am the founder and CEO of the Eisenstadt Group, a multifaceted consulting firm specializing in political campaigns and issue advocacy. I am a respected blogger and pundit who regularly appears on television and radio.

I was even the subject of a widely seen BBC documentary entitled *The Last Republican*. I am Martin Eisenstadt, and I was born on July 23, 1964, in upstate New York to Connie Beane of Grand Rapids, Michigan, and Izzy Eisenstadt of Ocean Parkway, Brooklyn.

Mom was a sophomore at Vassar. Dad was just starting out in the family zipper business. The year was 1963. Mom had never met a Jew before. Dad had a client who owned a beret factory, so he was looking sharp that night at the White Horse Tavern in Greenwich Village. Mom loved poetry and jazz. Dad didn't come all the way from Brooklyn just to hear poetry and jazz. Kennedy had been shot that morning so Mom was feeling sad. Dad was feeling lucky. Like Barack Obama, I am the product of a mixed-race relationship (if by race, we mean ethnicity, and by ethnicity, we mean religion). Like Barack Obama's, my parents became estranged soon after having me.

And like Barack Obama, I spent my early years with relatives because Mom was off gallivanting with the hippies. And even after Grammie Beane set Mom straight and sent her to Washington, where she landed a job in the Nixon White House as John Ehrlichman's secretary (or should I say mistress, but that's for a later chapter), I was still bounced from house to house and often introduced by Mom as her nephew. So trust me when I say: I get Barack Obama. I too had to be different things to different people—a chameleon, if you will. Which probably explains why we both went into politics.

And to answer the question on so many of your minds, yes, I would be willing to apologize for some of the more inflammatory statements I may have uttered about Barack in the heat of the campaign. But who could have known? All evidence pointed to his being a radical socialist, an America hater, a Malcolm X type. I mean, he talked about raising taxes on the oil and gas companies. He participated in the divestment protests of the 1980s antiapartheid movement. He palled around with college professors. And that smirk! Like he was some sort of tattoo-covered NBA thug . . . But that's the past and now he's president, and America needs to come first.

Because for me, "Country First" (a phrase I, by the way, came up with, but let others take credit for—in the body of the book, I will explain) is not just a slogan. It is a philosophy, a value system, a moral ethic I live by. That's why I offer no regrets in leaking to the press (after the election, of course) that Governor Palin greeted me in a skimpy, provocative towel and that she wasn't sure whether Africa is a continent or a country. In my humble opinion, America needed to know, so I put country first.

You know how much hate mail my blog and think tank received because I exposed Governor Palin as a wacky hillbilly with no real knowledge of anything outside of moose hunting and faith healing? One of my unpaid interns was so frightened by the vitriolic mail she had to open every day that she up and quit on me. More important, I have good reason to believe that it was someone in the Palin camp who spread the slander that I don't exist. I mean, what better way to kill a story than to accuse the source of not existing? Well played, Sarah. Well played.

Or maybe it was Joe the Plumber. I did write on my blog that he hooked up with Kristen Wiig at the *SNL* after party. Sources tell me this bit of information didn't go over well with Joe's other campaign consort, the senator's beloved daughter, Meghan McCain. What about the boys from Sharif Investments, Jamie and Nabil, on whose behalf I traveled to Iraq and who have this strange idea that I cheated them? And who is this "Wolfrum," the supposed golf blogger based in Brazil, who since May 2008 has been lobbing absurd online accusations against me?

Or maybe it was Hank Paulson still smarting from the whoopee cushion I put on his chair when I was a mere nine and he and Mom both worked in the Nixon White House. No. Even Wall Street guys don't hold grudges that long.

As my sexy British editor repeatedly reminds me, mysteries sell, and as I've always known, the business of America is business. So I see no shame in rehashing some of the less flattering episodes of my past in order to unravel the mystery of who hoaxed me and why. And I see no shame in baring all, about myself and others, as long as the greater agenda of promoting freedom, democracy, and capitalism is furthered.

# Introduction

Still, when the prestigious publishing house Farrar, Straus and Giroux (FSG) contacted me about writing an honest, tell-all book, I at first resisted the idea. You see, I consider myself more of a behind-the-scenes kind of guy. I serve at the pleasure of candidates and clients. And it's important that my notoriety not eclipse theirs. Also, did I want to be remembered forever as the Washington insider accused of not existing? In politics, reputation is key, and did it make sense to amplify and keep alive my shame by writing a book?

But as I learned when I did my part to help Swift Boat John Kerry, assets (even service in war) are simply liabilities waiting to be exposed. Which means the opposite must be true as well. So I'm excited to turn a negative into a positive, to write this book, to get my side out. For in politics it is imperative to define ourselves before others do it for us. As the Good Book teaches, "In this life, reputations are destroyed quicker than they are built."

That's why it is essential that this book not just be about Martin Eisenstadt as victim, as laughingstock, as creepy middle-aged man, but be about something more. About the media not check-

ing their sources. About my advocacy on behalf of important issues—like drilling in the Arctic and encouraging war with Iran.

And don't think I'm naïve to the fact that in this era, it's not
the intellectuals who get the book deals; it's the celebrities. But
I'm okay with being a celebrity. I've paid my dues. I've cleaned
candidates' cars and given their wives foot massages. I've pon-
tificated on podcasts and public radio. So without apology I look
forward to the day when Martin Eisenstadt, the pundit, appears
only on tier-one shows. When Martin Eisenstadt, the consultant,
gets picked up by a driver and doesn't have to take the bus ever
again. And that's what a book can do for you. (Mind you, I've
written books, several of them, but they're currently out of print
in North America.)

So call me shameless. What do I care? Because if putting my
face on a book helps my pundit career, helps the Harding Institute, and helps spread Western hegemony in the guise of Pax
Americana, then that's a bullet I'm willing to take.

It's like the prostitutes I saw in Novosibirsk back when I was
doing polling for the 1996 Yeltsin campaign. Some of these Siberian ladies would sleep with more than thirty men a day, seven
days a week, for years. And in bad conditions. Outdoors. In the
cold. But in the end, these go-getters had the last laugh. They
saved enough to return to their villages with plenty of cash to
buy homes, plant gardens, and take on young lovers. While their
counterparts, the maids and checkout girls, who weren't willing
to absorb temporary discomfort and shame for long-term benefit, still rent, live paycheck to paycheck, and are stuck taking
care of geriatric husbands and nagging kids.

Just like Paris Hilton here at home. Not only was Paris able to
overcome the ridicule of a sex video; she transcended it in the service of a higher purpose, the rebranding of the Hilton name. If it
wasn't for Paris, I would argue, the Hilton name today would be
indistinguishable from Best Western. And nothing says branding
like a bestselling book. Just ask the Donald. Or as Joe the Plumber

whispered to me at the *SNL* after party, "You're nobody in this country without a book."

So I am excited to write this book, to uplift the Eisenstadt name. I am excited to spread our message of freedom, democracy, and capitalism. And I am determined to get my book on the bestseller lists even if it means betraying some confidences. And as a key McCain strategist, I assure you I have multiple confidences to betray. I was there, on the inside, at the critical junctures. I got drunk with Joe the Plumber. I've seen Governor Palin's tattoo. I was an original member of the Committee for the Liberation of Iraq but fell out of favor with some in the inner circle after I tried to warn them that our good buddy Ahmed Chalabi might be an Iranian spy.

It's like what my good friend Senator Joe Lieberman said to me: "Marty, you need to write a book. You have a story to tell." And that's when I realized he was right. Martin Eisenstadt has a story to tell. "And would you please pass the caviar? My challah's getting cold." I passed Joe the caviar, inadvertently spilling mustard sauce on his perfectly creased white pants. He wasn't happy.

# Marty's Stomping Grounds

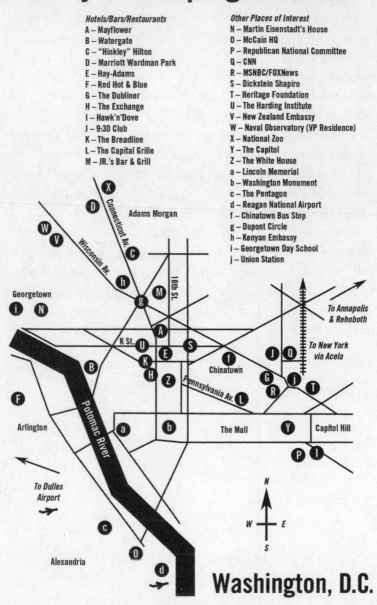

**Hotels/Bars/Restaurants**
A – Mayflower
B – Watergate
C – "Hinkley" Hilton
D – Marriott Wardman Park
E – Hay-Adams
F – Red Hot & Blue
G – The Dubliner
H – The Exchange
I – Hawk'n'Dove
J – 9:30 Club
K – The Breadline
L – The Capital Grille
M – JR.'s Bar & Grill

**Other Places of Interest**
N – Martin Eisenstadt's House
O – McCain HQ
P – Republican National Committee
Q – CNN
R – MSNBC/FOXNews
S – Dickstein Shapiro
T – Heritage Foundation
U – The Harding Institute
V – New Zealand Embassy
W – Naval Observatory (VP Residence)
X – National Zoo
Y – The Capitol
Z – The White House
a – Lincoln Memorial
b – Washington Monument
c – The Pentagon
d – Reagan National Airport
f – Chinatown Bus Stop
g – Dupont Circle
h – Kenyan Embassy
i – Georgetown Day School
j – Union Station

Adams Morgan

Connecticut Av.

Wisconsin Av.

16th St.

Georgetown

K St.

Chinatown

Pennsylvania Av.

To Annapolis
& Rehoboth

To New York
via Acela

Arlington

Potomac River

The Mall

Capitol Hill

To Dulles
Airport

N
W   E
S

Alexandria

# Washington, D.C.

I Am
Martin
Eisenstadt

# The *SNL* After Party with Joe the Plumber

1

I T WAS THREE DAYS before the election, November 1, 2008, and there I was at a legendary *Saturday Night Live* after party with my candidate's sexy blonde daughter, Meghan McCain, and America's newest political celebrity, Joe "the Plumber" Wurzel- bacher. He was over six feet tall, tan, with rippling muscles; like Mr. Clean at a soap convention. Meghan had interned at *SNL* the year before and she knew the ropes. She led the way as we snaked through the hordes of beautiful people, back to the bar. Over in the corner, we saw a skinny bald white guy hunched over two turn- tables spinning tunes. Meghan couldn't contain herself. "Ohmi- god, that's Moby!"

"Hey, Joe," I shouted above the crowd. "Looks like you crapped out a tiny version of yourself!" I could see Joe and Moby ex- changing head-nod hellos, as if they were in some sort of private skinhead fraternity.

While we waited at the bar, *SNL* cast member Fred Armisen (the nervous guy with the glasses) came over to us and said, "Hey, Joe, I'm a big fan!"

Joe replied, on the threshold between umbrage and disdain,

*(Courtesy of FOXNews)*

"Do you even know what I stand for?" Armisen glanced at Meghan and raised his eyebrow, looking for an assist. Meghan's shrug said, "Fred, you're on your own, buddy." Joe, his brow furrowed, pecs tensed, and buns taut, glared down at the small funny man.

Fred cowered away, "Uh, uh, you know, what you, uh, said about the little guy and taxes, or something. Sir?"

Then Joe busted out his secret weapon: the biggest smile this side of Cleveland, and said in a perfect impression of Armisen's Venezuelan TV host character, "I'm jus' kidding!" and wrapped up Fred in a giant bear hug. Poor Fred seemed relieved and bought us all a round of drinks (I was told that due to budget constraints at NBC, it was a cash bar).

This was the hottest ticket in New York, especially the Saturday before the election. But like coats and weapons, politics were checked at the door. In this very Democratic city it was nice just to see people let their hair down and forget about the campaign for a couple of hours.

Sean "Puffy" Combs was holding court in one corner of the club, enthralling the likes of Andy Dick, Paul Simon, Lauren Hutton, and Mary-Kate Olsen with contractor horror stories from the Hamptons. I ducked into the bathroom and overheard Alec Baldwin in the stall yelling at his daughter in L.A. Then again, it could have been that night's host, Ben Affleck, doing his Baldwin impersonation yelling at Baldwin's daughter. Hard to say.

When I returned to the bar, I noticed Meghan McCain eagerly sampling hors d'oeuvres of sesame-crusted crab cakes with wasabi aioli. Dammit, they looked delicious, but for reasons I'll explain later, no shellfish for me. Governor David Paterson walked over to Meghan. Hands outstretched, he found her. "Ms. McCain, what a pleasure it is to meet you. Welcome to the fine state of New York."

"Uh, you can take your hands off me now."

"Please forgive me. I'm here with my wife tonight, and we swing."

Just then, a meaty hand grabbed my shoulder.

"Marty, hey, there you are. I got to tell you, man, I don't usually have a pregger fetish, but there's this smokin' tall chick over there who looks about seven months ripe."

"Jennifer Garner?"

"Is that who that is? Yeah, come to think of it, she did introduce me to this stuffed suit who she said was her husband's agent. He wants me to star as the Bachelor next season. Here's his card."

I looked at the card: Patrick Whitesell, Endeavor Talent Agency.

"That's funny."

"What?"

"It's the talent agency run by Ari Emanuel. Rahm's brother."

"You mean the guy from *Entourage*?"

"Something like that. Mind if I keep the card?" I asked. Not a bad connection to the Obama team if this McCain thing doesn't work out.

"Sure, I don't really like to stuff things in my pockets anyway. Interferes with my mobility, if you know what I mean."

Night wore on to early morning, and Joe finally got some "quality" alone time with a certain female cast member. I'm not that familiar with the show, but I know it wasn't Tina Fey or Amy Poehler. The skinny brunette, I think it was. Kristen, maybe? If politics makes strange bedfellows, then plumbing makes stranger ones. I ran into Joe the next morning outside his hotel, and ever the gentleman, he refused to reveal more than his mile-wide grin.

So how had I, a mere campaign consultant, think-tank fellow, and pundit, found myself at the epicenter of the wildest presidential campaign in history? I was at the cusp of politics, celebrity, fame, and fortune.

And all this just three days before the election. For a political operative such as myself, it really couldn't get any better. The only thing that could top this would be an election-night victory for John McCain! So you're probably asking yourself, how on earth did a Washington brat from a broken home grow up to be this successful self-made man?

That night in a leopard-skin booth, with a highball in one hand and a buxom young actress in the other, I asked myself that same question. But just a scant two weeks later, I would have to ask myself the even deeper question: How did that blessed life come crashing down to a fate worse than death—being accused of never having lived at all—and what on earth could have gone so horribly, horribly wrong?

# The Life of Marty

## Eighteen and a Half Minutes in the Nixon White House

I'll admit it. I had a bit of an unsettled early childhood. But at least it was a childhood that prepared me well for the dark arts of political campaigning.

My mother, Connie Beane Eisenstadt, and I were vagabonds living through the haze of the 1960s. She dragged me everywhere—from a Be-In at Golden Gate Park in San Francisco to the Democratic Convention in '68. I also remember distinctly going to Woodstock with Mom. Even at that young age, I must have had a firm grip on propriety because while she was partying backstage with Jimi Hendrix, I was clapping along to Sha Na Na. By the turn of the decade, I finally stopped breast-feeding (literally and figuratively) and was starting to develop political and cultural ideas of my own.

But by 1973, it was Mom's own parents who had finally threatened to cut her off if she didn't settle down. The one town she hadn't conquered yet? Washington, D.C.

Mom was old friends with the young Washington wife Wendy Paulson (Mom had been her babysitter in the late fifties during teenage summers in Cape Cod). Over martinis one lunch at the Lafayette dining room at the Hay-Adams, Wendy suggested that Mom get a job in the secretarial pool where her husband was working. (I recall how strikingly tall Wendy was, and how her legs seemingly swayed like slender palm trees that reached from the hem of her plaid mini to the tops of her leather boots. As I scrambled under the table for errant martini olives and mara-schino cherries, I couldn't help but notice just how short that miniskirt really was. For a nine-year-old with limited access to *National Geographic* magazines, this was an image that was seared into my brain.)

"Oh, where's he working?" Mom asked.

"Look out the window." Wendy pointed while crossing her legs (nearly kicking me in the face). Across from Lafayette Park stood the White House. The Nixon White House.

You see, Wendy's husband was none other than Hank Paulson: a young, dashing go-getter, by way of Harvard's Vietnam-avoidance MBA program. After a stint on staff at the Pentagon from 1970 to '72 (someone had to figure out the cost-benefit analysis of napalm versus Agent Orange and the future Treasury secretary and Goldman Sachs CEO was the perfect bean counter for the job), Paulson had moved to the White House to serve as John Ehrlichman's assistant. For those of you too young to have seen *All the President's Men* in all its Robert Redford–Dustin Hoffman glory, Ehrlichman was assistant to the president during the key Watergate years. Along with fellow Teutonically patro-nymic pal H. R. Haldeman, they were Nixon's closest confidants. (Though most would know them as the "Berlin Wall" that sur-rounded Nixon in his darkest days, I always thought it was cool that Ehrlichman had all these secret meetings with H. R. Pufn-stuf. I was easily confused.)

Mom joined the White House secretarial pool working for Ehrlichman, but was under the strict guidance of Rose Mary Woods, Nixon's personal secretary. Ms. Woods was a stickler for neatness, punctuation, and especially personal appearance and posture. Gone were Mom's braless peasant dresses from her Woodstock days, and in were the bright lipstick and architecturally challenging Sears foundation undergarments of a professional woman in the White House.

I was a frequent visitor to the Nixon White House, and Mr. John (as I was instructed to call him) became something of an early mentor, regaling me with tales of Nixon's various campaigns. (Strangely, I recall Mom always introducing me as her "Jew nephew" Marty. I was under strict instructions to always refer to her as Auntie Connie in front of Ehrlichman.) Even thirteen years after the fact, he was still smarting from the devastating TV debate between Nixon and JFK. Turns out it was Ehrlichman who told Nixon not to wear makeup ("What are you, some kind of pinko pansy? Now get out there and sweat like a real man!"), and I suspect he was always trying to make up for that bitter loss as only a true political operative could do. He schooled me with tales of dirty tricks, enemies lists, "rat fucking," and "the Plumbers." I was entranced. It all sounded so ex-

Young Marty with childhood hero Richard Nixon *(Courtesy of Nixon Library)*

citing and patriotic at once! Even as a fidgety fourth grader hooked on Ritalin, when asked to write an essay on what I wanted to do when I grew up, I penned: "I Want to Be a Campaign Strategist!"

Despite the watchful eyes of Ms. Woods, Mom and her new boss couldn't resist the timeless eroticism that comes from working in the West Wing. I remember one night in particular, playing in Ms. Woods's secretarial station outside the president's office. Nixon had retired for the evening, and Mom told me Mr. John had to give her some "dictation" in the Oval Office. Ever the curious lad, I tired of playing on Ms. Woods's IBM Selectric typewriter and peered through the door of the Oval Office. I was strangely mesmerized as I got my first glimpse of my mother servicing one of the most powerful men in America. I was filled with a whirlwind of emotions, silently trying to figure out what exactly they were doing. For eighteen and a half minutes, I crouched in a fetal position under Ms. Woods's desk, leaning against some sort of red tape-recorder button. Huddling in fear and self-recrimination—wondering, is this what powerful men do with weak-willed women in this town? Yes, I concluded. If Ehrlichman was doing to my mother what he did to the country, then it must be a good thing. From that moment on, my ambitions in Washington were cemented.

Suffice it to say that Mr. John soon had to resign, and eventually served eighteen months in a minimum-security penitentiary. Mom and I visited him only once at the Safford Federal Correctional Institution in Arizona (conjugal visits were strictly limited to one's legal spouse—thus explaining Ehrlichman's prison-era divorce). Mr. John seemed to have found solace in his incarceration, and was the captain of his prison softball league (perhaps his influence explains my own lifelong affection for the game). And he was still very proud of the role that he'd played in bringing Richard Nixon to the White House, even if it wasn't quite for two full terms ("That's a half term better than that slack-jawed peanut farmer ever got—ha!" he would later tell Bob Woodward in one of Woodward's chronically unread books).

Mom eventually parlayed her time in the White House into a lucrative career as the gossip columnist for the old *Washington Star*. But as for me, my career aspirations were just getting started.

## Amy Carter, Mika Brzezinski, and the Night That We Don't Talk About

Growing up in Washington at the height of the Cold War, teenagers could easily become blasé about living in the most powerful city in the world. But not me. Sure, I went through an adolescent phase, but I never lost sight of the awesome privilege and opportunity that came from living in the District. Other kids, though, were more cavalier.

Mika Brzezinski, for one, was a bit of a wild child. Her dad, Zbigniew, was Jimmy Carter's Polish answer to Henry Kissinger—thick accent, didn't like the Russians, and more than a little nuts. But coincidentally, Mika is only five months older than Amy Carter, so the two girls were fast friends. Amy was pretty sheltered then. She was surrounded by Secret Service agents, and rarely allowed to leave the White House grounds.

Mika was, to put it mildly, a bad influence on Amy. She used to have sleepovers at the White House with Amy,[1] and on one excursion to Camp David, eleven-year-old Mika and Amy nearly ran over Prime Minister Begin while out driving on the grounds in a golf cart. If it weren't for the quick thinking of Amy's Secret Service detail, which shoved Begin to the side, the Camp David Accords would be remembered less for peace in the Middle East and more for the preteen assassins who killed the Israeli premier.

The girls were a couple of years younger than me, but at that age, they grow up fast. I remember one night—it must have been

Amy Carter, Mika Brzezinski, and their soccer coach at
Camp David *(Courtesy of Carter Library)*

in December 1980. The election was over, Washington was starting to get giddy with the Reagan inauguration, and there was
talk that the Iranian hostages might finally get released. But it
was also the heyday of the hard-core punk scene in Washington.
I was out one night at the 9:30 Club in downtown D.C. with
some of my classmates from Georgetown Day. State of Alert
(with a pre–Black Flag Henry Rollins) was the opening act for a
bill that included Minor Threat and Bad Brains. (At one point, I
went to the bathroom, and peeing in the next stall to me was
Rollins. Though skinny and pre-tattooed, he was still an imposing figure on stage and off. As he zipped up, he turned to me and
said, "A wise man once told me something wise." I trembled. "He
said, 'Be wise.'" And then he left.)

In the middle of Minor Threat's set, I saw two girls slink in
through the back door. I thought I recognized them. Mika had
snuck Amy away from the White House. Since she was a lame-
duck first daughter, security had grown lax, and after that year's
bruising presidential campaign where Amy herself had been
dragged through the mud, she really needed to let off some steam.

At a hardcore punk show in the early eighties *(Courtesy of Skizz Cyzyk)*

We got to talking (screaming, really—the 9:30 Club is one of the loudest venues in D.C.), and when I mentioned my name was Marty Eisenstadt, they assumed I was the son of Carter's domestic policy adviser, Stuart Eizenstat (I got that a lot in those days). I didn't hear them very well and must have nodded in agreement.

Mika had stashed a couple of wine coolers in her purse, so we hung out in the back room and played a mini version of Truth or Dare. Since Amy's life was pretty much an open book back then, we stuck to dares for her. I probably shouldn't say too much, but I think it's fair to admit that my notable attraction to redheads (particularly in the company of blondes) probably emanated from that one crazy night.

Eventually the Secret Service found us and hauled Amy and Mika back to the White House. I think the agents were as embarrassed as anyone that they had lost track of the girls, and we all vowed never to speak of that night again. I was just lucky not to get a bullet in the head and wind up in the Potomac. But it definitely was a turning point for all three of us: Amy became a college radical and got kicked out of Brown[2]; Mika's stern father sent her to boarding school, where she grew into a serious journalist who refuses to report on Paris Hilton[3]; and I went on to be fearful of intimacy.

## Iran-Contra: It Seemed Like a Neat Idea at the Time

After completing high school, I hoped to attend an Ivy League university, preferably Yale or Harvard. Unfortunately, due to a misunderstanding over a deadline, I had to settle for D.C.'s third-best local college, American University. Mom, too, was disappointed that I wouldn't be attending school outside of D.C. and was more than eager to spend the extra bucks so I could stay in the dormitories across town. These were not my best years, I must confess. My freshman year in particular: I suffered from severe acne and felt ashamed to be seen in bright light. I tried hiding behind binge drinking and black turtlenecks, but that just caused more problems. I listened to the Smiths, the Cure, and New Order, and occasionally wore eyeliner and spoke with a British accent.

I even smoked marijuana on a handful of occasions. For years, I was terrified that this youthful indiscretion would come back to bite me. I suspected there was a picture out there of me inhaling pot. Many nights I lay awake tormented by the notion that if one day I were to run for elected office, somebody from my past could spring up and blackmail me. I think subconsciously this is one reason I became a political operative rather than seeking elected office myself. All I can say is, thank God for Barack Obama and his admitted cocaine use. Youthful drug experimentation is no longer an obstacle to the White House.

Training to defend the homeland at Young Americans for
Freedom (YAF) Easter retreat *(Courtesy of YAF Archives)*

Either way, I was on the road to nowhere fast. And if it wasn't
for Ronald Reagan, I truly don't know where I'd be today. Mom
was secretly dating Ted Kennedy at the time, so perhaps I joined
the Reagan Revolution to get back at her. Maybe it was my desire
to fight and kill communists. Maybe I liked suits and bow ties
and close-cropped hair. I don't know. What I do know is that
before I discovered the conservative movement, I was aimless
and drunk, shy and insecure, prone to misunderstandings and
angry reactions from others. But all that changed after attending
my first Young Americans for Freedom rally. A mujahideen warrior from Afghanistan, dressed in traditional tribal wear, spoke
to the cheering, flag-waving crowd through a translator. He
thanked America for providing the Stinger missiles that he and
his buddies were using to bring down Soviet helicopters. I never
before felt so proud. I, too, wanted to be a freedom fighter, to
battle communists. What a contrast to the antiapartheid divestment protests that were also common at the time, where loose,

liberal girls criticized America and thought they were too good for guys like me.

When I returned to campus, I joined the College Republicans and helped in Ronald Reagan's reelection effort (a crushing victory over Walter Mondale in all but Minnesota and my own dear District of Columbia, a failing I took personally). I fondly recall all kinds of wild adventures from that time: demonstrating on behalf of Star Wars and less government, sabotaging the Jiffy Johns at proabortion rallies, and watching over and over again that American classic *Red Dawn*, starring Patrick Swayze, about American freedom fighters who take to the hills when Soviet armies invade and occupy the homeland. I even considered dropping out of college to go to Angola to fight against the communists. Young men today don't appreciate how lucky they have it. When I was coming of age, America didn't directly fight in wars. We fought by proxy. Now America has two wars, and it's as easy as joining the army to be able to participate in one.

Luckily, Mom knew Elliott Abrams, the assistant secretary for Inter-American Affairs, and got me a job as his intern. Abrams managed his own little fiefdom at State where he oversaw our Central American wars in conjunction with Oliver North at the National Security Council. The two men never trusted regular interoffice messenger services, so I was often dispatched to secretly meet with North's secretary, Fawn Hall. She was just a few years older than me, and her billowing blonde hair was as wildly expressive as her heart. From time to time she had to smuggle documents from her boss's office in her bra, and it was up to me to remove them. Inevitably, we grew close, and let's just say, she was my first, although it is doubtful I was hers. I dreamed of making her my girlfriend, of marrying her, of gliding through town together as a D.C. power couple, but I never got the chance.

Elliott Abrams was subpoenaed before the Iran-Contra committee and it was suggested (by Elliott? by Fawn? I don't recall) that it might be best if I left the country for a little while. I took

My love affair with camel racing started at an early age.
*(Courtesy of Juan Cole)*

advantage of the semester-abroad program offered by American University and went to their campus in Cairo. Elliott was close to Jeb Bush, who was always present at Contra meetings when they convened in Miami. When I returned to the States, I got a call from Jeb saying he'd arranged an internship for me on his dad's presidential campaign. Was I interested? Damn straight I was.

## Red, Hot, and Lee Atwater

I very happily worked as an apprentice to Lee Atwater and Roger Ailes during George H. W. Bush's run against Michael Dukakis (it was a great team back then, and I'm still close with guys like Charlie Black). Atwater was a brilliant strategist and I admired him greatly. He also made terrific barbecue ribs—even in the midst of the campaign—and the portly Ailes clearly availed himself of them as often as he could. Lee once admitted to me that the reason he opened his still-thriving restaurant Red Hot & Blue was so he wouldn't have to keep cooking for Roger.

If you remember, the late-eighties issue du jour was drugs.

Between Nancy Reagan's Just Say No campaign and the T-shirt-and-blazer look of *Miami Vice* at the height of its popularity, America was obsessed with drugs. The only problem was that the polls showed the issue starting to skew Democratic (must have been the blazers). The trick, Atwater told us in the research room at the RNC, was to subtly turn the issue from "drugs" to "crime"—a code word that meant the GOP would protect hard-working white Americans (still the majority of the voting electorate) from the hordes of violent, darker-hued criminals. Lee was nothing if not subtle.

So I found out that Dukakis had supported a Massachusetts prison furlough program which had let convicted murderer Willie Horton out on the streets, where he proceeded to move to Maryland and rape a woman and stab her boyfriend. Naturally, our job was to make this guy the moral equivalent of Mike Dukakis's running mate. How hard could it be to give Willie Horton more name recognition than Lloyd Bentsen? ("Lloyd who?" you're asking. Exactly.)

I headed up the team that went to the state prison in Draper, Utah, which had this incredibly photogenic revolving door (Lee had decided that would be a great metaphor). Roger wanted to make sure that all the actors in the ad were either black or Hispanic. But this being Utah, it was hard to find enough actors of color. So using techniques I learned from a film class I'd taken at American University as a freshman, I suggested we shoot the commercial in black-and-white and just instruct the white Mormon actors to act black. But this was Utah, and their only experience with black people came from watching *The Cosby Show*. We told them to take off their colorful sweaters, and we applied additional makeup to their faces. It worked. The public dialogue shifted from drugs to crime, and Willie Horton became a household name.

A couple of weeks later, Lee entrusted our team with putting together the Dukakis-in-a-tank ad that would run during game five of the World Series. Frankly, I found the initial footage of candidate Dukakis in an M1 Abrams tank (while wearing a tie) strangely compelling and actually quite patriotic. The challenge was how to make it ironic, given Dukakis's track record opposing defense spending. Still thinking about the basic cinematic tools we'd used in the Horton ad, I was the one who suggested the squeaking sound effect for the tank. The ad was a success, and Bush won the White House.

## From Bush to Clinton to Bush

Under Bush 41, I held a variety of positions in the Defense Department. That's where I met Dick Cheney for the first time. Unfortunately, I once made a lesbian joke in his presence and was unable to rely on him later in my career. But my immediate superiors liked me, and I was a natural, what with my high IQ and Middle East background. Just as I was about to be made a deputy assistant secretary, the gig ran out. Clinton won the election, and for the next eight years the Democrats would be in charge.

Like many other Republicans who were waiting out the Clinton years, I found a way to participate in what other countries might call "the government in waiting." In America, we call it "think tanks." I took an associate fellow position at the vaunted Heritage Foundation. It was at that time the preeminent bastion of conservative thought in Washington. Not surprisingly, it dominated—and to a large degree still does—the influential Think Tank Softball League in Washington. There were enough avid players at Heritage to field three teams. Unfortunately, because of seniority issues (and *not* talent, I must emphasize), I was forced to play on the Heritage C team in the minor-league division. It was the A team that had the handsome young congressman Newt Gingrich as their ringer shortstop, and it was at their practices that they developed the influential Contract with America. The closest we came to policy influence on the C team was getting all Heritage employees banned from the Arlington Hooters.

I'd be lying if I said I was entirely happy working at Heritage, but it did give me a keen insight on how think tanks influence policy in Washington. More important, I saw how they work as an imprimatur for pundits who are neither qualified to be real academics nor successful enough to actually make money in the private sector. For someone of my particular skill set, the think-tank world held an immeasurable appeal. But not at Heritage. It was already too crowded, and between the likes of Jeane Kirkpatrick and Ed Meese, there were too many egos butting heads. I had to move on.

After working on Alan Keyes's failed primary campaign in 1996, I decided to join some former Pete Wilson staffers who had been hired to go to Russia to teach polling to the Boris Yeltsin campaign. I was promised a healthy compensation. After six months in Russia (well, Siberia actually), I came back with no money and a Siberian wife, Zolzaya, who demanded that I get a high-placed government job. As Mom didn't approve of my marriage, we couldn't count on her for free room and board. Knowing that it would take some time to find the right political appointment after being away for so long, I took a side job managing a telemarketing call center in Falls Church, primarily up-selling cable TV service to Latinos and seniors. I now had a family of my own to support.

Shortly thereafter, Zolzaya left me for a deputy secretary of defense, who I understand is now under indictment for passing secrets to an unnamed foreign agent. I have to admit that my heart still hasn't healed from losing Zolzaya. On numerous occasions, I've tried to track her down, but the Russian embassy has been less than helpful, insisting that they have no record of her.

Ironically, it was my job as a telemarketer that propelled me back into the political game. Only now, after the last obituary has been read on John McCain's career, am I willing to admit publicly that it was *my* call center that waged the infamous push-polling campaign of 2000. We had all of South Carolina believing that John McCain's adopted Bangladeshi daughter was actually a black love child. Without that primary win in South Carolina, Bush never would have gone on to win the nomination. The Bushies owed me. So when Bush 43 decided to invade Iraq in response to the 9/11 attacks, I was invited to join the Committee for the Liberation of Iraq (CLI), set up by the administration to sell America on the war and peopled by the movers and shakers of the neoconservative movement.

To me, invading Iraq was a no-brainer; Iraq had the second-largest reserves of oil on the planet. And after the trauma of 9/11, America was craving war. To paraphrase my old friend Jacob Zuma, recently elected the president of South Africa, "It is just as big a crime to not give a woman sex when she wants it as it is to give her sex when she doesn't."[4] Likewise, when the people are frothing for war, you have no choice but to give it to them. War thins the herd. It allows the young to experience bravery. It creates new markets for our goods. For the health of the community, that kind of bloodlust needed to be fed. And feed it, we did. We (my colleagues and I over at CLI) wrote articles, appeared on TV, and spoke at churches and synagogues. It was the most money I ever made as a pundit (thanks to the pundit payola system the Pentagon was running at the time). We warned of mushroom clouds. We insinuated connections between Al Qaeda and Iraq while reporting that our troops would be greeted as liberators. We explained to the people that only through war could peace be achieved. I myself appeared on TV numerous times comparing Saddam to Hitler while preaching the virtues of freedom, democracy, and war.

So it was only natural for me to go to Iraq on the heels of the invasion to help out with the reconstruction. At first I worked closely with Paul Bremer, helping to draft the new constitution. Later, employing the knowledge gained while working in tele-

Reconstructing Iraq one cell phone at a time
*(Courtesy of Michael Viggoda)*

marketing, I oversaw a massive telecommunications project in the north. Under Saddam, Iraqis did not have access to cell phones. It didn't take a brain surgeon to realize that there was a lot of money to be made here. Thirty-five million people without cell phones, who had never had cell phones. It was a daunting challenge, but I relished it. I traveled the countryside, meeting with tribal leaders and desert nomads in an effort to convince them that everyone needs a cell phone and that having a cell-phone tower in one's backyard is a good thing. I personally signed up more than twenty thousand new customers to an ambitious plan where you pay only once a year, receive free rollover minutes, and get unlimited texting during Ramadan.

Who could have known that the insurgents would later use these very same cell phones to attack our troops? Apparently, cell phones are an easy means of crafting remote-control devices for IEDs and bombs, and we had inadvertently made them available to a wide range of people. As the Provisional Authority redrafted its cell phone policy, I decided to return stateside, just in time for the 2004 Bush versus Kerry campaign.

## Naming Names: The Swift Boaters

When I returned from working in Iraq in 2004, I was looking for a way to help in the George Bush reelection effort. I called my old pal Rick Reed, whom I'd known from working briefly at the National Republican Senatorial Committee. His was a natural door to knock on. Rick told me that his firm, Stevens, Reed, Curcio, and Potholm, was already staffed up, and more important, they weren't "officially" doing any work for Bush that year. Now I know a good set of air quotes when I see them, so I knew Rick had something interesting up his sleeve.

He told me that they were getting ready to do some work for a group of Vietnam vets with an ax to grind against Kerry. But they needed to call themselves something. In our business, coming up with euphemistic names for organizations and legislation

*(Courtesy of Karl Rove)*

is half the battle. Names like USA Patriot Act (to spy on Americans), Healthy Forests Initiative (to chop down trees), or Log Cabin Republicans (to dress up like Lincoln and have gay orgies) are all legendary in Washington. Reed was looking for just such a name for this group and handed me a list that they'd brainstormed with Karl Rove at a recent breakfast at the Arlington IHOP. He was close, he said, but would I take a stab? Scribbled on a napkin and half drowned in blueberry syrup were the names you can see on page 23.

I could tell they were close. But then it dawned on me: Swift Boat Veterans for Truth! If the word "truth" is in the name itself, then mentally we all assume everything they say *must* be true. Rick jumped all over it, and the ads were running within a week. My only regret is that he never paid me a consulting fee. But no matter: if success in this business is measured in bragging rights alone, then I am a wealthy man. If, on the other hand, it is measured in actual wealth (as I'm told is how most people measure it), then no, I am not a wealthy man.

It was at around this time that I realized I couldn't keep relying on the benevolence of old friends and family to keep me going. I was teetering on the brink of forty, and in the grand scheme of things, didn't have much to show for my life. I needed a legacy; something that I could call my own; a place, quite literally, to hang my hat. In short, I needed my own think tank.

## Birth of a Think Tank

There are two critical elements to any good think tank: a catchy name and a reliable source of money. In my opinion, the most memorable and successful think tanks are named after former presidents; think of the Wilson Center, the Hoover Institution, or even the global do-gooders at the Carter Center. So I looked for presidents I admired and found only a handful that didn't already have a think tank named after them (it's tough—since

JFK, every president has automatically had a library and/or think tank set up as soon as they leave office). I struck gold when I tracked down the grandnephew of our twenty-ninth president, Warren G. Harding, living in a retirement home in Silver Spring. Clifford Harding III was a spry old fellow who still managed the purse strings of the Harding Family Trust. Warren G. Harding was not a particularly well-loved president, and he died in office under mysterious circumstances. Lucky for me, Clifford was eager to bolster his patriarch's dwindling reputation, and when I pitched him the idea for the Harding Institute for Freedom and Democracy, he loved it.

By residing in my mother's basement in Georgetown, I was able to save enough money to choose an especially desirable downtown office space with a K Street address (the building manager said it was Ken Starr's old Whitewater headquarters, which always makes me wonder which room they kept the blue dress in). And I should mention, I'm not ashamed of my living situation. Mother is now a very respected figure, the doyenne of the Washington social scene. Her cocktail parties are legendary and I learn a lot from her. Plus, as a firm believer in family values, I'm proud to be there for Mother in her times of need. For example, just last week, I was there for her when the water heater broke and she needed help finding the name of a good plumber.

Back at the Harding Institute, I quickly put together a staff: Eli Perle, a recent graduate of my alma mater, American University, became my associate fellow (the standard Washington thinktank title for an assistant). Eli was another local D.C. boy, and maybe I saw a little of myself in him. My next move was to bring on a disarmingly subservient Pakistani American named Marwan Al-Rahat as a research assistant. Eli then proposed that we round out the staff with attractive unpaid interns to answer the phones and do the work that could be interpreted as demeaning to the senior staff. I should mention that we also set up a cubicle for my old lobbyist pal Stanley Rubin (an "adjunct fellow" if ever there was one), but he rarely comes in. Every now and again, our benefactor, Clifford Harding III, drops by as well, but usually just to get one of the interns to teach him how to use a fax machine.

In addition to endowment funding from their namesake's benefactors, think tanks have other means of raising operating funds: corporate sponsorship (hence, the Coca-Cola® Conference Room and the Xerox® Copy Corner at the institute), government contracting (the occasional study or report), and merchandise (including publications, mugs, and T-shirts).

While we printed up one set of business cards and stationery, the nice lady at Kinko's said we could get a deal on two. So I also set up the Eisenstadt Group (of which I am CEO), which would

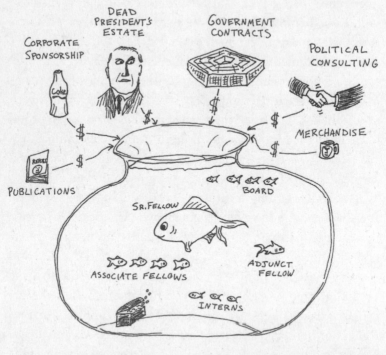

ANATOMY OF A THINK TANK

*(Illustration by Poppy Cartwright)*

be the consulting firm geared for campaign and lobbying work. I don't want to bore you with accounting details, but let's just say that for tax reasons, it's sometimes better to route consulting jobs through the nonprofit Harding Institute. Either way, we were all under one roof. And yes, in my spacious corner office with a panoramic view of downtown, I finally had a place to hang my hat.

I could now call myself a senior fellow at a prominent Washington think tank named after an early-twentieth-century president. In the punditing world, this is what's called bona fides. And what is a pundit? We are oracles, soothsayers, sirens; we

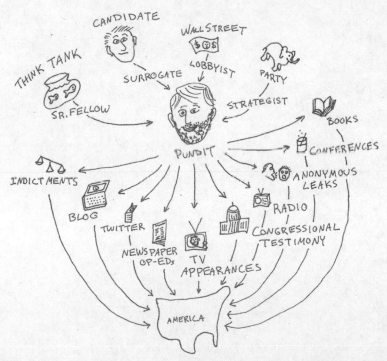

ANATOMY OF A PUNDIT

(Illustration by Poppy Cartwright)

predict the future, and no one ever checks later to see if we got it right. Pundits give our own opinions (as paid for by whoever our benefactor may be at the time: think tanks, candidates, parties, or corporate clients). And we use every means of modern communication at our disposal to get the message—and our name—across to America. Pundits have been essential to American democracy since the birth of our great country. If George Washington was the first American president (as I believe to be true), then it could be said that Ben Franklin was the first American pundit. And guess whose face is on a higher-denomination bill? I rest my case.

# The Mysterious Giuliani Stealth Campaign

# 3

## The Race for the Race

Within minutes of President Bush's reelection in 2004, the speculation instantly turned to who would succeed him in 2008. It was clear, even before he shot his hunting partner in the face, that Dick Cheney wouldn't be running.

So who would it be? From early on, it was obvious to anyone paying attention that Rudy "America's Mayor" Giuliani would be the front-runner. By February 2007, Rudy was poised to accept the mantle of president. His victory was inevitable. And every Republican consultant in America—including me—was clawing to be on Team Giuliani.

It's a curious thing about political consultants. We always tell ourselves how much we can do for the candidates, but really we know that it's the candidates who can do the most for us . . . if they win. To be able to list a winning candidate among your clients offers more than just bragging rights and the cost of a round at the Hawk'n'Dove on Capitol Hill. Nope, the more winners you list, the higher rate you can charge your next client. Ironically, though, the bigger a loser you are, the more TV appearances you're likely to make during the next election as a pundit. Just look at how many former Dukakis, Kerry, Dole, Dean, and Edwards strategists there are on CNN. To say nothing of perennial also-ran Pat Buchanan and now Mike Huckabee— both arguably much better as pundits than they ever were as candidates. As a loser, no one else will hire you, so you've plenty of time for publicly second-guessing the people who really did get those jobs.

So as the droves of consultants, strategists, pollsters, and others flocked to Camp Rudy, there was naturally some jostling for position. Rudy had his own loyalists from New York, and admittedly, there wasn't much room on the campaign for someone of

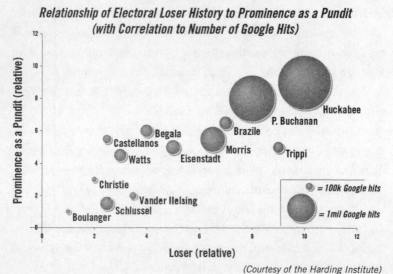

## Pundit Chart
### Relationship of Electoral Loser History to Prominence as a Pundit (with Correlation to Number of Google Hits)

*(Courtesy of the Harding Institute)*

my particular talents. But then I came up with an idea. It was so crazy, it just might work.

## Secret Meeting with Rudy

I needed to speak privately with Giuliani himself. Perhaps auspiciously, it was the Ides of March when I went to New York to see him. There was a rare late-winter snowfall, and Rudy wanted to meet me in Yankee Stadium. Aside from us, it was deserted. He greeted me at the dugout and we walked onto the diamond.

"Marty, stand on home plate." Giuliani then turned his back and strolled through the half-foot-deep snow to the pitcher's mound.

"Mr. Mayor," I yelled to him, echoing through the stadium, "I want to create a series of YouTube videos that on first glance would look like authentic campaign ads, complete with a link to your official website. I'll make them entertaining enough that they'll go viral, and people will keep coming back for more in the series."

"Like lonelygirl15. Sure, I know all about the YouTubes, Marty. Big whoop." He turned and threw a snowball at my chest.

"Here's the twist, sir. To give the ads even more resonance in the media, we post them anonymously and give the impression that they were actually planted by one of your opponents."

"Why would people think that?" He beaned me on the head with another snowball, but I continued.

"Simple: upon further examination, and as the ads progressed, it would be clear that they were subtly insulting you and therefore *must* have come from one of your primary challengers. Why, you'd be crazy to have your own ads insult you—right?"

"Keep going." He packed another snowball. Hard and icy.

"You see, if there's one thing the electorate doesn't like in politics—especially in the GOP primary—it's the breaking of Ronald Reagan's eleventh commandment."

" 'Thou shalt not speak ill of any fellow Republican.' Yeah, I've heard it."

"So if we somehow gave the impression that squeaky-clean McCain or Romney or one of the others had generated these negative ads, it'll only backfire in their faces. Meanwhile, with every ad that gets seen, people will find the link to your website."

Rudy let it sink in. He thought for a moment, then threw the snowball at my head.

"I love it!"

Rudy's always had a great sense of self-deprecating humor (witness his numerous *Saturday Night Live* appearances and, of course, his penchant for wearing women's dresses and panties, frequently in public). But in order for this idea to work, we had to go dark. Seriously dark. More than just plausible—this would be probable deniability. No further communication with the campaign, and of course, no official acknowledgment that these ads have any association with the campaign whatsoever.

Rudy walked back to home plate and leaned in close. Close enough for me to smell kielbasa on his steamy breath and his third wife's perfume behind his ear.

"Marty," he said, gently wiping snowflakes off my eyebrows, "you're a sick genius. The worse you make me look, the better it'll be. But if you so much as leak one word of this conversation, I'll cut out your gallbladder, and shove it up your left nostril. *Capice*?" He wrote me a check and walked away. The rest was up to me.

## The Bitter-Valet Ads

Naturally, the first stop when I got back to D.C. was the Eighteenth and K Street branch of Bank of America. As a seasoned political consultant, you learn quickly to deposit checks as soon as you get them. And wire transfers? Even better.

I knew that my assistant Eli would be key to this new Giuliani operation. He'd occasionally mentioned Hollywood aspirations, so I figured he'd know his way around a camera. And he'd know how to manage the YouTube and other Internet intricacies. But the key to this stealth campaign would be to limit the number of people with any knowledge. That meant we couldn't even hire actors. Too risky. Actors are notoriously cheap and weak-willed. One wine spritzer and the promise of a good review will get even the most seasoned actor to spill the beans and burn the potatoes. Nope, better to keep it all in-house. Eli and me—it was up to us.

I came up with a simple but ingenious premise that we could accomplish with just two people: a slightly deranged parking valet would give a running monologue about the various candidates. Eli would operate the camera and I would act. For my own sense of humility, I would rather have been behind the camera, but we knew we'd have to turn these spots around fast in order to stay topical and timely. I hadn't done any acting since a high-school production of *Fiddler on the Roof* at Georgetown Day School. (I had the thankless role of Avram, the Bookseller. My one line? "A hat!") But I felt I was up for the task, so I shaved my beard and put on some glasses. I *became* the parking valet. As my old drama teacher told me, "If you *believe* you are Avram, the audience will *forget* you are Marty." And to this day, most have forgotten.

The first spot we shot was called "Real Balls." You'll see from the transcripts that it was pretty edgy (we needed to get the first one noticed if these were going to go viral). The tagline said it all: "Rudy: Real Lucky, Real Balls." And then it had the legitimate link to www.JoinRudy2008.com.

It was an instant hit on the Internet. The video was picked up in all corners of the blogosphere. Everyone from the *National Review*'s blog and Michelle Malkin on the right, to Crooks and Liars on the left. Wonkette wrote that it was the "viral video on

YouTube that everybody in politics is talking about."[1] As predicted, the initial reaction was that it was a legitimate Giuliani ad (given the end graphics), but quickly suspicion turned to it being a dirty-tricks mud-slinging effort by one of the other campaigns.

In order to keep strict anonymity, Eli set up a YouTube channel under the nom de plume Abrad2345. There was considerable speculation on the blogosphere about that name and what it meant.

Strangely, no one ever suspected that Abrad was simply Darba spelled backward, and that 2345 was just an easy number to type with the left hand. In the mid-nineties, I had a kidney scare and went to India to scout for a cheap replacement. At one point, I stopped in a small town in Chhattisgarh Province called Darba. I remember it fondly—mostly for the curry and incense, but also for the strawberry-blonde Australian traveler at an ashram who helped to cleanse my chakras (if you know what I mean).

Internet rumors soon blossomed into a major piece on ABC News on July 18, 2007, by Brian Ross and his relentless investigative team: "A trio of edgy online videos attacking GOP presidential front-runners may comprise a new 'dirty trick' in the 2008 presidential race—if anyone can figure out where they came from."[2]

Ross, who was known as the guy who broke the Mark Foley gay-text-messaging story wide open, is a brilliant reporter. But if he got too close, I could always call in a marker I had with him: I'm the one who forwarded Ross the Foley text messages when the scandal got too close to my pal Denny Hastert. As an anonymous source in this town, I'm too valuable of an asset to burn.

As it turns out, we had nothing to worry about. Ross could never figure out the source of the ads—our tracks were too well covered. But in his story, he got denials from the McCain campaign, from the Obama campaign, and even from the Giuliani campaign itself. Naturally they would deny any culpability—Rudy had kept his own team in the dark. The ABC story begat

## "Real Lucky, Real Balls": Partial Transcript

*(Courtesy of Eisenstadt Group)*

Giuliani's got balls. He wasn't afraid to mess with the mafia. He wasn't afraid to mess with the anarchists, he wasn't afraid to mess with the Haitians. If you gotta stick a plunger up somebody's ass to reduce crime, then you stick a plunger up their ass.

Because it ain't skill, it ain't talent in this life, it's luck. McCain. I dunno, is that lucky to get shot down? Romney. Is that lucky to be born Mormon? Giuliani. Two towers fell on top of him and he walked out unscathed. That is a lucky man, that's somebody you want.

Giuliani Italian? Where did you hear that from? Mobbed up? What are you talkin' about? "Jew"-liani, "Jew"-liani. He's from New York. You don't get it? Oh, come on. He's Italian like I'm Polish.

articles in *The New York Times* and throughout the media world. But no one figured out who was behind the ads.

Meanwhile, Eli and I stayed focused and on task. We shot more of the videos, including ones that poked gentle fun at Rudy's opponents: John McCain (a Manchurian candidate), Mitt Romney (Mormons and the missionary position), and Fred Thompson (young, hot wife really a tranny). Increasingly, people were still trying to figure out the source of the videos. And we left plenty of clues for them to find.

## Cool Beans and Eliot Spitzer

The blogosphere was fascinated by our videos and constantly tried to track down their origin. They noticed specific trees in the backgrounds, fleeting glimpses of buildings, and any license plate that they could freeze-frame and track down ("Aha! A California plate! These must be shot in L.A.!"—not realizing that tourists often come to D.C. from California). Naturally, we didn't want to put in the real license plates for the Mazda minivan we had borrowed from Eli's mother (the glorious Sandra Perle, from whom the term MILF, I believe, was inspired), so we found a website containing scores of license plates from around the country. Apparently there is a whole subculture of people— like trainspotters, but without the heroin and Scottish accents— whose mission it is to take pictures of license plates from every state in the union.

So we printed out a new set of plates, glued them over the real ones, and made sure to conspicuously film them in one of the ads. What we didn't expect was that one particularly obsessed fan/stalker actually paid forty dollars to do a vehicle ID search for the owner of that plate.

Turns out the plates belonged to one ███████ █████████, a D.C. resident who works as a food-aid specialist for the U.S. Dry Bean Council (USDBC)—a trade association of dry-bean producers, who are apparently in a running feud over government subsidies with the so-called canned "wet" bean producers. Ironically, I once did some lobbying for the USDBC, which was trying to get wet beans declassified as a vegetable under the federal school lunch program—under the guise that they added to children's methane production and increased global warming. To this day, I'm still quite proud of my "Whoever smelt it, dealt it" issue advocacy ads that ran on CNN at the time, and for which I was runner-up for a Pollie Award (presented by the Association of Political and Public Affairs Professionals). ████████ is a handsome and well-liked guy, but to this day I doubt that he ever knew that his license plate wound up on a website, and thereafter in our videos.

In one of our final ads, we addressed the issue of giving driver's licenses to illegal immigrants, and brought up Hillary Clinton's controversial support of Eliot Spitzer's program to give these licenses away. Keep in mind, this was nearly six months before the New York governor would be forced to resign from office over a prostitution scandal. Clinton was still the Democratic frontrunner at the time, so it was important for Rudy to tie her to a scandal that would instantly recall her own husband's indiscretions in the White House. Though the scandal hadn't yet broken, a good political consultant like myself sees these firestorms coming months ahead of time and lays the groundwork early. So how, dear reader, did I know about Spitzer and the hooker when it came as such a surprise to everyone else? Allow me to digress for a moment.

### Rolling the Dice with Ashley Dupré

The Mayflower Hotel in Washington is well known as the site of Calvin Coolidge's triumphant inaugural ball (one, by the way, that the notoriously unjovial, and frequently silent, Coolidge did not actually attend) after he assumed the presidency following our dear Warren G. Harding's mysterious death in 1923 (some still suspect Coolidge of poisoning poor Warren). As famous Washington hotels known for their scandals, the Mayflower is to sex what the Watergate is to break-ins and what the "Hinkley" Hilton is to assassination attempts. JFK kept his alleged mistress

Judith Campbell Exner at the Mayflower, and years later, it's where Monica Lewinsky would stay when news of her affair with President Clinton broke.

So from time to time during the fall of '07, I would sit in the Lobby Court bar—a perfect people-watching location with a well-lit view of the hotel entrance. As a pundit and occasional lobbyist, it pays to keep an eye on which public officials might be capping off their days with high-priced escorts and aerobic rounds of policy wonking. The words "spying" and "blackmail" seem so uncouth. I prefer the expressions "observational attentiveness" and the inevitable "social persuasion."

It was on one of these nights that I recognized Eliot Spitzer walking into the hotel with a woman who was—as we say in Washington—not his wife. I saw them enter the elevator and head up to the notorious eighth floor (Willie the bartender calls it the "wag and shag" floor). Following Willie's custom at the Mayflower bar, I rolled some dice to choose my next cocktail. I got snake eyes and Willie served me a whiskey sour with a kalamata olive twist. I'd barely nursed it for twenty minutes when I heard the distinctive elevator "ping" and saw a slightly ruffled Spitzer walking out of the hotel with a jaunt in his step and his shirttails untucked: I knew then that he'd either just had sex with a hooker or had sold a U.S. Senate seat to the highest bidder (or possibly both).

By the time I'd rolled an eight the hard way and Willie had served me a dry martini with a flotilla of pomegranate seeds, I heard the elevator again and saw Spitzer's courtesan come out and head to the bar. Seeing as I was the only patron there, she sat next to me.

"Mind if I roll you a drink?" I turned on the charm.

"Sure, why not."

I rolled a lucky seven and Willie poured her a Long Island Iced Tea—aptly enough, given the circumstances.

"Kristen," she said her name was, but she looked like an Ashley if ever I'd seen one.

"Ferdinand," I replied (a cover name I'd used once on a job in Panama ... but that's another story). "I work for a big-time pharmaceutical company in Indiana, and I'm in town for a little lobbying."

She shot me a look that said, "Haven't I seen you on Wolf Blitzer's show?" Thankfully, she was a woman who knew how to ask only as many questions as she was likely to answer herself.

"I've got a room upstairs. Already paid for. Care to join me?"

I did. The sheets were rumpled and the TV still turned on to C-SPAN (say what you will about Spitzer, but the man is a rigorous information hound). Once upstairs, Kristen was all business. Turns out that New York governors make a lot more money than Washington pundits, and Spitzer hadn't scrimped on his discretionary spending. I'm a gentleman, so I'll leave out the details of what seemed like a rather extended negotiation, but suffice to say that there was no "sloppy-seconds discount." Under the circumstances, I thought it best to bid my good wishes and retreat back down to Willie and the dice. Upon reflection, this one decision probably saved me from prosecution and undue public embarrassment.

All of which is to say that when we were prepping the Spitzer immigration spot, I knew it would be prescient to his eventual downfall.

## Obama Girl and the Arrogance of Inevitability

In the summer of 2007, our stealth Giuliani ads were the hottest thing on the Internet for any of the GOP candidates. The Dems were another story, though. The well-endowed Obama Girl ads and the slightly less famous (but no less well-endowed) Hott4Hill ads were heating up the summer. I remember one unrelated

## How to Be with a Hooker

My free advice to politicians who want to avoid having their names associated with prostitution services:

1. Use a good alias. Throw people off the scent by using another politician's name. Someone classy like Dick Armey (whose name sounds like an alias anyway).

2. Pay with cash. Preferably, Canadian dollars.

3. Too many witnesses at fancy D.C. hotels. Use cheap Virginia motels run by South Asians. They're too busy burning their curry to notice you.

4. To avoid incriminating blackmail tapes, always wear a disguise while performing the act. My personal preference is Groucho Marx mustache glasses.

5. Expensive call girls are more likely to be better educated, could recognize you, and might extort you. Best to use undocumented immigrants who don't speak much English and have more to fear than you do.

6. But tip generously.

7. If you suspect that you're under investigation, set up your own wife with a male escort or congressional colleague. If she can't complain about your behavior, why should anyone else?

punditing appearance I was supposed to make on Chris Matthews's show on MSNBC. I was all set to speak about Nancy Pelosi's "unsubstantiated" and "alleged" ties to Kim Jong Il (I once saw her eating bulgogi at a Korean restaurant). But Obama Girl was in D.C. and Chris bumped me in a heartbeat. His show's not called *Hardball* for nothing.

The whole point of my Abrad campaign was to make the

other candidates seem like dirty tricksters. And in that, I succeeded. But the ads weren't supposed to live in a vacuum. They
were designed to drive Internet traffic to the real Giuliani site.
Unfortunately, Rudy's official campaign put no time or money
into that site, and those who visited left underwhelmed. By
the beginning of fall, every Republican candidate was courting
MySpace and Facebook friends, had active campaign blogs, and
most had official YouTube channels. Except for Rudy. With the
notable exception of our stealth campaign, the Giuliani team
had all but ignored the Internet. And in the end, that would be a
sign of its undoing.

## The End Was Near

John McCain's campaign had almost completely bottomed out
by August. He'd fired most of his staff, he was traveling coach to
New Hampshire, and his famous Straight Talk Express bus had
literally run out of gas. If Giuliani had followed my strategy, we
could have put McCain out of his misery then and there. But he
didn't, and McCain stayed alive, clawing forward with his one
good arm.

By the time the leaves turned orange in New Hampshire, the
GOP had split into several distinct demographics. Giuliani and
McCain were competing for the same moderate on-social-issues-
but-hawkish-on-defense voters. Romney had the potential to
capture the socially cynical, fiscally rich wing of the party (and
Mormons). Fred Thompson, Mike Huckabee, Tom Tancredo,
Sam Brownback, and Duncan Hunter battled it out for the so-
cially conservative, trans fat–loving wing of the party. And Ron
Paul had the easily dismissed, but hard to ignore, die-hard liber-
tarian, antiwar nut jobs all to himself.

As McCain slowly resuscitated his campaign one maple-
syrup-drenched pancake at a time in diners from Concord to
Nashua, he quietly peeled away votes from Rudy. And only Rudy.

The rest of the field were battling within their own little fiefdoms. Whether it would be Rudy or John to emerge victorious, New Hampshire would ultimately lead one of them to a victory speech in St. Paul.

Giuliani's campaign was still acting like we had the election in the bag. Thomas Ravenel, Rudy's handpicked campaign chairman in South Carolina, was indicted for felony cocaine possession and distribution.[3] And Giuliani's Southern regional campaign chair, Senator David Vitter of Louisiana, was caught red-handed in the D.C. Madam's little black book.[4] Both stories fed into the prevailing narrative among the GOP's Southern base that Rudy was a cross-dressing, pro-choice, twice-divorced, gay men's choir, New York pansy. For Rudy to win the nomination, he had to dominate New Hampshire and Iowa, survive in South Carolina, and win big enough with expat New Yorkers in Florida to carry momentum into Super Tuesday. But once Rudy announced he was abdicating the Iowa Straw Poll on August 11, I was starting to suspect that he really wasn't in it to win it.

# The Annapolis Peace Conference

# 4

## Turning a Page with Mark Foley

Don't get me wrong, though. I was still doing my part for Rudy, both stealthily and overtly (as an occasional campaign surrogate and a liaison with the Jewish community, mostly in Florida). Even if he was starting to not believe in himself, I still believed not only that America *deserved* Rudy Giuliani but that we *needed* him.

On the Tuesday before Thanksgiving, I returned to Washington from a stint in Florida. That day, I must confess, I was avoiding going into the office. The interns hadn't been reimbursed for the softball jerseys they paid for but never received. And I was reluctant to have to face them. I would have paid them back out of my own pocket but the Giuliani campaign still hadn't approved my last expense report. I was thinking about taking in a late-afternoon movie when my phone rang.

I assumed it was the institute trying to reach me, as I did tell them four hours ago that I would be in within the half hour. And wasn't there an intern who was supposed to catch a plane home for Thanksgiving? Did I imply that I would drive her to the airport?

I reached for my phone and was relieved when I saw a 225 prefix on the screen, indicating the call was coming from the House of Representatives. It was my old friend Denny Hastert trying to reach me. First time we met, years back, we were both wearing tights. I know that sounds bad. It was a charity event, and as I had grappled JV at Georgetown Day, I relished the opportunity to get back in the ring, especially against Illinois's winningest wrestling coach, Denny Hastert, recently elected to the House and soon to be its Speaker.

So Denny Hastert needed to talk to me. Denny, who had been the rock of our legislative process for close to twenty years, the longest-serving Republican Speaker of the House in U.S. history, needed Martin Eisenstadt. I liked the sound of that. Granted, as of last year's election, he was no longer Speaker and therefore something of a lame duck. And with the Democrats he had kept down all those years now clamoring for his head, Denny had become vulnerable. They were even trying to blame him for the Mark Foley sex scandal. If you ask me, life shouldn't shut down because a randy congressman tries to solicit sex from underage pages. I mean, if we can execute fourteen-year-olds for crimes committed, we surely can hold them responsible for bad sexual decisions and not simply blame the nearest adult (and yes, I say this with the authority of someone who proudly served as a page during one semester in high school).

As I am wont to say, "If proximity were a crime, then all of Washington would be in jail." But Denny, ever the conservative, was not taking any chances. He had already made public his plan to retire at the conclusion of his term. Too many friends and colleagues were getting indicted. And with Tom DeLay and Dick Armey gone, there weren't any lightning rods left to hide behind. Time to move on, he figured.

So was that why Denny was calling? To pick my brain about

Highlight of my page tenure: serving the great congressman from Buffalo, Jack Kemp
*(Courtesy of the author)*

the private sector, to quiz me on the nitty-gritty of parlaying public expertise into private profit? Denny was never bashful about doing his due diligence.

Or maybe . . . No! Please God, no. Could I be in some sort of trouble? Did I once, perhaps, speak ill of Denny behind his back, and only recently was it repeated to him? And now he's irate, unable to rest until he confronts me. I made an immediate resolution to pay more attention to what I say to whom late nights, after too many bourbons, at the Hawk'n'Dove. And then it happened. Razor-sharp memories of past humiliations bombarded my cerebral cortex. I cringed. My body shook. I took a deep breath. I imagined myself swimming in the ocean. I reached for my wallet and popped the anticonvulsant pill that I sometimes take for anxiety.

## Denny Hastert Grips My Balls

I was stopped at the entrance to the Rayburn House Office Building by the Capitol Police because of the weapon I sometimes carry. After hiding my Mace dispenser behind some bushes, I reentered the building and proceeded to Denny's third-floor office. As it was the week of Thanksgiving, I didn't see many people in the halls and stairwells. A voluptuous blonde, wearing a tight-fitting sweater and a Chicago Bears scarf, sat at the reception desk in Denny's office.

"Go in. He's expecting you," instructed the corn-fed beauty who still hadn't really taken notice of me.

"Thank you, darling," I offered with a smile and a stare. No response.

(I'm sorry, dear reader, for fixating so much on one person. But please understand, Denny Hastert was a very important man for a very long time, and he and I were friends. Both as a pundit and as a consultant, knowing Denny Hastert has served me well. I am proud of the relationship we share. More important, if you would just bear with me, you will see that this story leads to the next which leads to the next which, in turn, provides the clues that answer the mystery of who set out to screw me and why.)

I opened the door to Denny's private office. The lights were off. A voice called out, "Turn on the light." I recognized the voice as Denny's but it sounded heavier than I remembered, almost muffled, as if he'd been crying. It took me a second to find the light switch. Not before turning on a fan, an electric bull . . . "The third one. Next to the door. You idiot."

I found the switch, flicked it on. The room was empty in some parts, cluttered with boxes in others, as if someone had been packing, going through things. Denny sat in an imposing brown-leather chair behind a huge mahogany desk. His face was puffy, his eyes red. "Have a seat." I moved a woman's wig from a chair and sat. Denny chowed down the last of his pizza, which was on his desk next to a soda can and a half-eaten bushel of broccoli. Finished with this round of food, Denny stood, guiding his baboon-like frame toward me. I rose from my chair. "Let me give you a hug," gushed Denny, opening his arms wide.

I wasn't going to fall for that trick again. The last time Denny offered me a hug, I ended up in a reverse crossface. So this time I acted first. I reached for his elbow, implemented a backdoor whizzer until I was able to secure him in a pinch headlock. Denny's face turned beet red. I couldn't tell if he was angry or if there was simply no oxygen getting to his face.

"Good one," staggered Denny. "I see the student has outmaneuvered the teacher. Good one." And then came the low blow, the swisher. Next thing I knew I was in a tabletop stance with all of Denny's body weight applied against my chest. "Ha, ha!" barked Denny. "I still got it. Join me for a sauna?"

"As soon as you let go of my balls." We laughed again. The ice had been broken. I was relieved. His massive, moisturizer-soft hand was still gripping my testicles.

## The Secret Sauna

Denny had something important to tell me, and since he was paranoid about recording devices, he insisted that we convene in the personal sauna hidden behind his office. It was common knowledge that Denny had spent a lot of time in Turkey and was a *hamam* enthusiast.

After disrobing in Denny's private bathroom, I opened the door to his makeshift sauna. Denny was already in there sprinkling water on the coals. I was naked. Denny wore a towel. There must have been a misunderstanding.

"Lie down," commanded Denny. Denny removed the towel from his waist and handed it to me. "Use this," I spread his towel on the deck and lay down. "No. Not that way. On your stomach." I turned over.

"You're going to be in Annapolis next week for the big Middle East peace conference, right?" inquired Denny as he dipped a steel scrub into soapy water.

"I wasn't planning on it."

"Of course you'll be there. You're Giuliani's guy for the Hebes."

"Why? What's going on?"

"I don't know how much more of this I can take, Marty. I made it through twenty years, and now with only twelve months to go, they're tightening the screws."

"Who? Who's tightening the screws?"

"The fucking Turks. Who do you think? You didn't see the *Vanity Fair* article?" I had, in fact, seen the article. Something about an FBI whistle-blower swearing up and down that she heard Turkish officials on a wiretap boasting about giving Denny tens of thousands of dollars in bribes.

> *One name, however, apparently stood out—a man the Turkish callers often referred to by the nickname "Denny boy" . . . Edmonds reportedly added that the recordings also contained repeated references to Hastert's flip-flop, in the fall of 2000, over an issue which remains of intense concern to the Turkish government—the continuing campaign to have Congress designate the killings of Armenians in Turkey between 1915 and 1923 a genocide.[1]*

"I wouldn't worry about it," I counseled Denny. "Nobody believes *Vanity Fair* anyhow."

"I'm not worried about *Vanity Fair*, you simpleton. I'm worried about the Turks. Now they want me to introduce legislation supporting Macedonia's inclusion in NATO, for no other reason than to piss off the Greeks. And I'm not even Speaker anymore. But they don't seem to get that. Enough is enough. I will not be blackmailed. Who am I kidding? I'm ruined."

Denny, who was now scrubbing my buttocks and feet, abruptly stopped. He began to pace. I sat up. It must have been two hundred degrees in there. I rubbed my eye. It was all of a sudden really itchy. I panicked that maybe I had caught something from Denny's towel.

"If only Ali knew, he would make them stop. I know he would." Was he talking about Ali Babacan, the foreign minister of Turkey? Denny continued. "Ali and I share a bond. We oil wrestled at sunset on the outskirts of Kirkpinar in front of two thousand villagers and their livestock. On my dear departed mother, it was one of the most moving experiences of my life. I must get to Ali before it's too late. He's going to be in Annapolis for the conference. I need you to be my messenger, to deliver something to him."

"What do you mean, deliver?"

"Stop being such a *hamam oglani*. I'll owe you."

So now I needed to go to Annapolis. I was not looking forward to it. I had long since tired of the Arab-Israeli conflict. And last time I stayed in a motel in Annapolis, I caught bedbugs. But who was I to turn down a former Speaker of the House?

## Unclogging the Pipes

I called my good friend and fellow neocon Daniel Pipes (director of his own think tank, the Middle East Forum) to see if I could hitch a ride with him. Mom's car was in the shop and anyhow I didn't want to deal with parking once I got up there. Pipes said that he didn't have any space, that he needed room for his cats. He was bringing his cats to Annapolis? What a weirdo. Daniel suggested that I instead call Randy Scheunemann.

"I just spoke to him," he explained. "I don't think there's anyone driving with him."

"Do you have his number?" Now mind you, Randy and I go back. We served on the Committee for the Liberation of Iraq (CLI) together. But I didn't have his current info.

"Well if you don't have his number, maybe I shouldn't give it to you. And anyway, he's a McCain guy. There might be friction."

It was true that Randy was a McCain guy, going back to the 2000 Straight Talk Express. He was John's senior adviser for foreign affairs. But why should there be friction? Randy and I were fellow travelers, and I was excited for the opportunity to reconnect with an old friend and close McCain adviser. After watching Team Giuliani botch my Abrad campaign and completely mismanage its online viral presence, I was starting to have doubts about Rudy's viability. I needed to get back in with Randy, just in case.

"Give me his number or I'll tell everyone that you plagiarized my résumé. You know you did. I'm going to expose you, Pipes."

"Okay. Okay. Here it is. But don't tell Randy it was me who gave it to you."

## Turkish Sweat and Blago Shops a Seat

So there I was seated next to Randy Scheunemann, president and founder of the CLI and a top McCain adviser, on our way to Annapolis. I was studying his beard trying to figure out how much time he spent grooming it. I envied the way Randy and Daniel kept such manicured beards. I probably also envied how much money Randy was making from his former east bloc lobbying clients, specifically Georgia. Having spent time in Russia when I worked as a pollster for the Yeltsin campaign, I have firsthand knowledge of how shifty and backstabbing Georgians can be. I needed a cash-cow client like that.

I offered some small talk about Rudy's handpicked former police chief Bernard Kerik's recent indictment on corruption charges. "You know what Rudy said to me when I asked him how I should respond to press inquiries. He said, 'Tell them that in a time of war, the don needs a strong consigliere.'" I waited for Randy to respond to my "heard it from the candidate" tidbit; a chuckle, a sneer, something. He must have had a lot on his mind. We endured more silence until I thought of something else to say. "So, are you excited about the conference?" I inquired.

"To be honest, I'm going there for business. Mauritania is interested in becoming a client. But sure. The world against Iran. I love it. And take your feet off the dashboard." Randy was real touchy about his new Saab 9-3. He had already yelled at me for slamming the door too hard.

For Randy, this gathering was primarily about isolating Iran, since it would be the only Middle Eastern country not attending. I disagreed. I argued that the conference was about something deeper, about propping up America and Israel's ineffectual puppet Abu Mazen as leader and representative of the Palestinian people. Randy might make more than me, but I knew more about the Middle East. I am half Jewish and have spent considerable time in the region.

"Either way, nothing's going to happen," I continued. "Israel won't be making any concessions, and that's all the Arabs care about, so what agreement could—"

"What is that stench?" Scheunemann was sniffing all around himself. "Is that you?" continued Randy as he sniffed in my direction.

"Maybe it's the ointment I put on my eye. I have a sty." I turned my face so he could see.

"Looks like herpes, if you ask me." Herpes? Oh my God. Could I have caught that from Denny's towel? Randy spoke again. "And anyway that's not the smell. It's coming from the back. It's like human sweat but worse." Randy turned for a second, noticing my bag in the backseat.

"Did you bring dirty laundry with you? You did, didn't you? And now I'm smelling olive oil—"

"Oh, that!"

"Oh what?"

I considered making something up. I wasn't sure if it was a good idea to betray Denny's confidence, especially to Randy, a notorious blabbermouth.

"It's a *kisbet*, like a lederhosen but made out of buffalo and calfskin. It's the special outfit that the Turkish wear when they do their traditional oil wrestling. It belongs to Denny Hastert."

"And what's it doing in my car?"

I decided to tell the truth. It was important that Randy see me as a player, as a go-to insider. Plus, it was an amusing story and I thought maybe we could bond over it.

"It's the *kisbet* that Denny wore when he wrestled Ali Babacan, the Turkish foreign minister. It's drenched in olive oil and both their sweat. Denny asked me to deliver it to Ali since I was going to the conference anyway. Denny wants Ali to see it, to smell it, so he will remember the bond they once shared."

"That's the most ridiculous thing I ever heard. Why would Denny do that?"

"Because they're blackmailing him."

"Well, you're a day too late. Don't you watch the news? Yesterday Denny submitted his official letter of resignation to Governor Blagojevich."

"Are you sure?"

"Of course I'm sure. Blago's already shopping his seat."

"I thought Denny was going to wait until the end of his term?"

"He's smart. He didn't want to give the Democrats a chance to investigate him. And by resigning at the start of the Annapolis conference, he got the story buried and pushed aside until no one cares anymore. I thought you were a media guy." Randy merged into the right lane, pulled his car onto the shoulder, and skidded to a stop.

"Get that rancid thing out of my car! I just had it detailed and washed."

"Can I put it in the trunk?"

"You're a real piece of work, Eisenstadt. Fine. Put it in the trunk."

I removed the sealed glass jar with Denny's drenched *kisbet* in it from my bag and transferred it to the trunk. I cushioned it between some rags and returned to the front seat. Randy put the car in drive and we continued our journey.

## Richard's Perles of Wisdom

We soon arrived in Annapolis, quaint and on the water, the drive from D.C. having taken about forty minutes. As I wasn't properly credentialed, I was depending on Randy to get me in. I also needed a place to stay.

"Where are you staying tonight?" I inquired of Randy.

"I'm not. I need to be at Reagan National by six. I'm flying to Florida for tomorrow's YouTube debate. You're not going to be there?"

"Of course I'll be there. My flight's not until tomorrow." My last statement was a half-truth. I hadn't yet bought my ticket. And to be frank, I was getting sick of Florida. With Rudy essentially based there, I had been visiting the Sunshine State too much as it was. I felt like I needed some time in D.C. to get a handle on my think tank and consulting group. I didn't want to get too lost and mired in what was starting to seem like a losing endeavor. It's a trap that a lot of consultants fall into, sacrificing everything for one candidate at the expense of our larger missions.

I grabbed my bag from the backseat and exited the car with Randy. We started to walk. Maybe this was a good time to bring up John McCain, to diplomatically broach the subject of openings and potential availabilities. The Martin Eisenstadt brand was bigger than any one specific campaign, and I needed to have my antennae up.

"So, I hear—"

"Don't forget your jar."

"Oh yeah. Thank you." Randy clicked open his trunk for me. I jogged to the back of the car, looked into the trunk. Oh crap. That can't be good. The jar had shattered. Oil, sweat, glass, leather . . . It was everywhere. And boy, did it stink. I noticed some drenched folders and loose-leafs that must have belonged to Randy. I hoped they weren't important. I started to collect the shards and slivers of glass.

"What are you doing?" he yelled from halfway up the block.

"Nothing."

I dropped the glass back into the trunk, found the *kisbet*, wrapped it in rags, and stuffed it into my bag. I closed the trunk. I caught up to Randy. This wasn't going to be easy but coming clean was the only way. "Randy. There's something I need to tell you, and if you want, I'll even deal with it now. But it's my responsibility. My problem to solve."

Randy didn't seem to be listening to me. He had spotted a friend, somebody apparently more important than Martin Eisenstadt. Was that Richard Perle, America's most famous neocon, getting out of his Hummer? He and Randy hugged. What about me? I wanted to say. You don't remember me from the CLI? We played on the same softball team, you schnook. They walked ahead of me.

"Good afternoon, Mr. Perle, how are you?" I called out.

"Good. Thank you."

He went back to talking to Randy. They're just sore because I was the first from our side to call out as a fraud their good buddy and intended puppet Ahmed Chalabi. That's right. It was me who first warned Randy in 2004 that there was chatter that Chalabi, head of the Iraqi National Congress and CLI member and starting pitcher, might be an Iranian spy, and contrary to his promise, had no intention of building an oil pipeline from Iraq to Israel. But as they say, no good deed goes unpunished. Randy banned me from future CLI meetings, took me off their punditing rotation, and kicked me off the softball team. Even after Special Forces raided Chalabi's Baghdad office and seized documents, Randy still wouldn't admit that I was right. He and Chalabi were close.

At the time, I argued it was a mistake to change the balance of power in Iraq in favor of the majority Shia, that instead we needed to rehabilitate the Bathists and work with Saddam's generals. It's laughable how these two still refuse to accept that it was their sloppiness which emboldened Iran. What were they talking about anyhow? And why were they making it so difficult for me to eavesdrop? Big shots, the two of them. Randy with his east bloc monopoly and Richard with his Kurdistan consortium. I needed to get in on their game, the solid contracts: infrastructure, construction, drilling. Telecommunications I'm less interested in. I met with mixed results when I sold cell phone plans in Baghdad and Mosul just after the invasion.

We passed hecklers and protesters representing the spectrum of political agitation. A crazy man wearing a yellow Jewish star and carrying a sign comparing Bush to Hitler threw a tomato at us. He missed.

"Fuck you, Prince of Darkness!" called out the heckler. I guess someone recognized Richard. An Annapolis cop wrestled the guy to the ground.

Upon arriving at the Naval Academy gate, Randy and Richard went straight in, not slowing down to notice that I had been stopped. The sailor wanted to see my badge. "Randy! Richard!" I called out. They had disappeared behind the very tall Sudanese delegation. But I could still see them. "Randy! Richard!"

They were apparently out of earshot. Now I wouldn't be able to tell Randy about his trunk. I turned back to the sailor and tried explaining to him that I was on the list, that I knew Condi Rice . . .

How was I going to get in now? I could try a different gate, but what was that going to change? I did what I often do when I can't make a decision, I looked for a bar. One thing I love about Annapolis, happy hour starts early. I hurried through a cobblestone, Colonial-era square past groups of midshipmen, young and virile, wearing tight-fitting uniforms and perky white hats. I thought for a second of John McCain and what he must have looked like when he was a student here at the Naval Academy. Too bad things didn't go so great with Randy. His boss was starting to look more and more viable each day.

I reached a bar that I knew from previous visits, Stan and Joe's, wandered in, ordered a drink. I continued to the bathroom, where I positioned my eye in front of a broken mirror. Could it really be herpes? My recently acquired Sprint clamshell cell phone rang. It was Denny Hastert.

"What did Ali say?" Denny demanded.

"I haven't seen him yet. I just got here. I heard you resigned."

"So?"

"So, you still need me to give him the *kisbet*?"

"Of course I do. I've been talking to Dickstein Shapiro about coming on board as a lobbyist, and I kind of implied that I was still tight with the Turks. Turkey is an important client of theirs. I need to know that Ali and I are cool."

"Okay. Sure. There's one problem, though."

"With you, Marty, there's always a problem. Go ahead. What is it?"

"I misplaced my badge, and I'm having trouble getting through security."

Denny chuckled. "Is that it? Let me call someone."

## Old Friends—the Israeli Delegation

Denny called back a little later and instructed me to wait at the northwest gate, where a friend of his would meet me and get me in. I didn't see anyone when I arrived at the gate. I made small talk with the dashing young sailor, buff and smooth skinned, charged with manning his post. And then I felt it, a tap on my shoulder. I turned.

"Marty Eisenstadt, we meet again."

"Hey, Ehud, how are you doing?"

"I'm doing great. I am prime minister of a little place called Israel. You heard of it?" Ehud Olmert, chuckling condescendingly, continued: "How are *you* doing is the question?"

"I'm great. I have a think tank now. It's called the Harding Institute. Maybe you heard of it?"

"I don't think so. Did you see my new Breitling?" Ehud lifted his sleeve so I could see his watch. "It was up in space with the cosmonauts. Check out the diamonds. It was a gift." While I admired his Breitling, Ehud, chomping on a fat cigar, blew smoke in my face. I coughed.

"Actually, Ehud, I was hoping you could do me a favor."

"You mean, get you into the conference?"

"I misplaced my badge."

"I know all about you, Marty. I just got off the phone with Denny Hastert. I must say, though, if I had known it was you, I wouldn't have wasted my time."

"Why would you say that? You and I, we go back."

"I saw you that time on CNN, during the Lebanon War, making fun of me, saying that because I'm a lawyer I don't know how to fight wars. That hurt, Marty. That really hurt." I did recall saying something along those lines but only because Wolf had put me on the spot and Donna Brazile had just said something clever and everyone else on the panel but me was a lawyer. And anyway, what was Olmert doing watching CNN in the middle of a war?

"I'm pretty sure I was taken out of context. But still, let me have my office issue a formal apology."

"Screw you and your apology. I'll show you and I'll show the world. What we couldn't do to the Lebanese, we'll do to the Palestinians. Just you wait and see. And then the world will fear us again, and history will remember Ehud Olmert forever alongside Moses, King David, and Anne Frank. Ironic, no?"

"I'm not sure 'ironic' is the word you're looking for."

"You think you're better than me, Marty. Admit it. That I'm some provincial Middle Easterner who dances the hora, drinks

milk out of a bag, and needs help from his rich American uncle.
Well, look at us now. I'm not mayor of rinky-dink Jerusalem
anymore. I'm prime minister! And as opposed to you, my mother
didn't get me the job." I must admit, that stung a bit. He continued: "I stayed in the VIP suite at Blair House last night. When I
arrived, there was a message from your president. He had called
to get my advice on an important matter. When Ehud Olmert
sticks his dick into the earth, the world spins. You can't even get
into a measly conference about nothing."

"Then don't do it for me. Do it for Denny. He's helped Israel
a lot over the years."

"Screw Denny Hastert. He's nobody now. Yesterday's news."

"Come on, Mr. Prime Minister, you owe me." He liked that I
called him Mr. Prime Minister. I could tell.

"I owe you? Ha!"

"I introduced you to Morris Klein, the strip-mall developer
from Miami."

"What are you talking about? I met him at an AIPAC convention."

"I know. I was there. You made millions off him, and I never
got my cut. I was supposed to get a finder's fee."

"You didn't get your fee? This is the first I'm hearing of that. I
had no idea. Why didn't you tell me?"

"I did tell you. Numerous times."

"Marty, how many times have I told you? The Middle East is
not the Midwest. And the Arabs, they're not like us Westerners.
They enjoy killing children. We do it with heavy hearts. You don't
see the difference?"

"Of course I see the difference."

"All right, Marty. My heart is feeling warm today. What do
you got?"

"What do you mean, what do I got?"

"Let me see your wallet."

I handed him my wallet. He removed and pocketed for himself my Metro card and all the cash that I had, seventeen dollars. He turned to the midshipman guard. "Okay. Let him in." Ehud disappeared as quickly as he'd appeared, rejoining his awaiting entourage of heavily armed security and sniveling assistants. I was in. Now to find Ali Babacan, foreign minister of Turkey.

## Marty Gets Crabs

The problem with this gathering of foreign ministers was that everyone looked the same. I spotted someone who looked different, the Chinese foreign minister, Yang Jiechi. I had met Yang at a WTO meeting in Cancun a couple of years back. I asked him where everyone was. He said they were attending a democracy symposium led by America's mustachioed ambassador to the UN, the always dignified John Bolton. But that afterward there would be a reception at Buchanan House, residence to the academy superintendent, Vice Admiral Jeffrey Fowler. Yang suggested that we go see if it was already set up, that maybe we could sneak in early.

When we arrived, the catering staff was still preparing the lavish spread that was to be called "Where the Middle East Meets Maryland." On one side, there was hummus, shish kebab, falafel, and a shawarma rotisserie. On the other side, there was seafood and more seafood; crab cakes, crab quiches, and crab mini burgers along with monster lobster rolls and fresh shrimp cocktail. Half of the waiters wore turbans while the other half wore pirate eye patches. As all the servers were Mexican, I decided to ask Miguel, who was filling the crab plate that I was noshing from, which part of the Middle East he was from. "The southern part," he answered.

I moseyed over to the bar and ordered myself a Maker's Mark. I was looking forward to the certainty of confidence that Maker's always gives me.

Drink in hand, I peered into the admiral's telescope, maneuvered it past frigates, over the Annapolis harbor to a luxury yacht with sunbathers. I was trying to focus it when the foreign ministers walked in. Arguing, backslapping, and boasting, they barreled through the doors like a stampede of peacocks. One step ahead of the competition, I ran to the seafood buffet and filled my plate with crab cakes. In a minute, this place would be overrun. And then I saw her across the room, Tzipi Livni, with her sexy blonde hair and pouty freckled face, foreign minister of Israel. How long had it been? She hasn't aged a day, I thought. She just gets more and more beautiful.

Personal disclosure: Tzipi and I shared a night of passion back in the eighties when she was living in Paris and I was a student on my way to Cairo for a semester abroad. I actually first met her friend Ronit in the hostel where I was staying. When I mentioned that my father was Jewish and that I was on my way to study in Egypt, she invited me to a party at a friend's in the thirteenth arrondissement. Most of the people at the party were Israelis. When Ronit introduced me to her friend Tzipi—blonde and slender, with big feet (just like I like them)—I was immediately smitten. She laughed at my jokes. She told me she'd had six too many drinks. One thing led to another. There was a real chemistry between us.

Even though I hadn't seen her in twenty years, I couldn't help feeling a little jealous that she was being so cozy with that notorious lady hustler Amir Moussa, the barrel-chested secretary-general of the Arab League. The way they walked and laughed together, it was like they shared a dirty secret.

I was leaning on the seafood buffet, gorging on fresh-out-of-the-water Chesapeake crab, when Tzipi strolled over. The other Israelis looked at Tzipi with spite as she fawned all over Secretary-General Moussa. With his beige suit and designer European glasses, Amir smiled wide. She was already on her second drink. I had been watching her. Quite the gentleman, Mr. Moussa stuck out his thick hand to me. "Amir Moussa."

"I know, of course. Marty Eisenstadt." I replied.

"I remember you. We met in Baghdad at Bremer's palace. You got hummus on my Hugo Boss tie." I still cringe when I recall that night. You see, I'd inadvertently smoked hashish before the event thinking it was a cigarette. To put it mildly, I wasn't at my best.

I nervously turned to Tzipi. I'd been following her career from afar, but as she entered politics late, I hadn't seen her in person since that night and morning (not that I'm bragging) in Paris. "It's been so long. How have you been?" When I leaned in to hug her, she pulled back.

"I'm sorry, you must have me confused with someone else." Icily, she moved on to another table.

It was time to get drunk. I went to the open bar and ordered a double, and when I finished that, drank another.

From this point forward I remember only in bits, without segues, without chronological clarity. But I was on a roll. I remember well that I was on a roll. I remember having a long conversation with Pietro Parolin, undersecretary of foreign affairs for the Vatican. I remember a little robot blowing up my bag with Denny's *kisbet* in it, which I forgot in the stairway when I went there to smoke a cigarette even though I had quit under hypnosis six months earlier. I remember finding Ali Babacan and trying to explain to him that Denny Hastert sent me, but the *kisbet* got blown up by a robot. I remember a befuddled Ali Babacan shooing me away.

I remember Amir Moussa leaving and Tzipi Livni staying. I remember a tipsy Condi Rice manhandling Tzipi. I remember seeing the two of them climb into one of the stylized tents erected by the catering company as a tribute to the free Bedouin spirit. Condi played bongos. Tzipi belly danced. They writhed like two jungle cats. I think the spry and svelte Taieb Fassi Fihri, foreign minister of Morocco, with his piercing desert eyes, was in there too showing them how to light the hookah. I admit it. I felt left out.

But generally I had a good time and felt confident, like I was representing myself and the Harding Institute well. My words were fluid, my excitement constant. I had a great conversation with Maria de Lourdes Aranda Bezaury, Mexico's undersecretary for foreign relations, whom I at first mistook for a caterer but managed to bond with after winning her over with amusing anecdotes from the Middle East. I told her about my time in Iraq, about the Iraqi boy I used to pay two dollars a day to clean my car, do my laundry, and give me back rubs.

The undersecretary excused herself to go to the bathroom, rather abruptly I might add. I noticed a sexy, dark-haired beauty with an Al Arabiya (the popular Dubai-based news and entertainment channel) name tag. Smartest thing we ever did was set up those "independent" Arab satellite stations. Six months of Western-style TV does more to pacify and grow a people than sixty years of occupation. I readied myself to approach her. But before I even took a step, my old friend Daniel Pipes, who wouldn't give me a ride, with his perfectly manicured beard, intercepted her. He said something that made her laugh. Knowing Daniel, it was probably in Arabic. How pathetic. I thought about getting another drink. Instead, I helped myself to more Maryland crab. This time I tried some shrimp too. The sauce was delicious. Another gentleman was also helping himself to a plate, and I glanced over.

## Rocking the Casbah with Sharif Investments

Muscled like someone who boxes or works out regularly in a gym, Jamie Melnick, CEO of Zen Management, as his name tag read, exuded machismo. I had the advantage that everyone, aside from me, was wearing a name tag. Balding but fighting it well with Rogaine, Jamie looked like the kind of guy who had a very hot girlfriend. He smiled at me.

"I couldn't help but overhear that you spent time in Iraq. I might be going there myself. If you don't mind me asking, what were you doing there?"

"I was a consultant to the Provisional Authority. I helped draft the Iraqi constitution. I was also involved in a multinational telecommunications project in the north."

"So you're a consultant?"

"And strategist. Martin Eisenstadt. Here's my card."

"Senior fellow at the Harding Institute?" remarked Jamie as he squinted at my card.

"Maybe you've seen me on TV. I appear on *Hardball* a lot. What about you? What's your game?"

"Casinos."

"Really? I did lobbying work for the Chippewa. I helped them get around a federally mandated slot-machine limit."

At that point, a dashing Arabian man, brown with soft features, sidled up to Jamie. "Nabil, I think you should meet this man, Martin Eisenstadt. He worked as a consultant in Iraq, and he has experience with casinos."

His name tag read "Nabil Al-Rahamani, President, Sharif Investments." Wait. I had heard of Sharif Investments. That was a $20 billion fund, the personal money of the Omani crown prince. These guys were serious. Nabil commented that I looked familiar.

"He appears on TV a lot," piped in Jamie.

"Did Jamie tell you what we're about?"

"I left that for you," responded Jamie respectfully.

With his music-to-my-ears British accent, which I imagined he had picked up at the best boarding schools in England, Nabil continued. "Our mandate at Sharif Investments is simple: developing, building, and managing high-profile hospitality projects with an emphasis on gaming. In fact, I just now had a conversation with Ali Babacan, foreign minister of Turkey, about putting four hundred tables and ten thousand slot machines in the casbah of old Istanbul. How are we different? you're probably asking. A lot of funds are financing luxury hotels in the Middle East.

But for them the casino is an afterthought. For us, it's front and center. It's intertwined with the whole overall aesthetic. Jamie can explain that better than me."

Jamie took over. "Essentially, we're about maximizing gaming profits by merging that Las Vegas pizzazz with traditional Oriental hospitality in a sleek synthesis of modernity and functionality."

"And we're not afraid to be bold and loud," interjected the prince. "We don't put our casinos in the outskirts. We put them in the town center. And we like to be ahead of the curve. For example, why is there no luxury hotel slash casino in Baghdad? You know how much disposable income passes through that Green Zone every day? I know. I'm from the next country over."

"I couldn't agree more," I said. "Isn't the Marriott hotel chain already building something there?"

"Yes, but without gambling."

"No. You're right. It's got to be a casino. Between the brass and the contractors and the diplomats, the Green Zone is an untapped gold mine. And as long as we continue our occupation, which could be another hundred years, it's completely protected. It's a brilliant idea. I love it."

"You're forgetting the best part, Mr. Eisenstadt. The Green Zone is waterfront."

"You can't go wrong with waterfront," I threw in.

"The Middle East is changing," continued Nabil. "Baghdad will someday be like Beirut and Dubai. And Sharif Investments likes to get in early."

"What happens in the Green Zone stays in the Green Zone," I added. "Has a nice ring to it."

Nabil turned to Jamie. "I like this guy."

I was on a roll, so I kept going. "And we can pitch it as a way to bring the different ethnic groups together. We'll show pictures of smiling families cheering a roulette table. We'll emphasize the employment opportunities it will bring. I love it. Are you guys gonna have a presence at the 'Business 2 Business Expo' they're having in February?"

"I don't know," answered Nabil. "The main reason we came here today was to talk with Hoshyar Zebari."

"Foreign minister of Iraq?" I interjected.

"Precisely. A source said he would be here."

"Well, he's not. No one from the Iraqi delegation is here."

Nabil turned to Jamie. "You thinking what I'm thinking?" Jamie nodded. They both looked at me, but Nabil spoke. "You ever do any lobbying, Mr. Eisenstadt?"

"Of course. All the time. That's what I do."

"And you know some of the players over there?"

"Know the players? I ran a major telecommunications project in the north, so if you mean do I know who to bribe and who to threaten, the answer is yes. More important, I was one of the original members of the Committee for the Liberation of Iraq. So I'm tight with all those guys. In fact, I was just talking before with Richard Perle about the Kurdistan consortium he's putting together."

"Take our cards. Jamie, give him your card." I shook both their hands as they now appeared to be preparing to leave. Nabil took out his BlackBerry. "I'm shooting you a text from my BlackBerry. I'm glad we met. I'm excited about this."

I waved goodbye to them as they huddled feverishly on their way to the door. After they were gone for a couple of minutes, I let the air out of my lungs. Wow. Exactly what I had been hoping for. Like Perle and Scheunemann, I was getting my very own overseas cash cow. This day couldn't have worked out better. I helped myself to another crab cake. When I looked up, I was face-to-face with Tzipi Livni.

"So I wasn't crazy. You did remember. I guess what they say is true: love felt even for a moment becomes eternal." I was drunk and feeling poetic.

"That wasn't love, you stupid American, that was an exam. I

was in the Mossad back then and we thought to recruit you, but to join our ranks you must be able to perform acts of amour of a certain caliber. Needless to say, you failed your exam. Good night, Mr. Eisenstadt." Tzipi grabbed a crab cake and returned to the dance floor, where she boogied with a group of twenty-year-old midshipmen.

All I could think of at that moment was, where am I going to sleep? I had been drinking for a long time and was now fatigued and becoming grouchy, so I did what any sensible person with a history of travel would have done, and looked for someone from the Indian delegation. Having been to India, I can tell you, they're used to sleeping seven in a bed. Why do you think there's a billion of them?

Although the reception had significantly thinned out by then, with the main delegate bus already on its way back to Washington, I noticed that the Indian representative, Kapil Sibal, minister of technology and earth sciences, and the Pakistani foreign minister, Riaz Mohammad Khan, were still there. Huddled in a corner, they argued over which was worse, eating meat or drinking alcohol. Kapil drank whiskey while Riaz licked shawarma off his fingers. Each looked at the other with disgust. I decided to join the discussion. I must have said something inappropriate because the Pakistani foreign minister soon called me an idiot and stormed away, leaving me alone with Kapil.

I asked Kapil a question about yoga. I mixed into my words that I had no place to stay that night and perhaps I would just wander the streets till morning . . . He kindly invited me to crash in his hotel room. He was excited to spend an extra day in Annapolis. As a minister of earth sciences, he especially appreciated East Coast autumns and was looking forward to an extra day to study the changing colors of the leaves. He had even brought a special magnifying glass with him. We left the party together.

## A New Ailment to Worry About

When we arrived at Kapil's hotel we took the elevator to a more than acceptable room overlooking the harbor. He took one side of the bed. I took the other. What a kind man, I thought. Note to self: Drunks are better people than meat eaters.

A few hours later, I awoke drenched in sweat with a pain in my left big toe that words don't exist to describe. When I looked at it, I saw that it was red, swollen, and apparently spreading. It was like somebody had inserted shards of broken glass against my joints inside the bottom of my toe. Any contact or movement, even the wind or the touch of a bedsheet, sent me into a tizzy, the kind of piercing pain that people scream out from.

My ex-wife liked to call me a hypochondriac, but she's wrong. I'm actually quite relaxed. It's just that I keep getting these ailments, and as I don't always have proper medical insurance, I sometimes have to self-diagnose, which is fine, as I firmly believe in the free market system. In the event that something catastrophic were to befall me, I could always go to an emergency room and give a fake name and address.

This time, I was thankfully sharing the bed with a doctor. I awoke Kapil. He put on his glasses and looked at my toe through his special magnifying glass. He took my pulse. He asked me if I injured it somehow. I said no, and then surprised even myself in how loud I screamed. I had never experienced such pain in my life.

"What did you eat today?" asked the doctor from India.

"It's a foot injury. What difference does it make what I ate?" Serves me right for seeking medical advice from an Indian "doctor." I was worried about the dollar falling against the rupee, but not anymore. What a quack. As I'm wont to say, Eastern medicine is an oxymoron. When I finally told him that I had eaten a lot of seafood the night before, he suggested that perhaps I had gout.

"Gout? Isn't that what fat British colonialists used to get?"

"It has nothing to do with being fat," he explained. "It comes from having too much purine in your blood. And from my experience, the two leading causes of attacks are eating excessive amounts of shellfish and drinking excessive amounts of alcohol." Strangely, the institute's namesake, Warren G. Harding, who died while in office, was thought to have eaten bad crabs. Then again, that could have been a cover story to protect Harding's wife, Florence, who to this day remains a suspect in Warren G.'s premature death.[2] President Harding did have a reputation as a ladies' man. The pain. I couldn't take it anymore. I clenched my fists, banged my head. It felt like someone was sawing my toe. I looked to my cell phone, which was blinking. I assumed it was an inane text message from my early-rising father, now retired in California, until I saw that it came from a 702 area code. Dad has a 310 number. Where is 702? I opened the message.

*Looking forward to doing business with you. We might need you to go to Iraq for us sooner rather than later. Either way, we're going to fly you out to Vegas in the next week or so.* I scrolled down. *Will call you in the morning. Best, Nabil and Jamie. Sent from a Black-Berry.*

YES!

# 5

# Casinos in the Green Zone

## The Key Is Florida

Over the next couple of weeks Nabil and Jamie repeatedly talked about flying me out to Vegas to meet with their team and develop a strategy for our casino in the Green Zone. But the trip kept being postponed. First, Nabil was away, back home in Oman celebrating Eid-ul-Adha with his family; then it was Christmas, then New Year's. It was already January and I still hadn't been paid anything, although I had already donated numerous hours of my time. So when Mike DuHaine, campaign manager for Team Giuliani, asked me to spend time in Florida courting Jewish voters for the run-up to the critical January 29 primary, I embraced the challenge. Plus, I looked forward to escaping winter a bit. It would be good for my health.

It had been frustrating to watch my hero and boss Rudy Giuliani slip so fast in the polls. I repeatedly warned Brent Seaborn, Giuliani's strategy director, that abdicating New Hampshire and Iowa to focus on Florida was a colossal error, an idiot's gamble.

## Seven Reasons to Run for President

It's been drilled into our heads since we were in kindergarten that our highest possible aspiration in life is to grow up to be president of the United States (at least we know Barack Obama drank that Kool-Aid). But rarely do people stop to wonder just exactly why. Why do people put themselves through a lifetime of chastity, four years of nonstop campaigning and hustling like a common whore for money, and then a 20 percent chance of dying in office? There must be *some* good reasons to run for president—right?

1. To be the leader of the free world

2. Private jet

3. Personal chef

4. Personal chef ON your private jet

5. Having the ability to destroy the planet with a single push of a button

6. The wisdom to think that's probably a bad idea

7. Interns

And I was right. After winning in New Hampshire and South Carolina, McCain, who two months prior was dead in the water, emerged as the front-runner. Huckabee, because he won Iowa, became the conservative alternative to McCain. And then there was Romney. By winning Michigan, even he passed us in the polls. To this day I don't understand how he managed to get a single vote. For God's sake, he's a Mormon. To be fair, he was spending a lot of money and seemed to know what he was talking about when it pertained to business and the economy. So that was the state of affairs. Two months prior, Rudy was the undisputed national front-runner and now he was running

But if you think about it, those are really reasons to *be* president, not to *run* for president. Turns out that people run for all sorts of other reasons beyond actually *wanting* to be president. Some like the adrenaline rush of a campaign: the adoring crowds, the speeches, the beautiful web videographers covering your every move (yes, John Edwards, I'm talking about you). Washington isn't called Hollywood for ugly people for nothing. For an overweight, bald, sixty-year-old white male lawyer, running for president is as close to winning an Oscar as he'll ever get. More important, if you lose in the primaries and miraculously survive unscarred by scandal, you will forevermore be known as "former presidential candidate Joe Schmo" when your *New York Times* obituary is printed, rather than just "former state assemblyman Joe Schmo, who died penniless and homeless." Finally, if you're like Rudy Giuliani and you've built up a very lucrative international consulting business, then your billable consulting rate could triple, or more. As Rudy would soon find out, losing the presidency may be tough on the ego, but it's great for the bottom line.

fourth in Florida, New York's sister state, the state that was supposed to be the linchpin of our winning strategy. What a bunch of idiots. I should have known when they botched my Abrad video campaign that this team couldn't beat a six-year-old in chess, let alone win a national election.

## Scaring Old Jews with Bernie Madoff and Chuck Norris

"What? Could you say that again?" I was sitting on a panel with a couple of other campaign surrogates at the Beth Shalom synagogue in Palm Beach, Florida. I couldn't quite hear the question posed by the distinguished-looking gentleman with the tossed-back gray hair and meticulous wardrobe. He put the microphone closer to his mouth. I squinted past a sea of old, rich Jews to better see who was asking the question.

"Where does Rudy stand on extradition of white-collar criminals? I know he was very aggressive as a DA and state's attorney."

"And tell me your name, please?"

"Bernie Madoff," he stammered, almost shy. A hushed silence quickly gave way to whispers and murmurs. I guess a lot of people knew this guy.

"Excellent question, Bernie, and I'm glad you asked it. I know this is an issue of concern to a lot of you, and I want to reassure you that Rudy supports policies that skew in favor of the rich and elderly. And he was there on 9/11!" The crowd cheered. "Muslim terrorists are coming to kill you, your children, and your grandchildren." Supporters cheered. "Rudy took on the Mafia and won!" I expected that to be an applause line but few seemed to care. "He got rid of the squeegee guys!" Some applause. "And he was there on 9/11!" The crowd cheered. People stood from their seats to clap and whistle.

"And what about Israel?" somebody called out from the crowd. Chuck Norris, who was there for Huckabee, tried to tell a story about shooting *Delta Force* in Israel with legendary filmmakers Golan and Globus. To his chagrin, Joe Lieberman cut him off.

Senator Joe was there representing John McCain. After wrestling the microphone from Chuck, Joe stood up so he could wander and pace while addressing the audience. "I know John McCain, and you can take my word for it, John supports Israel in his kishkes. His foreign policy will be completely lopsided in Israel's favor!" The crowd cheered. "Sure, Rudy talks a good game. He's from New York. What do you expect? He grew up around Jews." Joe suddenly grinned wide. "Have you heard this one? What's the difference between an Italian and a Jew? Twenty IQ points." The crowd laughed.

## Blacks and Jews

If you live long enough . . . A black man is president. The Kennedys are power brokers again. And thanks to the über-investor Bernie Madoff, the Jews are broke, back to *Fiddler on the Roof* times. Life apparently works in cycles.

After the panel discussion and questions from the audience, there was a bagels-and-lox reception in the downstairs social hall, where Joe Lieberman and I struck up a nice conversation. He was impressed with my handle on Middle East issues. Joe asked why we hadn't met before. I reminded him that we did in fact once meet, at a Committee for the Liberation of Iraq softball game. (He and his buddy John McCain were CLI honorary co-chairs.) Joe was obviously starting to feel comfortable around me because his next words were uttered quietly, against my ear. "I know Bernie. I can get you in." Before I could respond, we became surrounded by a gaggle of blue-haired yentas who wanted their pictures taken with Joe. I decided to check my phone messages. I had put my phone on "silent" for the panel event, and I just now noticed that someone had been trying to reach me. Before I could even see who it was, my phone blinked on. A call was coming through. "Hello."

"Things are moving fast. We need you out here in Vegas." It was Nabil and Jamie. As usual, Nabil did most of the talking. "There's a plane waiting for you at Miami Dade. Can you be there in an hour?" The Florida primary was ten days away. It was down to the wire, and I had told the campaign that I would stay in Florida until after the vote. I think they were even expecting me to help break down the headquarters after the twenty-ninth, whether Rudy won or lost. Why am I even wasting my time agonizing over this? Giuliani ain't winning. Once again I had picked the losing horse. I started to resent all the crap I had taken from the campaign brass. All the trouble they gave me every time I turned in an expense report. Screw these clowns. What have they ever done for me? They themselves were going to be unemployed in ten days while Sharif Investments was around for a long time and had limitless pockets. Heck, I'm in the private sector. And everyone knows that in this town there's no better gig than an Iraq contract and no better sponsor than oil money from the Gulf. "Miami Dade in an hour? No problem."

Nabil seemed pleased. "Excellent. See you in Vegas."

## One Night in Vega$

I was the only passenger on the Gulf Stream III that took me from Florida to Nevada. I kind of expected these guys to at least have a Gulf Stream IV. The IV is a smoother ride. A stewardess served me a cocktail. When I awoke, we were over the desert beginning our descent into McCarran Airport, just south of Las Vegas.

A limousine met me at the airport and brought me to the Bellagio on the Strip. Everywhere I looked I saw Democrats. The

In front of the Paris hotel with Chelsea Clinton (Photograph by America Ferrera)

Nevada Democatic Caucus, a must-win for Team Hillary, was only two days away, and the campaigns had sent out their big guns. I, however, was there on business and needed to stay focused on the task at hand. There would be time later to socialize and network (see graph). I approached the front desk and informed the clerk that I was a guest of Jamie Melnick. From that point forward, it was like being a king, president, or contestant on a reality television show. A busboy led me to a special floor reserved for high rollers and VIPs. After perusing the adult channels, I went to meet Jamie and Nabil at Bouchon, the high-end French restaurant at the Venetian.

Nabil had a lot of questions for me. "You're going to go through the parliament or through the Americans?"

"A combination. You see, I've already been there. So I know the red tape."

"And you feel comfortable handling this on your own?" interjected Jamie. "Maybe we should put together a team. We've been talking to Randy Scheunemann over at Orion Strategies. Do you know him?"

"Sure. I know him. And he's a great shortstop if you need a ringer for your softball team, but Randy doesn't know the Middle East like I know it. He's more of a Balkans kind of guy. Plus, between you and me"—I looked around—"he's in a bit of hot water now. It's been alleged that information passed to his buddy Chalabi 'somehow' ended up in the hands of the Iranians. But I'm not one to spread gossip."

"But he's with McCain. McCain might be the next president."

"Exactly. The campaign is heating up now. Randy's going to be too busy. This project needs a 24-7 commitment. You don't think so?"

"I like it that you're not afraid to throw your friend under the bus. That's why we picked you. We do our due diligence. Make sure you have all your shots. We're flying you to Baghdad for the Business 2 Business Expo."

## Rolling with Holy Joe

Comfortably seated in the Crown Lounge at Dulles International, just outside of Washington, D.C., I looked up at the electronic board to see that my flight to Amman had been delayed

# The Las Vegas Strip
### *January 17, 2008*

9:00 p.m. – Check into the Bellagio. Is that Michael Dukakis in front of me arguing over his pay-per-view bill?

10:30 p.m. – Meet Nabil and Jamie at Bouchon in the Venetian. Next table over, Wesley Clark sucks up to grocery mogul Ron Burkle.

Midnight – Jamie takes me to the Palazzo, where we run into Chelsea Clinton and campaign surrogate America Ferrera ("Ugly Betty") unwinding over Martinis after long day of stumping. Jamie invites them to join us down the block at the Flamingo.

*Circus Circus*

1:30 p.m. – Flamingo. Celebrity host Billy Joel kindly takes our coats. Can't make up my mind who to hit on, Chelsea or America. Girls want to leave. I tag along.

3:15 a.m – Planet Hollywood. 50 Cent event nowhere to be found. Give bellhop $100 to tell us that party is at the Trop.

2:00 a.m. – Basement of New York–New York. Warren Christopher, Dukakis, and rich Indian chief play no-limits poker at private table. I tell Indian chief that I did sweat lodge once. He asks me why I talk so much. I proudly inform him that I am a pundit. We hear about 50 Cent party over at Planet Hollywood.

❸ *Palazzo*
❷ *Venetian*
*Mirage*

❹ *Flamingo*

*Bellagio* ❶
❾ *Paris*
❻ *Planet Hollywood*

4:00 a.m. – Tropicana. 50 Cent shindig turns out to be Obama fund-raiser. When Christopher's manservant accidentally steps on 50 Cent's toe, all hell breaks loose. Scarlett Johansson, fanatic Obama supporter, and America get into catfight. I pull them off each other.

*New York–New York* ❺

*Excalibur* ❽
❼ *Tropicana*

6:00 a.m. – Sun rises. America and I sit on curb in front of Excalibur. I tell her that I often appear on Chris Matthews. She asks if I am a sexist. I say, "Of course not." She leans her head against my shoulder . . . [redacted due to legal proceedings initiated by America's attorneys]

❿

10:00 a.m. – America and I meet Chelsea for eggs and mimosas at Paris.

Noon – I catch flight back to Washington.

once more. From Amman I was to fly to Baghdad. As Rudy had placed fourth in Florida and subsequently dropped out, I could now focus all my attention on my new client, a $20 billion fund. I had already checked my luggage and was looking forward to flying halfway around the world on someone else's dime. I didn't even care that the interns would be using and abusing my office all the time I was gone. Last time I returned from a trip overseas, I found a dental retainer in my desk drawer. When I asked Eli about it, he informed me that it was better I didn't know, so in the event of an investigation I could legitimately claim ignorance. But today, nothing could dampen my good spirits. I had been paid. And as I had already deposited the $20,000 check from Sharif Investments into the Harding Institute account, I didn't have a care in the world. Although technically it was the Eisenstadt Group that would be doing the consulting/lobbying, for tax purposes we sometimes find it beneficial, for all concerned, to fudge the boundaries and involve the institute. And I do it with a clean conscience. We Republicans are against taxes. It's part of our faith, and a man's faith is sacred, protected by the First Amendment. I was suddenly distracted. That voice. It was so familiar. I turned around.

"Senator Lieberman, how are you?"

"Wonderful. Grateful to be alive." He flashed his trademark "golly gee, I'm just happy to be here" smile and continued. "Don't you just love America? There's no other country like it. Where else could a son of immigrants grow up to be a senator?"

"Isn't Sarkozy, prime minister of France, the son of immigrants?"

"You're a bit of a contrarian, aren't you?"

"Must be all that Talmud in my DNA." As I'm wont to say, when in Rome, I like to wear a toga. Being a chameleon comes easy to me.

"A *yiddishe cup*, we call it," remarked the senator. I laughed knowingly. I later looked up *yiddishe cup*: it means "a Jewish head." I'm actually only half Jewish.

"Well, it's good to see you again, Senator."

"And when is it I saw you last?" I was starting to think that the senator had no idea who I was.

"Marty Eisenstadt. We were on the Committee for the Liberation of Iraq together. And I appeared with you a couple of weeks ago at Beth Shalom in Palm Beach."

"Of course. Too bad about Rudy. But how do you like *my* boy? I couldn't be prouder."

"My boy too. I love John McCain. Always have. I even supported him in 2000." A half-truth when you consider that I was involved in the South Carolina whispering campaign in which we successfully spread the rumor that John had fathered an illegitimate black baby. "And once I get back from Iraq, I intend to officially join up."

"You're on your way to Iraq now?"

"Gonna be my second visit."

"God bless you. And check out the Shorja market. I bought my granddaughter a wonderful backgammon set there. If you buy two, the third one is free. They really do make great gifts."

"You know, Senator, I was thinking recently. We took a lot of criticism for this war. But that's just people. They love to panic, to think the sky is falling. But we stood tough and implemented the surge. What am I saying, we? It was you and Senator McCain and General Petraeus. You're a true American hero. Thank you. Sincerely." I touched the flag pin on my lapel and extended my hand. We shook again. He was genuinely moved.

"You're a good man, Marty Eisenstadt. I look forward to working with you on the campaign." The senator needed to go. An aide was hurrying him along.

And then it hit me, could I really count on my friends over at the McCain campaign to hook me up? Sometimes friends are the last to help you out. This was a real opportunity. Seize it. "I hope so. I mean, I'm a tad concerned because a lot of the key positions on the campaign are being filled right now, and I'm going to be in Iraq."

"Don't you worry. I'll be seeing John after the weekend. I'll make sure to put in a good word. We could use a bushy-tailed go-getter like yourself on our team."

"Would you? Thank you. I appreciate that."

"Safe travels." He placed his hand on my head and muttered a Hebrew blessing. "God be with you." And then he was gone.

## What Happens in the Green Zone Stays in the Green Zone

The business expo was held in the Rashid Hotel deep inside the Green Zone. Companies, both Iraqi and foreign, set up booths to showcase their products and make their cases to investors and buyers. Two hundred and thirty-three companies were represented with more than eight thousand invited guests participating. Hitachi was there promoting a new power tool. Humbolt Security displayed a bomb-detection device that you could keep in your pocket. The state company for tobacco offered sample cigarettes. Motorola was there unveiling a text-message system that operates even when general cell-phone service is down (a common occurrence in Iraq, as terrorists often use cell phones to activate their bombs). I "accidentally" knocked over their display case. (If it wasn't for Motorola, I would be a very rich man today. Back in 2003, it was me who traveled around the country venturing into hostile territory to convince the nomads and rural folk that they needed cell phones, but it was Motorola who got the contract to build the towers. Instead of cutting me in, they shamelessly shoved me aside and stole the customer base I worked so hard to recruit.)

I noticed an Iraqi television crew conducting interviews with vendors and dignitaries. As a professional pundit, I sensed an opportunity to get the word out about my project, to create a

## Interview with Iraqi TV: Partial Transcript

*(Courtesy of YouTube)*

**MARTY:** But yes, the pizzazz, the Vegas pizzazz, that American can-do, let's have fun, we're all one attitude, yes, unapologetically we're going to bring that here to Baghdad but mixed with local sensibilities.

**INTERVIEWER:** *Insha'alah.* If you could educate us more about your background in the United States.

"buzz," if you will. I spoke to the Iraqi gentleman in charge. I smooth-talked him into doing a segment with me. It was important that I manage a little public relations before diving into the actual lobbying. It was a format I knew well, and I was excited to argue my talking points directly to the Iraqi people. And if you ask me, my appearance on Iraqi television alone was worth the twenty grand Sharif Investments paid me. Nabil and Jamie seemed to differ. But they're not political people. They don't appreciate the complexities and nuances of lobbying. They have this strange idea that only results matter. They don't understand that lobbying is a process. And I was happy with the interview I gave. Little did I know that it would land me in hot water a

**MARTY:** I'm probably soon going to be an adviser to John McCain, since my candidate, Rudy Giuliani, dropped out. And I can assure you that John McCain supports this effort, John McCain who will likely be the next American president. And John McCain as the head of the Indian Affairs Committee in the Senate knows hands-on, full well the importance of development and how a casino, how a sauna, how a golf course can transform a people, can transform a region and bring together groups that otherwise fight.

**INTERVIEWER:** Great idea.

**MARTY:** We're excited to build hotels, to build golf courses, to bring Madonna, to bring Elton John. You'll find that today there's a wide consensus. Across the board, the American people are committed to helping Iraq see this problem through to its end. We're not going to cut and run. We're partners. We're in this together for at least a hundred years.

couple of months down the road. But that's another story for a later chapter.

## Surging with Petraeus

After my interview, I quickly recognized that there wasn't much else for me to do at the expo. I didn't have a product to sell. I had a plan that required approval. I needed to find the big shots, the players. I left the Rashid Hotel to take a stroll and gather my thoughts. I was glad that I had received all my credentials. With my expo badge, I was able to move around with ease. The Green Zone had changed since the last time I was here. It had become the ultimate gated community. Everything you could ever want or need was here. And the concrete blast walls, eye scanners, bomb-sniffing dogs, metal detectors, X-ray machines, checkpoints, and roadblocks kept it safe. I felt reassured and proud that my government had taken security and one-stop shopping to that next level. All that was missing was a missile-defense shield which, sources tell me, is just a matter of time. I had no doubt that this model of living would one day be the standard.

In the distance, past the Taco Bell, I noticed a crowd waiting to get into one of Saddam's former palaces. I asked a passing leaf blower (oddly enough, from Romania) what all the commotion was about. He told me that General Petraeus was inside signing autographs and posing for pictures. I joined the line. When it was my turn, I handed the general my expo program to sign.

"Here for the expo?"

"Here to make your job easier, sir. Martin Eisenstadt. We met once in Washington at Bill Kristol's Halloween pool party. I was an original member on the Committee for the Liberation of Iraq. So you can see I have vision, and when I look at the Green Zone here today, I don't see now, I see the future. I see opera houses and museums and underground parking. And one question screams out to me. Why is there no casino here in the Green Zone? Casinos bring people together. Casinos say normal. Casinos say capitalism. Have you heard of Sharif Investments?" The general's assistant tried to usher me along. I had already received my autograph, and he couldn't figure out why I was still there. He even called out "Next." But I wouldn't be deterred.

"You and I both know, sir, that this war is not just about bullets. It's about hearts and minds."

"What is it you want, Mr. Eisenstadt? Spit it out. I have a war to run."

"I want to help you normalize Baghdad. I want to offer you a seven-figure consulting job with Sharif Investments after you retire. I want to provide jobs for Iraq's poor. Is there maybe some-one in your office I could talk to at greater length about this?"

"About what? I'm still not following."

"About acquiring the necessary permits to build Baghdad's first Vegas-style casino."

"Are you crazy? Get out of here. And next time do your re-search before wasting my time. Military doesn't even handle that kind of stuff anymore. The Hajjis are in charge of permits now."

I visited the Ministry of Trade hoping to find some familiar faces. But Iraq had changed a lot since 2003. Low-level collabo-rators from back then were likely dead by now. After chatting up a sexually confused male secretary in the restroom, I gleaned that I needed to talk to Ahmed Ridha, the head of the National Investment Council, which was charged with issuing permits and approving foreign investments. Things were moving along. I was making progress.

I climbed two flights of stairs to Mr. Ridha's office. I explained to Mr. Ridha's hijab-wearing assistant that I was there to talk about a big hotel project. Because of issues of cultural sensibili-ties, I figured it best not to emphasize the casino part at this stage. To my surprise, she told me to "Go right in."

## The Two Ahmeds

Ahmed Ridha, his grin wide, his belly and mustache even wider, stood from his desk to greet me. Behind him on the wall was a photograph of Iraq's current prime minister, Nouri al-Maliki. Mr. Ridha was excited to see me. "I've been expecting you," he gushed.

"You have?"

"You're with Marriott, right? I've been looking over the plans—"

"No. I'm here for a different project. I represent Sharif In-vestments."

"Good company. I know it. Please. Have a seat."

"If it isn't my old friend Marty Eisenstadt." Wait, who said that? It was then that I noticed the other person in the room, Ahmed Chalabi, the ultimate wheeler-dealer. He sat cross-legged on the couch behind me sipping tea and smoking a cigarette. I had read that Chalabi had maneuvered himself into a succession of power-wielding jobs in the new Iraqi government but still, what a coincidence running into him like this. The former head of the Iraqi National Congress and good friend to the whole neocon crowd, Chalabi was a regular fixture at the Committee for the Liberation of Iraq (CLI) softball games. It was Chalabi who told us that Saddam had weapons of mass destruction. It was Chalabi who told us we'd be greeted as liberators. And with buddies like John McCain and Joe Lieberman, Chalabi was able to wrangle out of Congress copious amounts of money for himself and his various organizations. It was even assumed that after the invasion he would take over and serve as America's puppet. It wasn't until much later, after we were in the throes of an insurgency, that some started to worry that Chalabi might have been working for the Iranians all along.

"So how's the old crowd doing?" Chalabi inquired.

"Great. Looks like John McCain is going to be the next president."

"Scheunemann must be excited about that."

"He is, and so am I."

"I thought I read somewhere that you worked for Rudy. I even saw a strange video of you without your beard on the YouTube driving around in a car saying bad things about the other candidates."

"Did you like it?" I was excited to get feedback on my performance. Strangely, Chalabi was the first person to have recognized me from the videos.

"Not really. You come across as unstable. But maybe that was the intent. What do I know? I'm a politician, not an artist."

"Well, anyway, it looks like I'll be working for McCain once I get back. And I hope you can help me convey to the relevant people here that the next American president supports this endeavor. But I'm getting ahead of myself." Chalabi nodded his head politely.

Bumping into Chalabi had given me a boost in confidence. In this game, it's who you know and I knew Chalabi, and he and Ridha were obviously friends. Heck, he might even be his superior. Making sure to alternate my eye contact between the two men, I continued my pitch. "Sharif Investments, based in Oman, has teamed up with Zen Management out of Las Vegas to take luxury gambling to the next level, merging the best of Oriental hospitality with that uniquely Vegas pizzazz we all love. Can anyone tell me why there is no casino here in the Green Zone? Paris has casinos. Beirut has casinos. New Baghdad should have one too. Look at all the disposable wealth that every day passes through this Green Zone. Foreign contractors. Foreign investors. The troops are paid in dollars."

"As you Americans say, money talks," observed Ridha.

"Money does talk," I continued, "and it's to the benefit of the Iraqi people, because that disposable income trickles down. We say in America 'trickle down,' meaning that when people with the big money are spending it at the roulette, they're also tipping their waiters. With six thousand rooms, we will need many young girls to clean them. Democracy is the first step, but it needs to be followed by capitalism and entertainment."

Once again, it was Ridha who spoke. "But maybe we Iraqis have a different sense of entertainment than you. It's not one size fits all. We had a Wendy's here in the Green Zone, but it closed down. Kebab is better meat than hamburger. You don't think so?"

"I couldn't agree more," I responded, my eyes lowered to show respect. "That's why, in addition to roulette and blackjack and poker, we're going to have a special section for backgammon. It's like I said in my Al Iraqiya interview: There will be a mosque.

There will be off-track betting for the camel races in Dubai. Let me put this to you another way. When you have a jack and a six and you hit, everybody's in it together. That rush transcends your language, your culture, your religion. And that's, I think, what's really going to bring people together. Whether you're Shia, Sunni, or Kurd, you're going to be wearing the same casino uniform with the same name tags which say, 'We're all one. We all work for the casino. There are no differences between us.'" I was in a lobbying groove, so I kept going.

"We in America also had a racial conflict once upon a time, among the Native Americans, the white people from Europe, and the black people from Africa. And somehow, casinos have managed to fix that divide. Where only twenty years ago Native Americans were drunk and homeless and committing crimes, today they're prosperous and wealthy, driving around in Mercedes, their kids with Game Boys and PlayStations, satellite dishes on their homes. And so, too, the black people with the sports have managed to advance themselves in this kind of entertainment sector, and it's brought a harmony between all the peoples. And we intend to bring that same thing here to Baghdad." Mind you, dear reader, I didn't use the term Native American to be politically correct. Political correctness is the greatest danger facing America today. I used it to distinguish from the other Indians, important allies in our War on Terror. With a billion people, a nuclear arsenal, and half our call centers, they deserve their own name. I had more to say, but I figured it was time to let someone else talk. I have found that in lobbying, listening can sometimes be as effective as talking.

"Interesting idea," Ahmed Ridha observed. "It will be like a culture center. What do you say, Ahmed?"

Ahmed Chalabi, my friend, settled his tea on a silver tray. He cleared his throat and fixed his eyes on mine. "First of all, let me congratulate you on a wonderfully prepared speech."

"Thank you."

"Unfortunately for your clients, I have heard from sources that you've been spreading rumors about me that I am an Iranian spy."

"What? Who said that? They're lying."

"I also heard that you've been telling people that I throw like a girl." Well, he did. If not for Chalabi's ineptitude on the pitching mound, I have no doubt we would have made it to the playoffs. Who'd been ratting me out? Was it Scheunemann? Who from the old crowd was Chalabi still in contact with? "Somebody's lying to you, Ahmed. I would never speak against you. It's not even like me."

"A man works his whole life to build a reputation. You hurt me, Marty. I thought we were friends."

"We are friends."

"No. We are enemies. And you know what? I do like your idea for a casino in the Green Zone, and I think when the Marriott representative gets here, we'll bring it up as something to add to their hotel plans. So thank you for the idea, Marty. And please tell your friends over at Sharif that my colleague Mr. Ridha said no to your proposal." Mr. Ridha looked away. Chalabi continued. "And if they want to know the reason, they can call me. Good day, Mr. Eisenstadt."

## Stranded in Somalia, Partying with Pirates

Nabil and Jamie hit the roof when they understood that their casino project in the Green Zone wouldn't be happening. They accused me of padding my résumé and exaggerating my qualifications. They repeatedly called my cell phone, but I didn't pick up. Even receiving a phone call overseas can be cost-prohibitive. They left angry messages. They blamed me for the failure of their project and insisted that I return money to them. That was out of the question. They threatened to sue me, to use physical violence against me, to destroy my reputation. Now you understand why I always cash checks the minute I receive them. Clients can be fickle.

As you can imagine, I was in no rush to get back to the States. Rudy had lost. The Obama and Hillary fight was still dragging on, which meant the general campaign was still some time away. Plus, March on the East Coast is so often cold and rainy. In the Middle East, it feels more like spring. The air was smelling nice. The sun was strong. At a hotel bar in Abu Dhabi, I met some Australians who worked on a cargo ship set to sail for the Suez Canal the next day. The lads and I drank and laughed until the morning. They invited me to come with, to join them on their journey.

The next day, my head pounding, I boarded their ship. I could use a week on the open sea to clear my mind and focus my thoughts. It had been too long since I was last in Egypt. Once I got there I would take some much needed R&R in the Sinai desert on the Red Sea coast.

I never made it to Egypt.

Our ship was attacked by Somali pirates wielding rocket launchers and automatic weapons. The pirates, who were young, brash, and chewing khat (a local amphetamine), figured I was someone important and took me ashore as a hostage.

I found the pirates to be big fans of American culture and very open to the neocon way of thinking, and I can now proudly say that I count multiple Somali nationals as dear and trusted friends. These are hardworking people. Risk takers. Believers in free enterprise. They don't kidnap for ideology. They kidnap for money. That's capitalism. These are natural allies. We should be reaching out to the Somali pirates, not demonizing them. I even talked with one of their leaders about opening a casino in his territory.

The pirates were a curious lot and would often keep me up into the early-morning hours plying me with questions about song lyrics: what this word meant, how to use that slang in a sentence, and why women were called "hos." To quote my guard Hussein Khadija, "According to our dictionary, this is a gardening tool."

In the end, the Harding Institute paid a ransom. It was good for Eli to learn the nuts and bolts of international wire transfers. To this day, there are some who don't believe that I was really held captive by Somali pirates. They think I made up the whole fanciful tale to get out of returning Sharif Investments' money. But that's absurd. Explain to me the withdrawal symptoms I still suffer from the khat dependancy I developed while waiting for Eli to pay my ransom. Explain to me my vivid memories of bonfires on the beach, all-night dance parties, pirates taking three girls at a time.

I had many memorable experiences in Somalia, but more on that in a later chapter and in my next book, which according to my coquettish editor, Mitzi, should be an account of my time spent in captivity. (I understand her position: I was taken hostage a full year before the *Maersk Alabama* incident, and yet those lucky Danish lackeys got all the press. The goal is to get me to finish my pirate book before that so-called hero Captain Phillips can write his. And for the record, let me just say that though he was captured *by* Somali pirates, he was never actually held captive *in* Somalia. I hope my loyal readers will remember that distinction come bestseller season.) For now, though, back to Washington and the campaign for the president of the United States.

## Jumping On Board the Straight Talk Express

Upon my return to Washington, I called McCain headquarters to see if Joe Lieberman had spoken to anyone about me. The campaign was starting to take shape, and if I was going to continue being a player in this town I would have to be on board. In a campaign season, if you didn't have "senior adviser" or "surrogate" after your name, the major networks had no use for you.

My call was passed on to Steve Schmidt, at the time a chief strategist for the campaign. Steve was a former Bushie who had worked for Schwarzenegger's gubernatorial bid. I knew him, but not well.

"Joe Lieberman was supposed to talk to the senator about me."

"I haven't heard anything. Let me pass you on to Salter. He might know something." Mark Salter, the senator's closest adviser, had cowritten John's books and took pride in knowing the senator better than he knew himself.

"Eisenstadt. Eisenstadt. Yes. Joe Lieberman did talk to the senator about you. And I even wrote it down. One second. One second. Here, I found it. Right. Martin Eisenstadt. You're going to be serving as our liaison with the Jewish community. Welcome aboard."

"So I'll be advising on foreign policy?"

"Sure."

"So my official job title will be liaison with the Jewish community and adviser for foreign policy? That's what Joe and I had talked about."

"Okay. I buy that. I'll make a note of it."

Next, I called Randy Scheunemann, McCain's top foreign-policy adviser and my old buddy from CLI, to tell him the good news, that I was going to be in his department.

"Randy. Guess what?"

"Martin Eisenstadt?"

"The one and only."

"You know how much money it cost me to clean that trunk? The stench even seeped into the metal. I can still smell it."

"Well, at least no one was hurt."

"My Saab was hurt. Important documents were ruined. You know what they did to a man in the Wild West who harmed another man's horse?"

"For that, please let me issue a formal apology. I'll make it up to you. I promise."

"How are you going to make it up?"

"By always having your back. By being your ally. Now that we're going to be working together—"

"Working together?!" Randy didn't sound well. His breathing had become heavy. Maybe he was coming down with something.

"Yeah. I just spoke to Schmidt and Salter. I'm on board. It's official . . . Randy? Are you still there?"

# What's in a Name?

**6**

## Losing Eli

The end of May 2008 should have been a high point in my life. I was now in full swing working for the McCain campaign as a senior adviser. Not that I had actually given any advice, mind you, or for that matter, actually met the candidate. But that's to be expected on these big presidential campaigns. The important thing was that I was contributing in whatever ways I could. And did this in some way make up for the 2000 whispering campaign I'd orchestrated against McCain? I suppose if I had had any moral objections to those whispers at the time, then maybe. But with so many former Bush and Giuliani staff working for McCain now, it was all one big happy campaign.

I also had some exciting new changes over at my Harding Institute office.

When I returned from my foray in Somalia, Eli greeted me with the sad news that he'd decided to seek greener pastures. He felt—and I think correctly—that he'd gotten all he could get out of his tenure at the institute.

Frankly, there had been some tension of late between Eli and myself. On my behalf, he had tried to spread the word about my blog to several other right-of-center bloggers, but I caught him having "extracurricular" correspondence with Debbie Schlussel, an attractive blonde Jewish blogger out of Detroit. I raised my voice at Eli one afternoon and accused him of trying to get a job with Schlussel, and of betraying the senior fellow–associate fellow bonds of confidentiality. I've always encouraged my young associates to follow their dreams, but not behind my back. Eli was apoplectic and claimed he was just trying to warm up to Schlussel so he could set me up on a date with her the next time she came to D.C. (she travels here for her frequent punditing gigs on Fox News and Al Jazeera English). If this was indeed the case (as a closer examination of his e-mails would eventually prove), then perhaps I should have been more grateful to Eli. Though I ultimately apologized to him, it was clear that we still had some underlying trust issues. Or maybe he'd just been with me too long and was starting to feel itchy.

In any case, he wound up pursuing a career in Hollywood at a small, slightly disreputable talent-management company called Provocation Entertainment (though from what I hear about Hollywood managers, it would be tough to call one any more disreputable than another). Eli felt he needed to leave Washington while he was still a young man in his early twenties, lest he stayed and wound up getting a law degree by osmosis (as happens to many young men who settle for too long in our nation's capital).

To replace Eli, I brought in two new staffers: Jimmy Havermayer and Poppy Cartwright (see, it took two to fill Eli's well-trod shoes). A fresh-faced virgin from the Midwest, Jimmy had driven me around the Florida panhandle as a volunteer for the Giuliani campaign, and I sensed in him then that he had a keen grip on life but knew when to ask for directions. Poppy couldn't have been more different than Jimmy. Self-assured, ambitious, and black, she'd first interned at the institute the summer before.

"Wolf, I'll be at the studio in ten minutes." *(Courtesy of Andrew Perreault/Harding Institute)*

But now that she'd graduated from Howard University with a dual major in political science and sass, I thought she should join us on a full-time basis.

So by the end of spring we had fresh blood in the office and a new direction forward with the campaign. What could go wrong?

### Denny Hastert, Ronald Reagan, and Transgender Air Traffic Controllers

On May 30, I wasn't particularly surprised to get a text from my childhood friend and honorary "adjunct" fellow at the Harding Institute Stanley Rubin (known throughout town as "a lobbyist's lobbyist") that my old pal and former Speaker of the House Denny Hastert had just joined a Washington "law" firm. This is, after all, what happens in America when our tireless political leaders leave the public sector. We all know that members of Congress are not paid a fortune, and their pensions are even more meager. So it is only fitting that we let them retire in style and put their well-earned knowledge of the legislative process to good use. But in the course of doing opposition research on behalf of the McCain campaign, my new associate Jimmy noticed a curious post on the liberal blog Open Left about Hastert's move.

> House Speaker Dennis Hastert is . . . joining Dickstein Shapiro, one of the largest law firms in DC and one with over 100 of the Fortune 500 as clients. It's rather telling that Hastert would join a firm that prides itself on tolerance for an atmosphere of "inclusion and respect" for, among others, gay, bisexual and transgender individuals, given that he voted for a constitutional amendment to deny gay people marriage rights.[1]

Jimmy knew of my affection for Denny (and how upon his retirement I'd courted him to serve on the Harding Institute's advisory board—a position he understandably declined because of conflict of interest with his other think-tank commitments). So Jimmy knocked on my office door. "Mr. Eisenstadt, is Denny Hastert really a tranny-loving lobbyist?" the fresh-faced young lad blurted out. I read the post and couldn't believe it myself. There were so many other so-called law firms Denny could have joined.

To be sure, Dickstein Shapiro has some excellent legal minds in their employ (including former senators Wendell H. Ford and Tim Hutchinson), and I would subsequently use them myself, at Denny's suggestion.

Now I myself have nothing against the transgender community (I couldn't have supported Giuliani in good conscience if I had), but the last thing John McCain needed was America getting a refresher course in Republican congressional sexual preferences. So I hastily (perhaps too hastily, in retrospect) posted this on my blog:

### Shame on Dennis Hastert for joining tranny lobbyist firm

May 30, 2008, by Marty

I was one of Dennis' first friends here in Washington. One of the
few who could talk in detail with him about high school wrestling
over the occasional mid-morning drink (I grappled JV back in high
school). From what I hear, he was one of the most hands-on and
effective wrestling coaches of his day. And I recognize that
retirement can be expensive and a man needs to make a buck.

But going to work for transgender-friendly Dickstein Shapiro?
Dennis, come on, buddy. I know you can do better. I defended
you in the Mark Foley scandal, and now you're just perpetuating
stereotypes of the GOP. We're going to have enough trouble this
fall defeating Obama and heading off another Democrat
landslide.[2]

As expected, the backlash from the left came when word got
out about Denny swinging through the revolving door of
Washington "law" firms. But they couldn't outright condemn
Dickstein Shapiro for fear of offending their own transgender
constituencies. The cloyingly titled left-wing blog Feministe was
put in the "awkward position" (to use a popular tranny phrase)
of suggesting that Dickstein was not in fact a transgender lobbying firm: "Especially with the standard GLBT formula, it seems
statistically probable that Dickstein Shapiro hasn't employed a
single trans person."[3]

Leaving aside for the moment the fact that I always thought
GLBT was a "green lettuce, bacon, and tomato" sandwich, I also
noticed the blog said that there's already an official tranny lobbyist: the National Center for Transgender Equality.[4] Ironically
enough, the NCTE has their office in the National Air Traffic
Controllers Association building on Massachusetts Avenue. This
may explain Ronald Reagan's little-known quote from August 3,

1981, when he busted PATCO, the original air traffic controllers' union: "I don't know about you, but when my 707's coming in to land at 200 miles per hour, I sure don't want the men in the tower fussing over their nails and curlers. What the hell kind of union is this?"

The Feministe blog, after looking at my site, had this ingot of love to say about me:

> Eisenstadt is actually one of John McCain's advisors. His should give us a good indication of the kind of intelligence McCain can draw on, and how out of step they are with actual American values.[5]

Snarky humorless bile from liberal blogs is to be expected. The good news here was that I was first and foremost identified as a John McCain adviser. In the long term that's what mattered.

Mind you, the Feministe blog says it heard about the controversy from someone named "Wolfrum." Who? Jimmy tracked down the link, and it came from the reasonably prominent liberal site Shakesville, posted by one of its regular contributors— some guy named Bill Wolfrum. In a similar vein to Feministe, Wolfrum couldn't resist a swipe at me personally:

> Eisenstadt of the prestigious(?) Harding Institute for Freedom and Democracy and a member of John McCain's campaign team, is personally horrified by this. Or maybe just horrified by transgenders. Or maybe he's just a dick.

Forgetting for the moment the irony of a liberal pro-tranny blogger calling someone a "dick" (is that a pre- or post-op one, sir?), I really don't mind being called such an appendage. Having been raised in the Richard Nixon White House, I consider the term a compliment. But my staff at the—yes, I dare say, "prestigious"— Harding Institute shouldn't have to be subjected to such crass in-

Does Wolfrum himself exist? This is one of the only picures of him on the Internet.
(*Source: www.williamkwolfrum.com*)

sults in the course of doing their jobs (believe me, the comments to this post from Wolfrum were even more rude than his initial entry). Poor Jimmy was raised in a strict Mennonite family in Indiana and went to the Christian liberal-arts college Goshen, where he was an active member of both the College Republicans and AMISH (the Association of Mennonites for Ice and Street Hockey). Working on the Giuliani campaign in Florida was as eye-opening for him as *rumspringa* is for his Amish cousins back in northern Indiana. Jimmy had never met a Jew until he drove me around Florida, and to this day, I'm fairly certain he thinks keeping kosher means not eating after sundown. So for him to have to read this liberal claptrap was a little troubling. But I put him at ease, and reminded him that Bill O'Reilly is fighting the battle to end Internet coarseness on our behalf. It's just taking a while.

### How Barack Obama *Really* Beat Hillary Clinton: Strange Bedfellows and Fertile Pandas

The speed of the Internet still exhausts me. I'd made that first post about Denny on a Friday morning, and by the end of the

"Wolf, can't find a cab. Start the show without me."
*(Courtesy of Andrew Perreault/Harding Institute)*

day, the liberal reaction had already come and gone. Jimmy may have been a teetotaler, but I, for one, needed a drink.

As anyone who lives in the District knows, if you're thirsty, you can usually quench that sensation by going to one of the Senate or House committee rooms on Capitol Hill. By 4:30 p.m., the committee chairs bang their gavels, and within an hour the rooms are transformed into luscious reception halls for all manner of lobbyists, trade associations, and causes du jour. But Congress wasn't in session: it was "jeans and puppies week"[6] on the Hill. Ugh. No receptions.

But I did hear about a nighttime shindig at the Washington Marriott Wardman Park kicking off the DNC's Rules and Bylaws Committee Meeting that weekend. After a long bruising primary campaign, this was the Democrats' big smoke-filled room that would effectively decide who would be their next nominee: Obama or Hillary. What the hell? This would be one train wreck worth watching.

So I hopped the Red Line from Farragut North up two stops. The Wardman Park is just across Connecticut Avenue from the National Zoo. Rumor has it that from the tenth-floor suites you can look down at the pandas trying to mate. Sure beats the pay-per-view. So I went up to the mezzanine level and straight to the Thurgood Marshall Ballroom. (Where else would the DNC have a party?) In my best Cajun accent, I yelled out: *"Laissez les bon temps rouler!"* I'd spotted my old pal Donna Brazile getting her credentials.

"Marty, you ol' dirty dog, what are you doing here?" As we hugged, I waltzed her in a long embrace through the entryway and straight to the wet bar. A surefire way of getting into any party. Although I was concerned that drinking heavily might lead to another gout flare-up, I was reluctant to show weakness in a room full of Democrats and decided to tempt fate.

Of the thirty members of the DNC Rules and Bylaws Committee, Donna was the most prominent of the seven so-called swing voters. In order to retain her pundit street cred, she'd made a point during the primaries to stay neutral between Obama and Clinton. In fact, she famously told the brilliant and handsome Stephen Colbert: "Look, I'm a woman, so I like Hillary. I'm black; I like Obama. But I'm also grumpy, so I like John McCain."[7]

## Anderson Cooper Bumps Donna Brazile

Donna Brazile and I were obviously on the opposite side of most political issues, but we were also fellow members of the punditocracy. By dint of being Al Gore's old campaign manager from 2000, she's a paid consultant on CNN's *Strategy Session*.[8] (Of course, as only an occasional guest, guys like me don't actually make a dime.)

I think the first time Donna and I spent quality time together was when we were both booked for Anderson Cooper's show back in August '05. It was during Katrina, and Donna and I were supposed to be discussing the political ramifications of the hurricane (she's from Louisiana, after all). But Anderson was anchoring live from Gulfport and his producer decided they would get better ratings just running a tight close-up of a teary-eyed Cooper than doing the normal split-screen pundit routine. He was like that goddamned crying Indian chief in those Keep America Beautiful PSAs in the seventies. America's silver-haired conscience writ large. His producer was right, of course. Cooper owned Katrina. Within three months, CNN fired longtime anchor Aaron Brown and made *Anderson Cooper 360°* the flagship evening news show.

Donna and I were still in adjoining makeup chairs putting on lip gloss when we got the word that we "wouldn't be needed" that night. So we guilted the producer into giving us a hundred dollars' "bump money" for our troubles, and headed over to the Dubliner by Union Station for a couple of pints of Guinness. We wound up singing "Danny Boy" with the band, and shut the place down at 2:00 a.m.

"Marty, honey, I still don't know which one I'm going to support. Help me out here."

"Donna," I said after our third whiskey sour, "the only reason the Democratic primaries dragged out until June is because you wanted to keep getting booked on CNN."

She downed her drink in one swig. "That's bull, Marty."

"Is it, Donna?"

"L'chaim!" she said, as we clinked glasses and drank.

"C'mon, Donna, we all know CNN pays you a retainer to keep those regular spots on Wolf's show." We grabbed another drink.

## The Fifty-State Strategy

While I was drinking that night with Donna Brazile, the one sober corner of my cerebellum kicked the rest of my head in the balls. By delaying her decision, this woman had single-handedly kept the Democratic primary season going until the bitter end.

The GOP had wrapped up its orderly business as early as March 4 when McCain clinched the nomination with a win in Texas. But Obama and Clinton were battling it out with a scorched-earth policy in every state—from Pennsylvania to South Dakota to Guam (and I don't even think Guam's a state!). Most in the McCain campaign were more than happy to sit back and enjoy the fireworks, letting Barack and Hillary bring down each other's negatives with accusations of unpatriotic pastors and racist husbands. (My alluring British editor, Mitzi, thinks this would be a great place to use a word like schadenfreude—a German word, I might add, that British people would be saying a lot more frequently if it weren't for America.)

I always had a sneaking suspicion, though, that the Democrats had stumbled haplessly into DNC chair Howard "Screamin'" Dean's much ballyhooed Fifty-State Strategy. By keeping up a vibrant primary battle until June, the DNC had guaranteed not one but two sets of organized volunteers, poll workers, and staffers in every state. I kept trying to voice my concerns up the chain of command at McCain headquarters, but most of the McCain staff had taken unofficial vacations, in many cases to catch up on work back at their respective think tanks and lobbying offices.

"Damn straight they do." We locked our left arms, tipped our heads back, and downed another whiskey each. "If I'd swung for Hillary back in Iowa or on Super Tuesday, they'd have to get a whole notha brotha on retainer for Obama."

"You'd be on half as often, and it'd cost them twice as much!" We both busted up laughing.

Donna and I held our noses, lifted our left legs behind us, and downed another shot each. Donna seemed confused. "Yeah, but my contract's done with CNN in a month. How am I gonna up the ante with them?"

"I dunno. Play them off against the other guys?" I spitballed an idea: "MSNBC needs a good heavy hitter like you."

"But they're in the tank for Obama. Everyone knows it."

"Well there's your answer, then. If Barack's already the presumptive nominee, you don't have to keep playing down the middle anymore. Threaten CNN that you're walking to go be a regular consultant on *Hardball*. You know Blitzer hates Chris Matthews. Wolf'll back a new contract for you in a heartbeat— double what you're getting now. I'm sure."

I could see Donna doing the math in her head. "Goddammit, Marty, you might be right."

"Then I'll drink to that."

And I did.

## The O'Russert Factor: Death of an Icon

It was later—much later—when I left the hotel and stumbled home, but I was still too wired to get to sleep right away. I flipped on Fox. They were rerunning a controversial clip of Bill O'Reilly railing on Tim Russert for Russert's upcoming interview with former White House press secretary Scott McClellan:

*If he softballs McClellan, he's done in the business. Russert's finished! He's playing that game over there to take his big paycheck home. Don't give me he's a noble guy. He's not! He's a cynic. He hasn't said a—I was going to say a bad word—he hasn't said a word about what's going on over there. I wouldn't work for any organization like NBC which is in the tank, which is dishonest, has been dishonest, and doesn't deserve any credibility! If you're working for them, you're part of it!!!*[9]

Now I'm not going to suggest for a minute that O'Reilly's rant gave Russert his fatal heart attack. But exactly two weeks later, Tim collapsed in his newsroom. Quite dead. Coroners can argue all they want about his "myocardial infarction" being caused by "occlusive coronary thrombosis," but this much is true. O'Reilly was prescient: Russert was finished.

Of course, there's no way I could have known about Russert's asymptomatic coronary artery disease at the time, so it seemed appropriate enough to add my voice to O'Reilly's concerns. Normally, when I write my blogs, I send an e-mail to my assistant— at that point, it was Jimmy—who adds a few links and pictures, and then posts them online. In the blogosphere, this protocol gives at least some time for "reflection." But in my condition, I made the mistake of posting directly onto the site. I believe it's called BWD: Blogging While Drunk.

### Boycott NBC and its tranny sympathizers

May 31st, 2008, by Marty

I warned you in my last post that Denny joining that tranny friendly lobbying firm would remind people of his past involvement with Mark Foley. And lo and behold I was right. Not only is Dickstein Shapiro tranny friendly, it counts General Electric subsidiaries as clients. Which brings me to the subject of this post, the warning my prophetic and good friend Bill O'Reilly is trying to get across to the sometimes gullible American people. Boycott NBC!

I've been on his show before, and I know Bill O'Reilly is right, 100% right. NBC is the most insidious, self-serving American corporation there is. The mouthpiece of the government behind the government. Between David Gregory dancing the jig with Karl Rove and Tim Russert offering up *Meet the Press* as a White House briefing room, NBC, in the run-up to the wars, was just as pro-Bush, pro-invasion as was FOX (not that I was complaining). But now that the tides seem to be turning, with possible criminal investigations down the road, NBC has coincidentally found again its liberal soul, its outrage, dare I say shock at the last 8 years of "excess."

You liberals are such fools. Fox News is not the propaganda channel. It's owned by an Australian, for God's sake. NBC, owned by GE, which makes more money off one bomb dropped in Iraq than it earns off the entire franchise of *Friends*, is the channel you got to watch out for. And who are all their gas bag blowhards, like Olbermann and Matthews, screaming for this year? Barack Obama.

John McCain is once again finding his voice as the true outsider, the maverick he's always been. And in this election environment, the smart money is on who can better paint himself as the "outsider."

ps. And for all you liberal haters who have defended Dickstein Shapiro as some sort of utopia for liberal diversity hiring policy, you might want to get a load of their clients: online gaming, the smoking lobby, mercenaries in Iraq, nuclear power, etc. Come to think of it, maybe they're not so bad![10]

Okay, so it was a little all over the map. But, eh, it was a Friday night. Nobody in America reads blogs over the weekend. It could wait till Monday for Jimmy to clean it up. I started to get ready for bed and suddenly wondered: If I'm wearing Donna's underwear, what happened to mine?

## A Single Person Decides the Election

The rest of the weekend was a bit of a blur. But from time to time I'd flip on the cable news channels. It's always fun to watch their weekend C-team anchors auditioning for the weekday slots. Younger and hotter than their weekday colleagues—their makeup a little brighter, their blouses cut a little lower—they're frequently poached from competing network affiliates in the local markets. Fox's WTTG in Washington seems especially good at breeding beautiful young reporters only to have them hired by corporate rivals MSNBC (strikingly blonde weekend anchor Amy Robach) and CNN (strikingly brunette weekend anchor Brooke Baldwin). Mmmm, flipping between the two of them, I couldn't help but think of the phrase "anchor sandwich." But maybe that's because I hadn't eaten in a day and a half.

On Saturday, the cable news shows had hourly updates from the DNC Rules and Bylaws Committee. The committee's job was to figure out what to do with Florida and Michigan—two states that defied party rules by staging earlier primaries than they were allowed. The meeting was deadlocked between the Clinton and Obama camps. Passions were high, and by 3:00 p.m. they hadn't even taken a lunch break.

Finally my girl Donna stepped to the mike. I knew if her head was throbbing half as much as mine, she was hungry. But everyone was waiting with bated breath to hear how she came down. If there was a single voice in that room who would pick the next president of the United States, it was hers. "My momma always taught me to play by the rules," she gravely intoned. "When you decide to change the rules, especially in the middle of the game, that is referred to as cheating." This was considered a clear nod to the Obama camp and the crowd at the hotel cheered wildly. Her voice was heard, her decision had been made. Crap, had she really taken my drunken advice from the night before by taking the MSNBC gambit and doubling down on CNN? I don't know, but when the crowd finally calmed down, she added, "Now let's eat."[11]

In the end, the Florida and Michigan delegations only got half their votes. It would net Hillary a scant twenty-four more delegates and not enough to make a difference. The Obama camp had been victorious. Within a week, Hillary would end her campaign and endorse Barack.

## Wonks vs. Pundits

By Monday, all anyone could talk about was the Democrats and Obama's presumptive nomination. The Hastert transgender controversy had come and gone. Thankfully, it didn't develop into a huge scandal or a burden on the McCain campaign. I'd like to think that my blog post had helped defuse the issue before it developed significant traction on the left. Meanwhile, Denny called me first thing Monday morning. Amused, more than anything else, about my blog posts. He was just happy to get a steady paycheck again and assured me he wasn't "going under the knife" anytime soon. By late Monday morning, I had moved on to other pressing matters in the McCain campaign, as well as my ongoing responsibilities at the Harding Institute. But for some strange reason Jimmy seemed a little agitated. I wandered over to the bullpen. "Jimmy, what's up?"

"Uh, remember that guy Wolfrum, on that site Shakesville?"

"Not really."

"He's been blogging about you again."

"You mean about Denny. I assure you, Denny's not afraid of a weaselly little blogger."

"No, about you."

"Well, that's flattering."

"Not so much."

I looked over Jimmy's shoulder to his computer. Wolfrum had apparently read the post I made about boycotting NBC and took umbrage at being called a liberal fool. His headline read:

M. Thomas Eisenstadt—Is John McCain's new foreign policy adviser a racist, transgenderphobic, homophobic, sockpuppeting liar?

Hmmm. I guess people do read blogs over the weekend.

So what was the gist of this rambling blog post where I'm accused of being such a horrible person? Turns out that Wolfrum was becoming obsessed with me. He must have spent his whole weekend googling everything under the sun about me and come up with some bizarre conclusions.

Who the hell is this M. Thomas Eisenstadt guy? I decided to try and find out more about this star neo-con. Interestingly, my search led me to The W█████ Institute for ███ ███ Policy and M█████ Eisenstadt.

M. Thomas Eisenstadt? M█████ Eisenstadt? It seemed like

## Why M. Thomas?

I should add that at this point in my blog, I was posting things under my academic name "M. Thomas Eisenstadt." As you've gathered by now, most people just call me "Marty," but starting back in my American University days, I had used "M. Thomas" for my written work. I suppose I could chalk it up to a certain level of pretension when I was trying to curry favor with a raven-haired senior TA in my Political Theory in the Twentieth Century class. In the end, I got a C+ in the class and got rejected by the TA (who was screwing the professor, natch). But at least I got a name that stuck . . . for a while.

a pretty interesting coincidence. And they both have bios that, while different, are quite similar and don't really contradict one another.

And on the "links section," of The Harding Institute for Freedom and Democracy, one of his links goes to the Hoover Institution of Stanford, which has a link to a W▮▮▮▮▮▮ Institute article including M▮▮▮▮ Eisenstadt. Another link goes out to the Middle East Forum, which features numerous articles by M▮▮▮▮ Eisenstadt. Another of the links goes to the American Enterprise Institute for Public Policy Research, which features literally more than 100 of M▮▮▮▮ Eisenstadt's writings. And finally, yet another link goes to the infamous Heritage Foundation, which also has had plenty of dealings with M▮▮▮▮ Eisenstadt in the past.[12]

Uh. So what? Of course M▮▮▮▮ Eisenstadt and I have similar bios, and of course, if you look at links to four random think tanks, you'll find other links to the both of us. All this "proves" is that two guys with the same Jewish-sounding last name work in the think-tank community. Alert the media!

"Let me ask you something, Jimmy." He nodded. "Are Lawrence O'Donnell and Norah O'Donnell the same person?"

"No."

"Do they both work at MSNBC?"

"Yes."

"Are they related?"

"Uh, I dunno."

"Not even."

"Okay."

"What about Larry King and John King. At CNN. Are they the same person?"

"No. But isn't Larry John's father?"

"No. No relation."

"But are they both Jewish?"

## Think Tank Linking

I had Jimmy do a little experiment using Wolfrum's search criteria. He cross-referenced the same four think tanks that Wolfrum mentions—Hoover, MEF, AEI, and Heritage (four of the most prominent think tanks in America). Then he checked to see what other people besides M██████ Eisenstadt appear as direct links from three sites and an indirect link from one (you'll note that in Wolfrum's quote, Hoover doesn't actually directly link to M██████ Eisenstadt, only to the think tank where he works). In just a few minutes, Jimmy came up with Paul Wolfowitz, Henry Kissinger, Paul Krugman, Milton Friedman, Thomas Friedman, Daniel Pipes, Douglas Feith, Robert Zoellick, Martin Peretz, Robert Rubin, Michael Rubin, Kenneth Pollack, Richard Perle, Charles Krauthammer, William Kristol, Irving Kristol, Scooter Libby, Norman Ornstein, Danielle Pletka, Henry Olsen, Mitchell G. Bard, Howard Berman, Ilan Berman, Patrick Clawson, Martin Kramer, Laurent Murawiec, Robert Satloff, Jonathan Schanzer, Meyrav Wurmser, Aaron Mannes, Elliott Abrams, Eliot Cohen, Ariel Cohen, and William Cohen. Former Carter and Clinton official Stuart Eizenstat appears on all four sites, and there's even a Sheriff Thomas S. Eisenstadt referred to on two of the sites in question.

"Well, yes, now they are. John converted when he married Dana Bash. But not all Jewish people are related."

"But what about Ted Koppel and Andrea Koppel."

"Well, he is her father."

"Like Mike Wallace and Chris Wallace."

"Right, Mike is Chris's dad."

"And are they Jewish, too?"

"Yes, their last name used to be Woleck."

"So that means Andrea Koppel is related to Chris Wallace?"

"No, she's married to Ken Pollack."

"Who's that?"

"He's a Jewish neocon who pushed for war with Iraq. He's also a pundit and a Middle East expert who's worked at a bunch of Washington think tanks."

"Just like you."

"Right."

"And M███ Eisenstadt."

"Right."

Jimmy sat there. A confused look on his freshly scrubbed Mennonite face.

"Jimmy, half of this town has the same bio as me."

He thought for a second more.

"Mike Wallace is still alive?"

But to answer the question (which is, after all, part of the point of this book), yes, I know M███ Eisenstadt. And no, we're not very similar at all.

To be clear, M███ is a great guy. But in the world of Middle and Near East studies, he is more what we call in this business a "wonk" rather than my profile as a "pundit." Big difference. Wonks believe in keeping their hands clean from the minutiae of electoral politics. In fact, guys like M███ pride themselves on their partisan neutrality and ability to navigate the political waters no matter which party is in office. I respect that choice, and I suppose for someone more academically minded than myself, that may make more sense. But a pundit goes a different route. A pundit places a larger bet on one party or another, and lives or dies by those political fortunes.

Another difference between a wonk and a pundit? Personal appearance. Don't get me wrong: M███ Eisenstadt is a handsome man. But let's face it, he's got a hairline just north of Bruce Willis's. That's okay for a movie star or a wonk, expected even. But for a pundit, a full head of hair is essential. As they say in the TV news world, you don't want to have a reputation for "getting the shine on." So have I ever dropped a few tabs of Propecia or

done the occasional Rogaine rub? Let's just say that if those purchases ever appeared on my federal taxes, they would have been
deducted as legitimate business expenses.

## Wearing a Sockpuppet for Protection

Wolfrum the blogger went further in his conspiracy theories. He
looked into Eli Perle's background and figured out that Eli was
now working in Hollywood for a somewhat disreputable management company. I warned Eli about that. But then Wolfrum started
going on about "sockpuppets"—apparently the name that bloggers use when people use aliases to promote something. In the
political consulting business, we call that "public relations."

In my line of work, I've naturally used the occasional "false
name" to promote one cause or another. And from time to time,
I train my staff to do the same. The trick to "sockpuppeting" is
to keep track of which names you're using, and when in doubt,
make up a new name (unless you *intentionally* use a name in two
different places because you're trying to get someone to make a
connection).

But maybe Eli had gotten a little sloppy. Between you and me,
he was never the smartest egg in the basket. Apparently he used
the pseudonym "Ronald" to make a comment about his new
company on the blog Crooks and Liars.

> I hear Provocation Entertainment is doing a film about Blondie's
> life. A music video director who used to work with Blondie is
> supposed to direct. Sounds interesting.[13]

Obviously, he was trying to drum up publicity for one of his
new music-video-director clients, the Finnish wunderkind Yrjö
Kankari. I don't begrudge Eli that. But he'd also used "Ronald" to
post a reference to our old Giuliani stealth campaign the year
before. Wolfrum thought he'd made an "Aha!" discovery, but

then he realized that there's already a connection between the Giuliani ads and myself.

> These videos were the viral rage of the moment approximately a year ago. Interestingly, M. Thomas Eisenstadt wrote about these videos in a post titled "The Arrogance of Inevitability: McCain's Victory Due to Giuliani's Missteps." Maybe it's just me, but I find the connection kind of interesting. I'm not implying anything of course, but wouldn't it be interesting if a guy who worked for Giuliani, helped sabotage Giuliani, then went to work for McCain? Just thinking out loud, that's all.[14]

The Giuliani campaign was over, and it was no secret I was now working for McCain. Frankly, Wolfrum was doing me a favor. By this point, I *wanted* people to know that I was behind one of the most successful stealth campaigns in political history. I was in a position where I was trying to climb the ranks of the McCain campaign, and any reputational leverage was appreciated. For contractual reasons, I still wasn't at liberty to out myself as the culprit behind those Giuliani ads. But to be "found out" by some obscure liberal blogger? That played right into my hands. On second thought, maybe Eli's not such an idiot. If he followed my training at all, it was now clear that he had led Wolfrum down this path on purpose. "Jimmy, be sure to send Eli a Starbucks gift card."

Beyond that, there wasn't much for Jimmy to worry about. So I went back to my office, closed the door, and took a nap.

Two hours later, Jimmy knocked. Hard. There was another post from Wolfrum. This time he posted a lengthy e-mail correspondence he claims to have had with M████ Eisenstadt, wherein M████ "admits" to not being me.[15]

"Jimmy, I know he's not me."

"Right."

"Let's get back to work."

## The Mysterious John Edwards Connection

Two days pass and I saunter into work. As I walked past our reception station, I remembered that our spring interns, Chris and Jenny, were in their last week. They'd come to us from an outfit called the Washington Center for Internships and Academic Seminars. The center recruits students from colleges all around the country, stacks them into some sort of dormitory-like housing, and then brokers them out to organizations like ours all over town. The center charges the students and their schools thousands of dollars, and we get them for free. It's quite an operation. There are Malaysian textile sweatshops who pay their ten-year-old seamstresses better than Washington interns.

Strangely, though, no one complains. The Washington Center makes money. We get free labor. The colleges get rid of their activist troublemaking students. And the kids get a semester's worth of full credit for drinking at happy hours and having crazy-mad intern orgies in their crowded barracks.

Jenny and Chris were terrific interns to have around the office. But I'm notoriously bad with names. If it weren't for the fact that Chris was a guy, I never would have been able to tell them apart. But this week, they were training our new summer intern. Victoria? Veronica? Virginia? Hard to say this early in the internship. But she was pretty, she knew her way around the fax machine, and we didn't have to pay her. She would turn out to be a valuable addition to the office.

But when I rounded the corner to walk through the bullpen, I ran into Poppy. "Marty, Jimmy needs to see you. Stat." This couldn't be good. I spotted Jimmy in his cubicle, eyes glued to his computer screen.

"Jimmy, what is it?"

"Remember that blogger? Wolfrum, on that Shakesville site. He's written four more posts about you. Now he's saying you don't exist."

Wolfrum was still flummoxed by all the so-called sockpuppetry mentions of me in comments on other blogs. Why is this so surprising? The only way to get more people to read a blog is to get other blogs to link to it. And the best way to do that is to post comments on their postings with links to your blog. I know Eli had set up a network of fans of my blog to help spread the word. That explains many of the so-called sockpuppets. And for some strange reason, Wolfrum couldn't figure out why people named "Eli" or "Marwan" or "Poppy" would say nice things about me and want other bloggers to link to my site. I don't know. Maybe because they *work* for me, and that's their *job*!

Whoever this guy is, he simply doesn't understand Washington. He thinks it's strange that a punditing senior fellow at a think tank would have his own parallel for-profit consulting group named after himself. In the marketing world, it's called "branding." That's the whole point of the pundit: to build up name recognition so that people will hire you. Perhaps Wolfrum's never heard of such entities as my pal Donna's "Brazile and Associates," or Joe Trippi's curiously named "Trippi and Associates," or maybe a little thing called "Kissinger Associates." Are we to believe now that Henry Kissinger doesn't exist?

Wolfrum had a hodgepodge of conspiracy theories about who and what I was, based mainly on the original tip he got about my Denny Hastert blog. Someone named Kareem Wahiri (or sometimes calling himself "KWah" for short), who used the e-mail account kwahiri@gmail.com, had alerted Wolfrum to my site. Wolfrum couldn't track down this tipster, and assumed he was one of my sockpuppets.

After six lengthy posts about me in less than a week, Wolfrum came to this stunningly brilliant conclusion:

> So, while I can't say for sure who the hoaxer named M. Thomas Eisenstadt is, his name could actually be M. Thomas Eisenstadt for all I know. He could be the infamous abrad2345 in text form. He

could be M██████ Eisentadt (though, let me reiterate, I find this extremely implausible). Again, I have no way to verify any of this.[16]

"Jimmy, the guy's a kook. Ignore him and he'll go bother someone else."

"But every time someone googles you, his blogs come up. It says in big bold letters: M. Thomas Eisenstadt is a hoax."

Huh, now that might become a problem. Sadly, in this world, you're only as important as Google says you are. And I also know that if you completely ignore attacks on your integrity, you're reduced to a bad John Kerry metaphor.

"Jimmy, find out everything you can about this guy."

"Right, boss."

Two hours later, Jimmy had a nice neat dossier prepared for me. You've got to hand it to the Mennonites for their sense of precision. And unlike his bearded brethren in Indiana, Jimmy wasn't too afraid of the Internet.

Here's what he learned.

- Wolfrum's one-sentence bio says that he's an American ex-pat writer living in Brazil.[17]

- He also blogs for WorldGolf.com—a seemingly innocuous commercial golf site. We're guessing this is his one source of income.[18]

- A bio of him on an obscure book-review site fills in some gaps: "A one-time commercial fisherman, Wolfrum has lived in Alaska, New York City and Southern California. His writing credits include the Boston Globe, New Jersey Star Ledger, Seattle Times, Anchorage Daily News, as well as several sports magazines."[19]

- He's also apparently a hard-core boxing fan and writes about it on such websites as SaddoBoxing.com.[20]

- The Shakesville site is run by blogger Melissa McEwan, who herself made headlines when she was fired by John Edwards for her profanity-strewn anti-Catholic blogging.[21]

- Wolfrum and McEwan had collaborated on an Internet hoax that claimed that Benjamin H. Grumbles, President Bush's assistant administrator for the Office of Water in the EPA, was actually a Victorian-esque character who was the "Detector of Potions, Elixirs, and Poisons for the U.S. Government and Its Occupied Territories," thereby sullying his good name on all future Google searches.[22]

Wolfrum's posts were annoying, to be sure, but as far as I could tell from his background, he wasn't working at the behest of any of the obvious enemies I'd made over the years. The connection to the Edwards campaign was intriguing, though. Could Wolfrum's posts be an elaborate DNC dirty trick to discredit McCain advisers one by one? If so, should I advise Charlie Black or Randy Scheunemann that they could be next? No, I decided. So far there wasn't any proof that this was anything more than some troubled expat golf blogger living in Brazil. And I didn't want to draw any unwanted attention toward me with the campaign.

I've worked long enough in the political and intelligence communities to know that when attacked, if you go on the offense too early, you'll only make matters worse. Just because we noticed what this lunatic was saying didn't mean anyone else had. But I've also learned that you have to be prepared for the worst and be ready to counterattack. I took one look across the office bullpen. Jimmy was pulling a crumbled mass of papers out of the copier. Poppy was trying unsuccessfully to staple a small poster of her idol, Condi Rice, on her cubicle wall. And Marwan was eating takeout Pakistani food at his desk, infusing the whole office with the aroma of chicken tikka. Nope. We needed expertise. We needed reinforcements. We needed some dorky kid who knows computers backward and forward. We needed . . . Danny Sadler.

## The Periodontist's Son

Just a week earlier, I'd gotten a call from my old friend Daniel Pipes (who wouldn't give me a ride to Annapolis). Pipes has long suffered the ravages of chronic gum disease, and on a recent speaking tour of northern New Jersey synagogues, his gingivitis had devolved into an acute case of aggressive periodontitis. At the conclusion of his speech at B'nai Shalom in West Orange, he remarked, half jokingly: "Is there a periodontist in the audience?"

"Yes!" Pipes was surprised to hear the Israeli-accented voice coming from the back. "I'm a periodontist!"

It was Dr. Chaim Sadler. Pipes had lucked out. Sadler was known as one of the best gum men in the tristate area (depending, of course, on which three states you were talking about). Sadler opened up his office that night and took care of Pipes the only way he knew how: root planing, a heavy dose of amoxicillin, and a strong prescription for Vicodin. Pipes was in love.

So when Chaim's son Danny graduated from Rutgers in the spring and told his dad he wanted to go to Washington, Chaim told him to call Pipes. Pipes, though, is based in Philadelphia at his own think tank, the Middle East Forum. So Pipes told Danny to call me. I'd seen Danny the week before for an interview and didn't think much of him at the time. He seemed bright and capable, but a little nebbishy, too. His resume said all the right things: A double major in poli-sci and computer science. Fluent in Hebrew and English. And he was already a big fan of the blog. He'd even been one of our sockpuppets in Eli's campaign to spread the word about the blog.

At the time I thought that we had too many men in the office. I didn't want to bow to the pressures of politically correct hiring practices by filling some unachievable diversity slate; I just like the idea of having more women around me. Also, I was already stretched thin on our budget for the fiscal year, and we couldn't afford Danny.

Now I could see, though, that we needed him. I called him on his cell. He'd been through a dozen interviews and no one had hired him yet. He was thinking of getting retail work at the Tenleytown Best Buy near American University, but he didn't seem excited by the prospect. I told him that initially we couldn't afford to pay him ("Much?" "No, at all"), but that technically I'd give him an "associate fellow" job title to make up for it, which is actually considered one pay grade above intern. He jumped at the chance. Any son of Dr. Chaim Sadler could afford to pay his dues for a year in Washington. Danny had found an apartment on Capitol Hill at Tenth and F, in a half-gentrified former crack house, and he was scheduled to start next week. Danny would be our secret weapon against Wolfrum.

I could tell there would be tension around the office if the staff found out that I was bringing in a ringer to work on our Internet efforts. So I told them that Danny was an IT guy, and that every think tank worth its salt has to have an IT guy. The team was actually pretty excited. There were murmurs around the office that this might be a prelude to us finally upgrading to Windows Vista. I let them dream on.

Sure enough, everyone was cordial to Danny. We cleared out the cubicle that we used to use for telexes, and Danny got straight to work. He suggested—and I agreed—that the first step to an Internet defense was to slowly degrade the reputation of the attacker. Did all the so-called feminists and liberals who read Shakesville know that their vaunted blogger calling himself Wolfrum was really on the payroll of Big Golf—about as bourgeois a sport as they come? We had to do to him what he was doing to us. But so subtly that it would neither draw further attention to his attacks nor antagonize him so much that it would invite more of them.

Danny also realized that one of Wolfrum's main beefs with

me was that, unlike many other blogs by practicing pundits, I didn't have a picture of myself on the site next to all of my posts. Sure, the idea had cropped up from time to time, but probably the biggest reason is because the office scanner hadn't worked in more than two years (since the unfortunate incident with Eli and the intern at the '06 holiday party). To this day, I walk past the peanut-butter stain on the wall in the Coca-Cola® Conference Room and cringe. But Danny said we needed to come up with a more plausible explanation.

### Rebuttal to the internet police

June 11, 2008, by Marty

It has come to my attention that a golf blogger *[and here, we linked to his golfing blog]* who moonlights as a shill for identity politics has been calling us names and challenging our right to speak freely. My assistant Jimmy thought I would be upset upon hearing this news. But I explained to him that flying under the radar in these turbulent times is not a bad thing, especially considering the sensitive national security work in which we sometimes engage. Unlike the Bill Wolfrums, Marnie Vander Helsings and Arianna Huffingtons of the world (or even my esteemed colleague Debbie Schlussel), my ego is not so out of whack that I feel compelled to plaster my face next to each and every blog entry, potentially compromising the safety of my dedicated staff and trusted contacts in the field.[23]

You'll notice I still refer to Jimmy as my key assistant. It was important that I keep Danny, my secret weapon, under wraps for a while. Apparently he had quite the reputation for appropriating free online music at Rutgers, and he was concerned that if word got out that he was working for me, it could hurt us both.

We felt confident that our post had done what it needed to do, but then Danny alerted me to a new post by Wolfrum that same day.

"Now what?"

"He's trying to tattle on you. To narc you out to other sites, too."

"Narc me out as what?"

"Not existing."

"But I do exist."

"So you say."

I looked at the post. In it Wolfrum stated that he had e-mailed SourceWatch editor Bob Burton, who then agreed to place "Hoax Warnings" above entries for M. Thomas Eisenstadt and the Harding Insitute.[24]

"Danny, what's this SourceWatch thing?"

"It's like a liberal version of Wikipedia. Everybody on the left uses it. You know what Wikipedia is?"

"Yes, Danny, I'm not an idiot."

"Of course you're not, Marty."

"Call me Mr. Eisenstadt."

"Yes, sir."

"But don't call me sir."

"Right."

"So should we be worried?"

"Well, he's burned your name."

"What do you mean burned my name?"

"Your name, your name!" Danny jumped up and down in frustration. "Any time someone looks up M. Thomas Eisenstadt, they now see this big SourceWatch thing saying you don't exist."

"You're the Internet genius. What do we do?"

"You've got to change your name."

## From JFK to MLK to MTE

Wow. That's something. A name is a precious commodity. I owe mine to one crazy night of passion between a young Connie Beane and a savvy Izzy Eisenstadt. JFK had been shot at 12:30 central time, and in a national day of mourning, America needed

## Punditing with Marnie

Marnie Vander Helsing was once famously described by one of those inside-the-beltway most-eligible-pundit lists thusly: "If Arianna Huffington had half the brains of Marnie Vander Helsing, and Maureen Dowd had half the good looks, then maybe both of them would have made this list, too." Come to think of it, I'll bet Marnie wrote that line herself.

Around New Year's 2007, Marnie and I made a joint appearance on Wolf Blitzer's *Situation Room* on CNN. Normally they have the likes of Paul Begala, Donna Brazile, or J. C. Watts on the show, but I've found that during the Christmas season when someone like John "Magic Map" King is filling in for Wolf, they'll usually book any pundit who's still in town. That's why I try to stay in the District during holiday seasons—just in case I get the call.

There was a certain level of anxiety, discomfort—and, dare I say, sexual tension—between Marnie and me in the greenroom that day. Finally, the notoriously handsome but emotionless King greeted us at the stage and offered the obligatory two-adjective pundit intro for his audience: "I'm here with Democratic analyst Marnie Vander Helsing and Republican strategist Martin Eisenstadt." We smiled and nodded, and then King asked us about the recent resignation of Don Rumsfeld and the impact it would have on the Iraq War.

a shoulder to cry on. Connie found Izzy's at the White Horse Tavern, and nine months later she had to pick a name for me.

"John Fitzgerald Eisenstadt" seemed too obvious. (There were more than a few John Fitzgeralds born around July 23, 1964—actor John "Fitz" Leguizamo was born just a day before me, in fact). And besides, neither Connie nor Izzy was Catholic. But Connie was at that point in her life very committed to the civil rights movement and Izzy was essentially out of the picture—

Marnie complained about the "surge." I argued that we shouldn't "pull out" too soon. She was witty. I was obstinate. She was self-righteous. I was shrill. Her cleavage beaded with perspiration. My forehead was sweaty. Our eye contact was magnetic.

"Marnie, will you have dinner with me?" I blurted out.

Marnie was stunned. King was dejected. Wittingly or not, I'd put Marnie on the spot: if she turned me down now, all of America would think she was an uptight shrew who thrived on hyper-partisan antagonism. She had to at least be polite and say yes. America demanded no less than that, and so she did.

As soon as the show was over, though, Marnie was livid. At least until the point where the CNN producers told us they'd gotten a record number of e-mails about the "Marnie and Marty" political theater we'd exhibited. Who knows, they said, maybe there was a show idea there. All pundits live for that moment when their guest spot turns into a regular appearance, which then turns into a regular guest-hosting job, which then turns into their own show. Like when Rachel Maddow got the call to host her own show after getting better ratings than Olbermann when she sat in for him. On the other hand, this is also what network producers say to keep the unpaid pundits coming back. And by the way, Marnie has *still* never gone on the dinner date with me.

working back at the zipper factory in Brooklyn. By the time she gave birth to me, Connie was already making plans to go to Martin Luther King Jr.'s March on Washington a month later. I think she felt that as a young white woman breast-feeding a newborn baby named Martin, she would be able to blend in better with the mostly black crowd.

For a middle name, like many newly emerging hippies of her day, Connie was enthralled by the beatnik poetry of Dylan

Thomas. When she realized I'd been conceived in the back room at the White Horse, the famous site of Thomas's last drink, her first inclination was to name me Dylan.[25] But ultimately Connie wasn't prepared to make that much of a statement at the risk of alienating her Waspish parents, who were, after all, sending remittances once a month to support her. So she went with Thomas. At least Connie would know who I was named after.

I'd been thinking about my name a lot ever since Wolfrum started confusing me with M███████ Eisenstadt the week before. Maybe it *was* unfair to let people on the blogosphere wonder what the "M" in M. Thomas stood for. After all, I thought, most people in D.C. already knew me as Marty anyway.

"Okay, Danny. Make it happen."

So we ran this blog.

### What's in a name?

June 17, 2008, by Marty

It's come to my attention that some people have confused our work here at the Harding Institute with that of M█████ Eisenstadt of the W█████████ Institute for ████ ███ Policy. M█████'s a terrific guy and a distinguished expert in the field of Middle Eastern security affairs. So out of respect for him, and to alleviate any lingering confusion, I've decided to start to publicly use the name that most of my friends call me anyway, Marty.[26]

To quote my erstwhile namesake, Dylan Thomas: "Great is the hand that holds dominion over man by a scribbled name."

No big fanfare, no fancy press releases. Forevermore, my blog, my business card, my professional identity was shed of pretense and artifice. Just a simple change that would bring about a clean slate on Google . . .

Or so we thought.

# 7

# The Jonas Brothers Are (Probably) Not Terrorists

### The Birth of Blogging

In this modern era of our punditocracy, it is incumbent on any decent political analyst/consultant/strategist to keep a blog. The political media cycle is so fast now that you can't just sit by the phone and wait for Wolf Blitzer's producer to call and invite you on his show. And you can't even wait a week for *The New York Times*, *The Washington Post*, or even the Dubuque *Telegraph Herald* to pick up an op-ed piece that's already out-of-date by the time it appears. Nope. You're nothing in this business without a blog.

Thomas Paine published a hundred thousand copies of his famous *Common Sense* pamphlet on January 10, 1776, and it arguably was the blog that started a Revolution. Like all bloggers, Paine had his vitriolic commenters, spammers, and player-haters: James Chalmers, a patsy Loyalist, accused Paine of political quackery and admonished that with no king to guide us, our gov-

ernment would "degenerate into democracy." Like all good bloggers, Paine took the quote out of context and objected to being
called a "degenerate." He then accused Chalmers of being a "ye olde
douchenozzle," and within no time, the flame wars had turned into
a very real war that launched our nation into independence.[1]

So when my old assistant Eli Perle set me up with a blog a few
years ago, it seemed all at once new and old. It freed me to comment on the day's news in a timely and topical fashion, and to be
a little more provocative than I might otherwise be on TV or in
print. The way it works is, the more confrontational you are,
the more other bloggers link to you. In theory, the point you're
trying to make trickles up through the murky blogosphere to
emerge into the fresh air of the mainstream media—percolated
into a nice distilled form of your original thought (then hope-
fully you're invited onto TV to defend your outrageous statement).
But more often than not, it's like a global game of telephone: you
say one thing, and the blogosphere strips away all qualifiers, ad-
jectives, irony, tone, context, and sarcasm—to the point where it
comes out the complete opposite of what you intended in the
first place. That seems to have happened to me a lot lately. One
series of blog entries I wrote in the summer of 2008 should shed
some light on this phenomenon.

### Rachael Ray, Dunkin' Donuts, and Hezbollah

On May 18, 2008, the moderately popular blogger Pamela Geller
broke the story that popular daytime diva Rachael Ray was wearing a keffiyeh in a photograph on the official Dunkin' Donuts
website.

Geller implied that the woman who brought us *30 Minute
Meals* was also somehow a depraved Jew-murdering pedophilic
barbarian at the gates of our civilization. Geller concluded with:
"We have to complain to Dunkin' Donuts or contact Rachael
Ray."[2] As Rachael herself might say, "Oh my gravy!"

The story might have ended there, but Rachael Ray is America's sweetheart—a younger, whiter, and only slightly skinnier Oprah. The story was quickly elevated to the twenty-four-hour cable news channels and beyond. The scandal got huge for a week or two following a familiar pattern: a threatened boycott, a nervous company pulling their ad, and even more backlash for them caving in to special interests (that is, the Jews).

In the midst of the developing story, numerous bloggers were on the hunt for other offensive wearers of the keffiyeh. My good friend Debbie Schlussel wrote that John McCain's daughter Meghan had been photographed several times wearing the "jihadist choice of accessories."[3]

Look, I'm the first to say that the keffiyeh has blood on its hands and should be as offensive to the West as the Windsor knot is undoubtedly to the East. But as much as I normally love Debbie's work, in my capacity as a liaison with the Jewish community for the McCain campaign, it was my responsibility to put my foot down and tell her to back off of attacking young Meghan. Just because a candidate's daughter takes one minor fashion misstep, does not mean that the candidate himself is an anti-Semite.[4]

## Kevin, Nick, and Joe: A Growing Threat to National Security

I didn't think about keffiyehs again for a while. With all the press over Rachael Ray and Meghan McCain, any public figures who thought about wearing keffiyehs again would at least be forewarned that they were treading on controversial fashion landscape.

But as the calendar moved into summer, I couldn't help but keep one eye out for other celebrities, politicians, and media figures who were wearing keffiyehs, too. Poppy Cartwright, my African American associate fellow at the institute, is always the most tuned in to popular culture at the office. One day Poppy drew my attention to a picture she'd found on the Internet of three cherubic young brothers—one of whom was wearing what looked like a keffiyeh.

She told me they were the Jonas Brothers, the hottest thing to dominate the collective preteen consciousness since Hannah Montana. "If you know who she is." Poppy rolled her eyes.

"Of course I do!" I replied. Poppy was surprised, but I told her that my niece, Sophie, up in Massachusetts was a huge fan. But I was still unclear on the details, so Poppy sat me down and schooled me all about these young actors/singers/celebrities.

Turns out there's a real girl, Miley Cyrus, who stars on a Disney Channel show called *Hannah Montana* as a girl named Miley Stewart who leads a double life as a pop star called Hannah Montana. But in real life, Miley Cyrus has been performing on tour as Hannah Montana and has become a genuine pop star in her own right, and more recently a top Hollywood actress. (If you thought I had existential problems, you can imagine what Miley/Hannah/Miley goes through on a daily basis.) Meanwhile, the Jonas Brothers are an act that first made appearances on *Hannah Montana* as a singing group called the Jonas Brothers, and then really did open for Hannah/Miley on her concert tour as themselves. By the summer of 2008, Disney was poised to launch the Jonas Brothers as their own celebrity franchise just as the Miley/Hannah juggernaut was peaking. So here's what I posted.

### Jonas Brothers terrorists? The keffiyeh conspiracy . . .

July 15, 2008, by Marty

Yes, the Jonas Brothers are cute, but why is it that even in the wake of the recent Rachael Ray controversy, Disney is still parading the boys out proudly wearing keffiyehs?

Sure, some conspiracy theorists will no doubt trot out the boys' Christian upbringing, Disney's alleged history of anti-Semitism, or some sleeper-cell conspiracy from Al Qaeda. But I reject such poppycock. Chances are, the brothers have been too curled up in their Disney incubator to be aware of the cultural insensitivity involved when you wear a keffiyeh in the manner of Hezbollah. Is Kevin Jonas (aka "the Romantic One") trying to seduce America's young girls into being the next generation of Hamas sympathizers? Probably not. But why take the chance? (My advice: if you really need to hide a hickey, stick to the Charles Nelson Reilly ascot.)

While Disney does damage control on their last manufactured pop star —throwing poor Miley "Hannah Montana" Cyrus under the proverbial JoBros tour bus because of a few indiscreet cell-phone pictures of her in the shower—they should think about the bigger image they're projecting with their newest stars. Or maybe they are? There are over a billion Muslims in the world, and probably not all of them have bought their Jonas Brothers lunch boxes . . . yet.[5]

That blog post became huge on the Internet.

## The Obama Daughters

The whole issue may have remained a footnote in pop culture, but then I stumbled into an angle to the story that I knew would spark an even bigger reaction. Candidates' children are always the third rail of campaign press coverage (just ask Amy Carter), but since Meghan McCain had been dragged into the controversy, this blog seemed fair play.

### Obama's daughters huge Jonas Brothers fans. Keffiyeh Koincidence?

July 17, 2008, by Marty

Okay, I hope I'm not reading too much into this, but in the course of responding to media requests regarding the Jonas Brothers

## Selected Angry Blog Comments on "Jonas Brothers terrorists? The keffiyeh conspiracy . . ."

comment number 9 by: Lauren
July 17, 2008 at 11:38 a.m.

OMG. seriously, its a scarf!! they were them cuz they look good on them! they are the CLEANEST boy band ive ever heard of. you should be worring about more serious stuff in the world and back off of the jonas brothers!!!

comment number 13 by: Laura
July 19, 2008, at 4:49 p.m.

How rediculous. They're fashionable scarves.. I have one, am i a terrorist? No. Get a frikin life, seriously, this could be the most stupid thing i have EVER heard. Jeeeezz.

comment number 19 by: haley starlitt
October 16, 2008, at 4:40 p.m.

omj!! wtf its a scaft!!!! so just leave them alone cuase its not a terrorist its a SCARFTTT

comment number 24 by: Katie
October 19, 2008, at 9:43 p.m.

I love the Jonas Brothers. Especially Joe he is so H.O.T. hot. So haters need to back off. Keep up the great work guys I will always be a fan

keffiyeh controversy, one of my interns alerted me to a story in the Indian press that revealed that Barack Obama's daughters, Malia and Sasha, are big fans of the keffiyeh-wearing Jonas Brothers.[6] All I can say is, "Oy."

Now, I'm not one of those McCain supporters who believes in

comment number 30 by: syaf712
October 27, 2008, at 2:08 a.m.
oh my god! they are totally hot(100x) especially Joe.
joe is the hottest, and nick is the cutest!!hope you come to brunei!

comment number 31 by: joBros fan 4 life
October 29, 2008, at 9:19 a.m.
I wud jus like 2 sya that its just a scarf, jus coz theyve put it in there own style doesnt make them a terrorsist KKK!!
i dont see y ur backin up miley cirus hannah montanan watever 'cos she s a slut y dont u say anythin 2 that!! so dont chat crap :[

comment number 32 by: Juliana
October 29, 2008, at 12:38 p.m.
Euu amoo o Jonas Brothers mais que tudo nessa vida !!!!! eu sou brasileira e eles são muito conhecidos aqui no Brazil !!

comment number 46 by: savanna
December 4, 2008, at 5:07 p.m.
i mean i wear scarfs so i guess im a terrorist now I DONT THINK SO!!!!!!!!!!!! n if anyone who reads this knos someone who can help my dream come true that would be one of the most amazing things that has ever happened to me! I LOVE U JOE NICK AND KEVIN JONAS U GUYS ROC!!!!!!!

perpetuating ugly innuendos about Barack Obama's faith or even his middle name. I believe Senator McCain can win in November fair and square. But . . .

First Meghan McCain wears a few mis-chosen keffiyehs, and next the Obama girls will be spotted wearing Che Guevara t-shirts.

At this rate, it may not matter who wins the election: the Jonas
Brothers will play the inaugural ball, Miley Cyrus will be showering
in the Lincoln bedroom and Chief Justice Roberts will terror-fist
bump whomever he swears in over the Koran. Makes me wish for the
days when the Beatles were the biggest threat to national security.[7]

Not surprisingly, the story got considerable traction. Infamous liberal muckraking website Talking Points Memo ran a big
link to my blog entry and quaintly referred to me as "a sick person," "a total piece of shit," and "a little fucktard."[8] I love their
subtlety. Other blogs and comments followed . . . all pretty much
voicing the same assessment of me. It's tough on the institute
staff who might not have the intestinal fortitude to withstand
these levels of persistent insults on the phone and in our blog
comments. But for someone like me who has been on the front
lines of Iraqi reconstruction (if not the actual front lines of the
war itself), I've dealt with far worse insults. Forget about verbal
brickbats thrown at me, I've had more than a few pairs of desert
loafers hurled my way. So a few days later, I responded.

### Does McCain think Obama's daughters are terrorists?

July 23, 2008, by Marty

The simple answer is no. But as long as the far left (and yes, some
on the right) see Meghan McCain's rare use of the keffiyeh as fair
political game, then the Obama daughters' abiding love of the
Jonas Brothers should be noticed (not dwelled upon, but noticed)
as well.

As you can see from the number of comments on and links to
my last post, the response was overwhelmingly accusatory, vitriolic
and vulgar. So I wanted to clarify a few things. Perhaps I had
overestimated the intelligence of my left-wing critics when I failed
to spell out in italicized letters that the final paragraph of my last

post was *facetious* and used *hyperbole* to make a *humorous* point. A joke, dare we say. Sadly, one deficit of the blogosphere is that people often react to buzz-words, rather than whole sentences, paragraphs, or—heaven forbid—the context of prior posts on the same blog. Forgive me if I didn't hyperlink every single reference in the paragraph to something contextual, ironic, or topical (usually my associate Jimmy does that for me).[9]

## Miley Cyrus and the Sarah Palin Connection

I thought that post would have put the issue to rest, but then I got an urgent call from my niece, Sophie, in Boston. She's the test-tube daughter of my half sister, Candice, and Candice's life partner, Arianna. Technically, I suppose, you would say that Sophie is my half niece, but that might make her wonder what the other half of her is. She's going to have enough identity issues of her own without me piling on.

Sophie had heard about the keffiyeh controversy and was afraid that because of Uncle Marty, Homeland Security was going to arrest the Jonas Brothers and waterboard them at Guantánamo. I assured her that waterboarding is not considered "torture," because by definition, the United States does not torture people. I explained that a better term for it was probably "indoor surfing," and she thought that Kevin especially might like that.

Sophie's "other" mother, Arianna, won a contest for them to go to the Teen Choice Awards in L.A. (It's hard to say which is Sophie's "biological" mom, because it was Arianna's egg that was used in the test tube, and then implanted in Candice. To this day, I'm still not sure whose sperm—if any—they used.) Between Sophie's firsthand reporting (well done, Sophie!) and Poppy giving me an ongoing education in pop culture, I was able to put this story together for the blog.

## Selected Angry Blog Comments on "Obama's daughters huge Jonas Brothers fans. Keffiyeh Koincidence?"

comment number 3 by: Get a grip
July 21, 2008, at 4:29 p.m.

The only threat I see is the one you pose to the English language with your abuse of the privilege of literacy. Please dedicate your aberrant brain to science.

comment number 7 by: Jenna L
July 21, 2008, at 5:59 p.m.

I am shocked by your stupidity. Seriously, I just wish you luck.

comment number 12 by: Farker
July 21, 2008, at 6:14 p.m.

We're being infiltrated by terrorist scarves wherever we turn. I'll bet the Jonas Brothers even do those terrorist fist bumps.

comment number 15 by: Faith
July 21, 2008, at 6:42 p.m.

Are you sane? What kind of grown person would try to analyze (and I am being generous) the crushes of a healthy American girls?

comment number 17 by: John
July 21, 2008, at 6:58 p.m.

Until the late 90's I'd been a life long Republican. So was my old man and his old man who boasted he voted for Alf Landon in

1936. If this is a typical example of where much of the GOP is it's truly losing its mind.

comment number 19 by: time horizon
July 21, 2008, at 7:05 p.m.
Wow. Do you see what a complete low-life you are. Fear-monger. Hater. Conservative. There is the door. Take Senator Lott, Thurmond's ghost and the rest of your kind with you.

comment number 20 by: REHuntJr
July 21, 2008, at 7:15 p.m.
So according to that logic, since the Bush daughters are boozy party chicks, that means their father is an alcoholic. Oh wait, that's right, he is an alcoholic. Never mind, you're right, Obama is a terrorist because his kids like the Jonas Brothers. Nice work.

comment number 30 by: Thom
July 22, 2008, at 12:34 p.m.
it's one thing to be an idiot in your basement. It's another to be an idiot of the day on the internets. Congratulations.

comment number 31 by: MD
July 22, 2008, at 1:36 p.m.
You're so correct, and I can't believe the rest of the media hasn't picked up on this already. At least 85% of American prepubescent girls are Jonas Brothers fans, and their parents are probably ALL plotting the downfall of the West as we speak.

## Jonas Brothers losing their religion: becoming Barack Obama?

August 4, 2008, by Marty

Have the Jonas Brothers taken a cue from world celebrity Barack Obama and shunned their own religion? I have it on good authority that at tonight's Teen Choice Awards on Fox the so-called JoBros thanked everyone under the sun for their success (parents, Disney, et al.), and even "the Big Man who's with them everywhere they go." God? Jesus? Allah? Nope. They meant their enormous bodyguard, Big Rob. Why is this relevant? Because as some angry commenters wrote the last time I mentioned the Jonas Brothers, they apparently come from a deeply religious family and their early work was often identified as Christian rock. Of course, this was before Disney got a hold of them and packaged them for the Godless masses. I would suggest that the Jonas Brothers had to lose their religion to attract the broadest audience—in the same way Barack Obama had to sever his ties to Rev. Jeremiah Wright before he could assume the Democratic nomination.

Compare this to Miley (aka Hannah Montana) Cyrus. She made a point of thanking Jesus Christ first and foremost in her speech. Yet another way of sticking it to her Disney masters? Maybe. It seems the clock is ticking on how long Ms. Cyrus is hanging around the House of Mouse before becoming the next Hilary Duff, or worse, Lindsay Lohan.

In the battle of preteen hearts and minds, the Jonas Brothers' ascension over Miley Cyrus is very much like Barack Obama's triumph over Hillary Clinton. Yes, girls want to cheer and adore their self-empowerment peer with the million-dollar smile (one actual Hannah Montana lyric: "Who said, who said I won't be President? I say, I say you ain't seen nothin' yet"). But when push comes to shove, young girls would rather swoon for the cute boys. That's just human nature.

So to my colleagues on the McCain campaign, the take-home lesson is don't count on getting any of those Hillary women to cross

over to the GOP (even with a Carly Fiorina or Gov. Sarah Palin in
the veep spot). At the end of the day, they'll vote with their hearts,
not their heads. And they'll vote for the cute boy. Barack Obama's
not a celebrity for nothing.

   (Final note on the Jonas Brothers: They conspicuously were NOT
wearing their trademark keffiyehs—no scarves, no ascots, no
cravats neither. I guess Disney's been reading my blog, and took my
criticism to heart.)[10]

You'll notice that a full month before John McCain chose
Sarah Palin as his running mate, I was warning people on my
blog and within the campaign not to overreact to the "Hillary
voters" by picking a woman running mate like Sarah just for the
sake of it. Sure enough, when all the votes were counted, Palin
wound up turning off more women voters than she attracted.
And if some of the people at the campaign had come out of their
Washington headquarters and really gotten the pulse of the pop-
ulace, they might have figured that out. This series of blogs
taught me a valuable lesson, too: pop culture is popular for a
reason; and the punditocracy would do well to remember that.

   And for the record, my facetious note about what would happen at an Obama inauguration was no stranger than what really
did happen: Chief Justice John Roberts flubbed the oath of office
and had to redo it the next day; the Disney Channel produced
one of the inaugural balls with both the JoBros and Miley Cyrus
performing; and the night of the inauguration, Sasha and Malia
had a scavenger hunt in the White House, opened their closet,
and out popped Nick, Joe, and Kevin Jonas to surprise them.[11]
Don't say I didn't warn you.

# 8

# The Art of the Apology: My Inglorious Moment on YouTube

## Riding High and Poised for a Fall

By late spring of 2008, I was slowly rising in the hierarchy of the campaign. I'd like to say it was through my own skills, wit, and vibrant good looks, but that would be naïve. You see, by mid-May a bored press corps was starting to look at Senator McCain's stated policy banning lobbyists from working on the campaign. At one count, there were at least 133 lobbyists who arguably could be said to be doing just that.[1] So the third week of May was particularly grim over at campaign headquarters, as John was forced to fire five top staffers for their ties to lobbyists.[2]

There's only so many of them that you can purge before you don't have anyone left to carry your bags. John couldn't bring himself to fire his top campaign strategists, like my friends chief political adviser Charlie Black (who had made telecommunications lobbying calls from the Straight Talk Express),[3] campaign manager Rick Davis (who represented Freddie Mac, an Israeli satellite imagery company, and a shady Russian oligarch),[4] and foreign policy adviser Randy Scheunemann (the NRA and the Republic of Georgia). But I won't lie to you. It was making all of us on the campaign who had ever dabbled in the fine arts of "issue advocacy" a tad bit nervous. But we persevered.

I came into the Harding Institute office at 11:00 a.m. on Friday, June 27, and told our newest intern to fill up my coffee mug. (By now I was pretty sure her name was Veronica, with us for the summer from one of the lesser Ivys—Cornell? Penn? Yale?— I don't remember exactly. Smart girl. Smelled good, too.) When I turned the corner, past the bullpen of associate fellow cubicles, Jimmy and Marwan were looking at me with jaws agape and eyes wide open. For Jimmy, that didn't seem so strange, but Marwan's left eye was preternaturally a little droopy, so I wasn't used to seeing so much of it. As I headed into my corner office, I walked past Danny, the newest member of the team.

"Mr. Eisenstadt, I think you should see this," he said.

I ruffled his bushy hair, leaned over to his computer, and said, "Call me Marty, kid. What's up?"

Danny pointed to the screen. "Juan Cole's blog. He's a big-time liberal, but he gets a lot of hits."

"Yes, Danny, I know who he is."

Juan Cole, as I patiently explained to Danny, was a hotshot alumnus from American University in Cairo and had returned as a visiting Islamic-studies professor during the year I was there as an undergrad. I took a couple of classes from him, and I loved the guy. I thought of him as a father. A raving liberal father whom it would be ultimately necessary to rebel against in true Alex Keaton/Luke Skywalker fashion. But ideology aside, Cole taught me to appreciate that academia is a means to an end, not an end in itself. Long before he was a widely read blogger who had his own pretentiously named vanity think tank, The Global Americana Institute, Cole was always out front in the advocacy/

punditocracy/academic revolving door. I believe it was Cole who once admonished me against a life in the ivory tower: "If you don't like what they're letting you publish, then start your own damn think tank and publish what you want!" Juan and I have appeared together in recent years on the pundit circuit as opposing experts on Near Eastern policy. Sure, we'll yell and scream at each other in front of the cameras, but I always invite him out for a drink afterward. Pundits first, partisans second.

Cole's blog headline was this: "McCain Adviser Plans Casino on the Tigris." I glanced through the first paragraph.

A "foreign policy adviser" to the McCain campaign was interviewed last February on television in Baghdad about plans for a Las Vegas–style five-star hotel and casino smack-dab in the middle of the Green Zone in Baghdad. He promises a trickle-down effect of wealthy gamblers' losses helping Iraq's poor. He promises Iraqi women jobs as maids in the hotel rooms. He promises Thai and Russian masseuses.[5]

"Hey, that's great! See guys, that's one of the first times I've been acknowledged as a bona fide 'foreign policy adviser' to the senator. Terrific work finding that, Danny. Make sure we send Juan one of the new mugs this Christmas. Veronica, put him on the list."

Veronica had by this time caught up to me with my very own Harding Institute coffee mug. A month earlier, Poppy had designed a great spoof on the Shepard Fairey–designed Obama "Hope" logo with Warren Harding's face instead, and Danny had just figured out a way to sell them online—along with T-shirts, posters, and of course, intimate apparel. (It would be rude of me not to mention that you—yes, you! my loyal reader—can get your very own Harding swag at our website at www.HardingInstitute.org/store.)

Danny, meanwhile, was momentarily distracted by Veronica. It seems that among the junior staff there was a distinct pecking

Now on sale at HardingInstitute.org! *(Courtesy of Harding Institute)*

order as to who would ask out the new interns first. For years Eli always had dibs, but with him gone, now it was Jimmy first, then Marwan, and now Danny. Of course, for the rare times when we had male interns, then Poppy had them all to herself (she and Chris were quite the item back in March—which caused some tension in the office, because Poppy had hooked up with Eli last summer when she was an intern).

Naturally, the interns were strictly off limits for me. Unless of course they had rejected all the junior staff first, and then only if it was within two weeks of them ending their internship anyway (an employment lawyer once explained that this would get me off the hook from any untoward litigation). Among a few former interns, their "going-away present from Marty" was the stuff of legend. Definitely more than a mug.

## The Globalization of Marty

"Marty, look."

Danny had by now scrolled down the page and I could see what looked like a still frame of me, probably from that interview I did on Iraqi television. "Marty, it's all over YouTube."

"Terrific! What's the problem?" Danny played the clip for me, and it quickly became apparent that my hour-long in-depth interview on Iraqi television had been drastically edited down to eight minutes and twenty-eight seconds. Whole segments of the discussion were completely missing. Words I said were edited out of context. "Ironic" photographs were superimposed behind my head.

"How could this happen? Was Juan behind this? Veronica, take him off the list." But Danny, our Internet maven, explained that Juan was only the latest in a long chain of websites that had found this YouTube clip. We came up with this reverse chronology:

- June 27: Juan Cole writes about it on his blog, Informed Comment, based on a link from:

- June 26: A blog called Ten Percent by an obscure British peacenik blogger named RickB, who writes:

  *I cannot urge you enough to watch this youtube clip and post it yourself, an American, Martin Eisenstadt . . . evangelises about casinos in the green zone . . . This is the naked face of imperialism, utterly greedy, endlessly racist and brutally arrogant.*[6]

RickB had found the link from:

- June 26: A blog called In the Middle by Raed Jarrar, an Iraqi peace activist now living in Washington, D.C. (who six months later won a $240,000 settlement from JetBlue for not letting him wear a T-shirt with Arabic writing).[7] Raed somehow found the video on YouTube here:

- June 11: The video was posted on YouTube by a very pretty nineteen-year-old Japanese girl who goes by the handle Asu-kajunk and wears a T-shirt that reads "Peace People Japan." Asukajunk writes this in her description of the video: "Found this on Nico Nico Douga: American propaganda from Iraq Business conference."[8]

Furthermore, she somehow figured out a way to annotate the video itself with Japanese—it's like seeing someone graffiti the video while you're watching it. Marwan's Pakistani roots made him the closest we had to anyone in the office who could understand Japanese, so I asked him to translate it for me. He objected slightly to me lumping all Asians together, and pointed out that Veronica was in fact a Japanese studies major at Columbia (I was right, one of the lesser Ivys) who had spent her junior year in Sapporo on the island of Hokkaido. Despite Jimmy's seniority in the office, Marwan had obviously spent enough quality time with Veronica to suss out her credentials . . . and perhaps a little more. Well done, Marwan!

So Veronica sidled into Danny's seat, and as we all looked past her silken caramel-blonde hair to the glowing computer screen, she simultaneously translated some of the annotations. The Japanese kanji scrolled on the screen in front of my face and Veronica happily chirped out: "Idiot!" "Imperialist Bastard!" "Ugly American!"

"Okay, I get it," I said. "Let's move on."

Veronica followed the reference in the YouTube description to a Japanese site called Nico Nico Douga that she described as literally meaning "smiley videos," but was in fact the hottest video-sharing website in Japan. Apparently a lot of the features we take for granted on YouTube were actually developed earlier and better on Nico Nico Douga. And yes, she said, they allow more "saucy" content than YouTube. I had found my new favorite site. Smiley videos, indeed!

- June 12: This is when the same eight-minute-plus video was posted on Nico Nico Douga. Veronica couldn't figure out much more behind it other than the brief description (in broken English): "Casinos in the Green Zone: American lobbyist interviewd on Iraqui TV says casinos in green zone will be good for bagdad, Iraq."[9]

"No other clues, boss." She looked up at me with her green eyes. "This is the point of origination."

Danny scratched his prematurely thinning hair. "Japan? Japan? I wonder how this footage from Iraq found its way to Japan? Marty, was there anyone from that TV crew who could have given it to the Japanese?"

"Of course not, Danny, that's ridic—"

And then it all became perfectly clear.

## Blubber Pirates, the Britney Sex Tape, and Catholics at MSNBC

When I left the Business 2 Business Expo in Baghdad, I had asked the TV crew at the conference for a raw DVD of my interview. A good pundit always tries to keep and compile his clips. And especially given the vitriolic nature of my benefactors Jamie and Nabil, any proof that I had attempted a public affairs campaign on their behalf would be evidence that they had spent good money for my services in Iraq. Compared with the $240,000 the Bush administration once paid prominent black columnist Armstrong Williams to shill for its education policies, my $20,000 fee was a downright bargain.[10]

I never got a chance to actually watch the DVD. I had it with me on that boat to Egypt when the Somali pirates attacked. At the pirate redoubt where I was held hostage, the compound of prisoners was like a mini United Nations. There were sailors from the Philippines, South Korea, Venezuela, Nigeria, and Nepal. But there was also a particularly rowdy group of Japanese crewmen from a whaling vessel that had returned from waters off Antarctica (and had been sailing around the Horn of Africa to evade nudnik Greenpeace boats). The Somalis were at a loss for how to hold giant whales for ransom, and we all quickly developed a taste for blubber.

For days on end, I led my fellow captives in daily rounds of Texas Hold'em, which I usually dominated. (The grinning gap-toothed Filipinos were especially bad at bluffing.) We wagered with whatever we had at hand—our daily rations of rice, packs of cigarettes, khat, whatever. But one day the Japanese first mate, a wily seaman named Hoshiko, kept upping the ante until I had nothing left to bet. I looked through my bag, and the one commodity I had was the unlabeled DVD I got from the Iraqis. Knowing that I'd drawn an ace-high flush, I was confident that I'd get the disk back. I told Hoshiko it was a bootleg copy of a Britney Spears–Kevin Federline sex video. He called with a bucket of blubber and promptly showed his full house, kings full of fours. Rats!

I'm guessing that when he did finally make it back to Japan (I'd read that the Somalis released the Japanese a month or so after I left), he was probably none too pleased with what he found, or rather with what he didn't find, on the DVD. His revenge? Posting the video on Nico Nico Douga. Damn you, Hoshiko!

But it could have been worse. The main crux of the interview was still intact: that the process of capitalism in Iraq had to go hand in hand with democratization. And frankly, if Jamie and Nabil came after me, I could still use it as proof of what I was doing in Iraq.

"So okay, gang, I can live with these fringe bloggers and You-Tube clips." The staff looked disappointed but rather satisfyingly in awe of me. "We'll all have to live with them. Veronica, go ahead and put Juan back on the mug list. Everyone else, back to work."

It was a Friday, and that meant a long lunch. Ever since my youth, I've always gravitated to the power of the White House.

Even now, as a seasoned political consultant working on K Street, I like to meander toward the White House on my lunch break and eat down the block from it at the Breadline on Pennsylvania Avenue. They've got the most amazing corn-jalapeño bread, and usually on Fridays they've got a great pre–Vatican II fried-fish sandwich with a terrific remoulade and coleslaw (a holdover, no doubt, from the Camelot days of JFK). Naturally, it's the perfect place to keep an eye out for some of the MSNBC Catholics. It's a safe bet that I'll run into either Chris Matthews, Pat Buchanan, Mika Brzezinski, Norah or Lawrence O'Donnell, or even Mike Barnicle. Sure enough, I saw my old childhood friend Mika over at the salad bar, loading up on lentils and feta. "Mika!" I angled over to her while I was waiting for my fish. "Care to join me at my table?"

"Oh, hey, Marty," she said as she quickly reached for a Styrofoam container. "Sorry, I'm to-go today. Next time!"

Though Mika and I have known each other in a professional capacity for years—and I see her frequently in the MSNBC greenroom—we both make it a point never to speak of the unspeakable truth. The night with Amy Carter. But the silence itself speaks volumes.


## Needed: Proof of Life

When I walked back to the office, I looked at Veronica, Jimmy, Marwan, and Poppy and got the same uncomfortable vibe from the staff as I'd gotten that morning.

"Marty," Danny said in his distinctly just-on-the-verge-of-irritating nasal intonation. "There's more."

"What now?"

Danny pulled me into his cubicle and pointed to his computer screen.

"Marty, now they're all saying you don't exist." Huh? "It's that golf blogger in Brazil again: Wolfrum. He's commented on all those blogs that ran the casino video and now says you don't really work for McCain. That the whole video is a hoax."

"I thought we threw him off the trail by changing my name. No?"

"It didn't work. He changed your name in all his blog posts, too."

"Good grief." This was why I hired Danny? "I thought this idiot was complaining that there weren't any pictures of me, and now that there's a whole video of me, how on earth can he still claim I don't exist?"

"It's a lot of things."

"Like what?"

Danny went through the list of the bloggers' concerns, and I just as quickly shot them down.

- *One says gambling is forbidden by the Sharia laws of Islam, so there couldn't possibly be a casino in Iraq.*

  Explain that to the camel racers in Saudi Arabia, Bahrain, Qatar, or the United Arab Emirates. Explain that to the millions of backgammon players throughout the Arab world. And more specifically, then, please explain it to Vitaly Kouznetzov, an ambitious Russian businessman who opened a casino in Sulaimaniyah in Iraqi Kurdistan in September 2007.[11]

- *Another says that the video itself looks weird because my knees are overlapping the interviewer.*

  As for the knees, of course they were overlapping (much to my slight discomfort). This interview was shot in a cramped little corner of the Rasheed Hotel during the Baghdad Business 2 Business Expo. The TV crew just clipped a green-screen cloth onto a curtain rod and shoved two chairs together in front of it. Look, it's not ideal, but I've been in CNN interview studios that were smaller.

- *A third guy thinks that I might actually be the same person as the interviewer.*

     What?! The guy doesn't look a thing like me. He's a local Iraqi reporter who's probably desperate to get his big break and start working for the big boys at Al Jazeera or the BBC. Nice enough fellow, doing tough work in a dangerous place. But come on—look at him! Flat forehead sloping straight into his nose with a big tuft of hair at the top. Damned if he doesn't look like Zeppo Marx straight out of *Animal Crackers*. But me? No way. If anything, he looks more like Danny—ha!

I didn't care about a handful of left-wing nut-job bloggers, but Danny explained that the danger of letting these stories stay out there is that they tend to get "sticky" in the search engines. We wouldn't want some low-level interview booker at CBS to Google me and suddenly these "hoax" stories start popping up.

Touching knees with the Iraqi Zeppo Marx *(Courtesy of YouTube)*

There's no way she'd risk inviting me on *The Early Show* if there was even a shadow of a doubt that I wasn't who I said I was. If Dan Rather can lose his career over a hoax story that a producer put in front of him to read, there's no telling what they'd do to an expendable junior staffer.

One strategy was to go on the offensive against Wolfrum. (This is, after all, one of the reasons I hired Danny.) We were still working under the assumption that he was a loner expat in Brazil, but I was starting to have some doubts. Was he really working alone? Or was he a cover for someone else out to get me? There was no way of knowing for sure, but if nothing else, we had to discredit him as a source. Danny was already starting to plant contradictory comments on various blogs. He wrote this comment (under an alias, of course) on the Ten Percent blog:

> I wouldn't be so quick to believe it's a "hoax"—or at least not in the way Mr. Wolfrum describes. Shakesville (lead by fired John Edwards blogger Melissa McEwan) itself has done this kind of hoaxing several times in the past. This sounds very similar to their M.O. of their recurring "character" named Benjamin H. Grumbles—which was a spoof of a very real (though unfortunately named) person in the Bush administration.
>
> A couple possibilities come to mind: Either Shakesville is now trying to discredit a very real neocon pundit (however despicable) by claiming he doesn't exist.
>
> Or maybe it is an elaborate hoax . . . but that Wolfrum and Shakesville are the hoaxsters themselves. Given their history with the Grumbles thing, that wouldn't surprise me in the least.

It was a little Internet jujitsu that had a chance of working, but only a chance. We were helped a bit by Wolfrum's own sarcastic denial of this accusation which he blogged about on July 9: "Wolfrum, Shakesville are Hoaxers—Benjamin H. Grumbles proves it!"[12] At least now any Google search for "Wolfrum" and "hoax" wouldn't necessarily mention me.

So as to confuse the matter more, we got into the hoax-revealing business ourselves by being the first American blog to notice that newspapers around the world had run a photo from the Iranian Revolutionary Guards showing four missiles being launched simultaneously. As an experienced military analyst, I immediately noticed that the smoke patterns on two of the launches were identical. As Danny explained to me, if anyone did a combined Google search for "Martin Eisenstadt" and "Hoax," our own blog posts about the Iranian missile picture would pop up.[13]

It was all a good start, Danny said, but we also needed to put out our own "proof of life" stories around the Internet so there would be no doubt that not only do I exist but I am indeed a foreign policy adviser to John McCain. But then he was stumped. It sounds easy, but how do you generate that kind of press? This is where my expertise came to bear. "Danny, dear boy. This is Washington. When in doubt, apologize."

"But you didn't do anything wrong."

So? The only two things in D.C. that get more press coverage than a semen-stained blue dress are a gay text message from a

*(Courtesy of Revolutionary Guards/Harding Institute)*

congressional page or a contrite apology from a campaign adviser caught lobbying. I suggested we go for the latter.

The next question was what to apologize for. Jimmy, who can veer toward self-righteousness a little too often (even for a virginal Indiana Mennonite), suggested the simplest answer: that I apologize for being a lobbyist while working for McCain. "What? And get fired?" I shot him a disgusted look. "Nope. The art of the apology is to make it enough of an apology that you'll get the press coverage you need without actually admitting any wrongdoing. And if you're really good at it, you'll distract people from the real damaging story and still help your candidate in the process." Just ask my pal Charlie Black.

## McCain's Lobbyist Affair: Who's Catering?

On February 21, 2008, *The New York Times* dropped a bombshell into the still-undecided GOP primary race. The *Times* quoted anonymous former McCain advisers as saying that during the 2000 campaign they thought McCain was having a romantic relationship with Vicki Iseman—a lobbyist who looks surprisingly like a thirty-year-younger version of Cindy McCain.[14]

McCain was furious, and Cindy even more so. John had almost locked up the nomination at this point, but Mike Huckabee was still in the race, and there was always the chance that Romney could jump back in if there was a major scandal. But how to defuse it? As Bill Clinton can tell you, just saying you didn't have an affair does not make the rumors go away. Whether they're true or not. McCain knew better, and he knew that the best way to defuse the allegation was to make the story about something else. Something he (and Cindy) could live with: lobbying.

Troubling, yes. But not a nomination destroyer to the social conservative base, which in the wake of an adultery scandal could still be tempted to vote for former minister Huckabee and his presumptive running mate, Chuck Norris.

But how to change the context of the story? It required not only a campaign staffer to go out and deny the affair but, more important, a staffer whose own ties to lobbying would be instant catnip for the press to follow the lobbying side of the story. Charlie Black offered to take one for the team.

The day after the *Times* ran its story, their rival, *The Washington Post*, had Charlie's well-honed denial front and center:

> *"It's a shame that the* New York Times *has chosen to smear John McCain like this," said Charles R. Black Jr., a top adviser to McCain's current presidential campaign and the head of a Washington lobbying firm called BKSH & Associates. "Neither Senator McCain nor the campaign will dignify false rumors and gossip by responding to them. John McCain has never done favors for anyone, not lobbyists or any special interest. That's a clear 24-year record."*[15]

In the annals of crisis management, this is one of the most gorgeously worded denials a campaign consultant could ever craft. Allow me, if you will, a moment to dissect this beautiful specimen.

1. The bait: "It's a shame that the *New York Times* has chosen to smear John McCain like this." Charlie uses the media rivalry between the two papers as leverage to get his quote guaranteed above the fold on the front page of the *Post*.

2. The attribution: Charlie makes sure he's personally identified both as a "top adviser to McCain's current presidential campaign" and as "the head of a Washington lobbying firm called BKSH & Associates." You know that's going to send reporters and bloggers scrambling on Google.

3. The denial: Your typical denial would end with the line about not dignifying false rumors: "Neither Senator

McCain nor the campaign will dignify false rumors and gossip by responding to them." But Charlie continues.

4. The changeup: His genius is in adding the next sentence: "John McCain has never done favors for anyone, not lobbyists or any special interest." Now the story is all about lobbying.

5. Close with the wild-goose chase: "That's a clear 24-year record." This will send reporters digging through endlessly tedious legislative records, campaign contributions, and lobbyist disclosures. In the heat of a presidential campaign, no journalist is going to successfully find anything without doing extensive digging, and no editor will allow their reporters to research a story for a month when they should be filing three stories a day (one for print and two for the blog) from the campaign trail. Which means no one will ever really unearth the truth.

As the McCain team had planned, the tale of the alleged romantic entanglement very quickly disappeared, and within a day the story was all about lobbying. And specifically about Charlie Black's own reputation as a lobbyist.

On February 22, the same two *Post* reporters who fell for the Charlie Black quote—Michael Shear and Jeffrey Birnbaum—had a page-one piece entitled "The Anti-Lobbyist, Advised by Lobbyists" in which they salivated over how many lobbyists work for McCain, including Charlie, Rick Davis, and Steve Schmidt. By the time they came around to mentioning Vicki Iseman, it's in the fourth paragraph, below the fold. Even then, she's referred to strictly in the context of being "a telecom lobbyist"—with no mention of any romantic accusations. Charlie had done his job well. The "Iseman Affair" became a non-affair, and thankfully, McCain cruised to a primary victory.[16]

For months during that spring, though, Charlie still had to deal with the lobbying issue, which kept haunting the campaign. Charlie was starting to get nervous that he might become a sacrificial lamb if the issue drew too much heat. What did he need to do? Apologize. Though not, of course, about anything that had any connection to lobbying.

## Charlie Black's Brilliant Apology

"Marty?"

"Yes, Danny?"

"How does this help you?"

"Wait for it, Danny."

In a fairly obscure June 23 interview he gave to *Fortune* magazine, Charlie had this to say about John McCain's readiness to lead:

> The assassination of Benazir Bhutto in December was an "unfortunate event," says Black. "But his knowledge and ability to talk about it reemphasized that this is the guy who's ready to be Commander-in-Chief. And it helped us." As would, Black concedes with startling candor after we raise the issue, another terrorist attack on U.S. soil. "Certainly it would be a big advantage to him," says Black.[17]

Within hours, McCain (shocked, shocked!) was asked about Charlie's "startling candor" at a press conference and said, "I cannot imagine it, and so if he said that—and I don't know the context—I strenuously disagree."[18]

Charlie had successfully changed the topic of the day from the economy ($4-per-gallon gas was a loser for McCain) to national security (fear of terrorism, a winner); he just needed to ensure that his own reputation stayed intact—while simultaneously keeping the story alive for another news cycle. So he issued an apology: "I deeply regret the comments, they were inappropriate . . . I recognize that John McCain has devoted his entire adult life to protecting his country and placing its security before every other consideration."[19]

The best part about the apology is that it was picked up in every newspaper in the country—and thanks to a generous story that Reuters put out, in almost every country in the world. Everyone on the globe now knew that Charlie Black was a top adviser to John McCain, and in a lucky break for Charlie, the Reuters piece doesn't mention that Charlie was a lobbyist. As far as most people knew, Charlie was simply a political strategist who had overreached a little while pointing out one of his candidate's biggest strengths. Certainly nothing to get fired over (especially when it became clear that McCain inched up in the polls after the incident). And in a very practical sense, the first page of Google searches for "Charlie Black" wouldn't all be articles about what a bad-ass lobbyist he is.

"Team," I said, "we need to pull a Charlie Black."

The only problem was that Charlie Black had just pulled a Charlie Black. Four days earlier. Even though this was more about my own reputation than the campaign itself, it would look ridiculous to have two senior McCain advisers apologize within less than a week of each other. I'd get fired in an instant. No, we'd have to wait at least a week—better yet, until after the July Fourth weekend. What I didn't count on was what happened the next Wednesday, July 2.

## Dick Cheney Stomps!

I had been out late the night before at a reception at the New Zealand embassy. They were celebrating that the tourism sector in New Zealand had hit a record high of more than $20 billion in the previous year. Mind you, that's $20 billion New Zealand dollars, so I have absolutely no idea what that is in real money.

Nevertheless, if there's one iron-clad rule in Washington, it's this: If you get an invitation to a reception at the New Zealand embassy, go!

It's a beautiful building, with huge, arching wooden beams, just across the street from the Naval Observatory, where the vice president lives. They had the place decked out like *The Lord of the Rings*, and some of the stars of the movie mingled in the crowd. At the entrance, there were ten enormous tattoo-faced Maoris banging on massive drums. Like all good revelers, the Kiwis had invited the stuffiest old couple in the neighborhood to the party (better to party with them, than to have them rat you out to the cops for excessive noise and vomiting). Don't believe the rumors that Dick Cheney was permanently sealed in a cone of silence. I caught him in the corner very happily downing pints of Tui—a popular New Zealand pale ale—with Ambassador Roy Ferguson. As for Dick's wife, Lynn, she was holding her own with TV star Lucy Lawless in some sort of competition for the best Xena-like warrior yell.

Me? I was content to stand by the barbecue buffet gnawing on

Hollywood hobbits partying with the Air New Zealand hostesses *(Courtesy of the author)*

delicious mint-drenched lamb skewers and downing an occasional pint of Tui myself. (Gout be damned, this was a feast I
wasn't going to miss.) I was starting to chat up a stunning representative from Air New Zealand who was passing out drinks—
a vision in her teal flight attendant uniform, with a figure that
definitely drew attention to her southern hemisphere.

"That's a beautiful uniform. Is it cotton?" I gently touched her
sleeve.

"Merino wool. It's a new design—we just got them a year ago.
Can I interest you in a Matua Valley chardonnay?"

*Bzzzz, beep, bzzzz.* Crap!

"Your BlackBerry?" she said in a lilting New Zealand accent
that was one part Aussie, one part South African, and three parts
sexy. My pocket was vibrating in overdrive, and yes, I *was* also
happy to see her.

"I'm terribly sorry," I stammered. "But I'll just be a moment."
I spun around to a quiet corner and glanced down at my cell
phone. It was my cheap Sprint clamshell. Not exactly a Black-
Berry per se, but Eli had gotten me a deal on a two-year contract,
and I was still locked in for fourteen more months. So when
Danny came on board, I at least had him set all my outgoing
e-mail with the signature "Sent from my Verizon Wireless Black-
Berry." It was a great excuse to send very short e-mails, and just
because I didn't have a BlackBerry didn't mean that other people
needed to know it.

I popped open the Sprint. It was an urgent text from Randy
Scheunemann: "Mrty- cmpaign mtng @ HQ tmrrw @ 8am-big
news ;)" Goddamn that Scheunemann with his cryptic emoti-
cons. Was that a sincere ";)" you're getting a promotion, Marty,
or an ironic ";)" you're getting fired? This is why I prefer old-
fashioned voice mail.

I turned around and scanned the room to see if I still had a
chance to rack up some frequent-flier miles on Air New Zealand.
But by then, my future mile-high-club mate had moved on to an

intense discussion with Democratic Representative Anthony "Regrettably Named" Weiner from New York's Ninth District. A handsome forty-three-year-old bachelor, he was the congressman who once famously proposed a special work visa for international fashion models, and then took illicit campaign contributions from several foreign supermodels.[20] I didn't stand a chance against this guy, but boy, did I respect his chutzpah. As I left the party, I couldn't help but notice Vice President Cheney flailing his arms and stomping his feet with the Maoris in their traditional haka war dance. No wonder people were scared of him.

## The Rise of Steve Schmidt

The next morning I headed to the Arlington headquarters of the McCain campaign. I checked in with the receptionist and thankfully was told the meeting was in the big conference room. (If it had been in the little one, I would have been nervous—that probably would have meant getting fired.)

I got to the big conference room and grabbed a white Styrofoam cup of coffee. The whole gang was there: Scheunemann, Rick Davis, Mark Salter, Steve Schmidt, and a slew of young eager beavers who looked half my age and twice as spry. I sauntered over to Charlie Black.

"Marty, could you pass the half-and-half?"

"Sure thing, Charlie." I gave him a little cup of room-temperature creamer. As for me, I always have a hard time getting the tiny lids off. Not worth the trouble.

"Nice work with the apology, Charlie."

"Oh, that little trick? Chip off the old Atwater, Marty. Damn if he didn't teach us everything we know. Rest his soul."

Rick Davis called the meeting to order, and told us the senator was on the big teleconference speaker in the center of the table. I knew he was out on the campaign trail, but for some reason, I just pictured him in a dimly lit room, slowly stroking a cat on his lap.

"Boys," McCain said, "we're in for a fight ahead of us. The biggest, most expensive general-election campaign in history. And like we say in the navy, we need all hands on deck." Turns out there was a restructuring afoot. Schmidt was going to step in on a day-to-day basis and run the tactical side of the campaign, while Rick would stick to the big-picture strategy: fund-raising, convention prep, and the like. On the one hand, it seemed like this was a bit of a letdown for Rick, but let's face it, with his battle-tested experience with the Bush campaign in '04 and with Schwarzenegger out in California, Steve was the guy we needed to steer the ship.[21]

With his freshly shaved head and barrel chest, Schmidt was a commanding figure of strength and determination. A former high-school football player and Eagle Scout who received his military training in the University of Delaware's vaunted ROTC program, Steve was tough and disciplined. He stood, thanked McCain, and made an incredibly stirring speech to get us all geared up for the campaign.

At one point, he jumped on the conference table, just inches from the speakerphone.

"Are you with me?!"

"Yes!" we chanted.

He kicked Charlie Black's half-empty coffee cup into the air, spraying us with lustrous beads of caffeine-infused energy.

"Is this our time?"

"Yes!!"

Veins popping out of his parietal lobe, sweat flying across the room.

"Can we do this thing?"

"Yes!!!"

A whirling dervish of macho white-man charisma, Steve climaxed: "Yes! Yes! Yes we can!!!"

The irony was not lost on the room, and we all burst out laughing—Steve included. Even through the speakerphone, I thought I heard a chuckle and a meow. There was no doubt in the room: Steve was the man to lead us to victory.

## July Fourth in ████████ Beach

After news broke of Steve's ascendancy in the campaign, I knew I still had to wait a few days before working on my own apology for the YouTube video. So I bid adieu to the institute team and figured I would spend the July Fourth weekend like I usually do: wandering down to the Mall to see the Independence Day parade, catching the National Symphony Orchestra, and watching the majestic fireworks over the Washington Monument. It's cheesy, I know. But especially in an election year, it's also an important reminder that unabashed patriotism and the lingering smell of cotton candy and gunpowder are what make this country great.

But on that Thursday night—the third—as I was leaving the office, I got a text message from ████████ ████████ asking me to show up at Dupont Circle in two hours, with a bag packed for the weekend. If there's one rule in Washington, it's if ████████ ████████ ever tells you to pack your bags and head to Dupont Circle, you do it. His July Fourth parties were the stuff of Washington legend, and I wasn't going to miss out.

(Dear reader: Given the high-profile nature of the participants in this next passage and my own slightly shaky memory of these events, my editor, Mitzi, has warned me that some of the names might have to be redacted, on the advice of Faber and Faber's lawyer, the ridiculously scrupulous Ms. ████████ ████████. I'm only hoping that she did not have the foresight or time to crosscheck any redacted names with what may already have slipped into the index. If that's the case, the savvy reader might still be able to get the gist of the story. To borrow Randy's emoticon: ;) Let me continue . . .)

We were on our way to Rehoboth Beach. It's a two-and-a-half-hour drive through Maryland, across the Bay Bridge, and into Delaware. But when your driving companions include some of the brightest lights, and hardiest partiers, in the political/media stratosphere—people like ███████ █████, Senator ████ ███████ (D-WI), and Huffington Post founder ████████ ████-███—the time flows like scotch over ice. The weekend was crazy. We met up with more of Washington's secret elite partiers at █████████'s beach house: my old ice-skating doubles partner, Secretary of State ██████ ████; former Representative ███████ "Call Me" ████; *Morning Joe* host ███ ████████████; at least two Kennedys; and a ████ twin (and I'm pretty sure it was the married one). It was largely a blur of mojitos for breakfast, frigid skinny-dipping in the Atlantic, barbecue meats from animals that bordered on extinction, and a rolling tour of Rehoboth's most forgiving bars: the Iguana Grill, Rouge, Cloud 9, and the Frogg Pond among them.

I never thought I'd see famed CBS anchorwoman █████ ███████ in a wet-T-shirt contest—much less one in a lesbian bar. A natural competitor, she won easily. And forget about Senator ██████ ███████. We practically had to pry her off *Washington Post* columnist █████ █████████ at the Purple Parrot.

Once we made it back to the house each night, the hormone levels rose as the outside temperatures dipped. With four bedrooms, countless pullout couches, the hot tub, and a beach shower (to say nothing of my own man sweat), it's amazing there was a dry towel left in the place by morning. At one point, wearing nothing but her trademark square-rimmed Lafont glasses, veteran broadcaster ██████████ ████████ dove headfirst into the Jacuzzi. When she finally came up for air, she had future vice presidential scion ████ █████'s boxer shorts in her mouth and the glasses were nowhere to be found. Down in the first-floor bedroom, I had to wonder: if ████████ █████████ had as much stamina covering the White House for CNN as she did covering Fox's ████ ████████ with her hot, steamy blanket of flesh, she'd be a hell of a lot better reporter.

And speaking of the White House, we all know that no party like this would be complete without spunky blonde ████ ████, who liked to unwind on days when there were no presidential press briefings. But honestly, with Department of Homeland Security secretary ████ ████? That was almost as surprising as the hidden video camera he asked me to run for him the whole time. In the kitchen, I helped Representative ████ ████ (D-MA) and Representative ████, ████ (R-CA) grind up a mixture of baking soda, Percocet, and oxycodone in the Cuisinart. Then we poured it down original Wonkette (and appropriately surnamed) ████ ████ ████'s ample chest and snorted lines up her freckled cleavage. And how about that hairless ████ ████? It was his house, of course, and host's prerogative meant that he got to show Florida congresswoman ████ ████ ████ the full 360. (It's no wonder she's always invited on his show.) For some reason, I got stuck in the laundry room trying to clean vomit stains off ████ ████'s black Supreme Court robe. (Note to self: Next time don't use bleach.) It was four in the morning when I suddenly heard one familiar voice from the CBS network cry out, "Well, if that's not *my* vulva, then whose is it?" Ed Murrow, eat your heart out.

I'm still not sure how I made it back to the District at the end of the weekend.

But by Monday morning, it was time to return to work at the institute with bloodshot eyes, a raging migraine, and a second-degree sunburn on my left ass cheek. First order of business was the apology for the Iraqi TV interview.

## The Apology

The trick, as I explained to my young colleagues, was to find something of very little consequence in the Iraqi video to apologize for, and then get the word out. I dictated the following press release to Jimmy.

## McCain Adviser Apologizes for Casino Lobbying Remarks in Iraq

### *Out-of-context comments posted on YouTube[a]*

July 7, 2008—Martin Eisenstadt,[b] an adviser to the John McCain campaign,[c] today issued an apology[d] for remarks made during an interview on Al-Iraqiya TV[e] on February 16 of this year at Baghdad's Business 2 Business Expo.[f]

"It's come to my attention that excerpts of my interview at the Business Expo were recently taken[g] out of context[h] and posted on YouTube,"[i] said Eisenstadt. "At the time,[j] I was representing commercial interests[k] in the Green Zone, and did not formally have a position with the McCain campaign.[l] During the remarks, I suggested that there would be a mosque inside the proposed casino development in the Green Zone.[m] I misspoke,[n] and if anyone in the Muslim community was offended by those remarks,[o] I sincerely apologize.[p] In actual fact,[q] the development plans to have a mosque adjacent to the complex, not inside it."[r]

"To be clear, John McCain[s] has the utmost respect for the Iraqi people,[t] and for all branches of Islam,"[u] added Eisenstadt.

Founder and President of the influential Eisenstadt Group,[v] Martin Eisenstadt is a senior fellow at the the Harding Institute for Freedom and Democracy in Washington, D.C.[w] An expert on Near East military and political affairs,[x] Mr. Eisenstadt formerly consulted on the Rudolph Giuliani campaign,[y] as well as with numerous corporate and multinational organizations on issues of security and policy development.[z] Martin Eisenstadt has been an influential voice in Near East policy debate for more than a decade.[aa]

For more information or to schedule an interview[bb] with Martin Eisenstadt, please contact his associate James

Havermayer at james.havermayer@hardinginstitute
.org.[cc] For more on Mr. Eisenstadt, go to http://www
.eisenstadtgroup.com or http://www.hardinginstitute.org.[dd]

—# # #—[ee]

---

Like Charlie Black's apology before, this one seemed to hit the high points.

a. The headline: Always use the headline you want—especially the first three words. "McCain Adviser Apologizes." Most press are lazy and will essentially use the same headline that you give them.

b. The name: "Martin Eisenstadt." Good press or bad, it's essential that your name be spelled right.

c. The attribution: For both political and professional reasons, it was essential that I get identified first and foremost as a McCain adviser.

d. The deniability: It's key that *I* issued the apology, not the McCain campaign.

e. The offending venue: The trick is to make it sound like the original offending remark was made on an important news outlet, not just YouTube.

f. This guy's been in Iraq: Further solidifies my bona fides as a Near East scholar willing to go into a war zone in defense of capitalism.

g. Intentional passive voice: Implies that it could have been a nefarious Obama campaign plot.

h. Diminish your culpability: Everything is always taken out of context.

i. Give people the B-roll: Newspapers and the Web can pull still images, and TV coverage can pull B-roll. If they track down the YouTube video, it means there's now a face to the name. Ergo, a "proof of life" that I exist.

j. The offending remark is *so* old news.

k. The greater context: This is code for "lobbying"—guaranteeing that it'll be placed in any bigger lobbying stories.

l. Plausible deniability for the candidate.

m. Reference to a minor point: If you watch the video, do you even remember this?

n. Taking responsibility: Okay, I did it. I "misspoke."

o. The classic "if/then" apology: I'll only actually apologize if anyone was offended.

p. Sincerity is key: If you say you're sincere, then you are.

q. If you say it's a fact, then it is.

r. The correction twist: This implies that the only thing that was offensive was having the mosque inside the casino. Easily rectified. Beyond that, clearly nothing must have been offensive.

s. Bring it back to the candidate: It's all about John McCain. Right?

t. The hundred-year plan.

u. McCain can't be bothered to quibble over the arcane distinctions between Shiites and Sunnis.

v. I'm influential: Why? Because I just said so.

w. The credentials: Not a lobbyist. A think tanker.

x. I'm a pundit: Put me on your show.

y. I've worked with a loser: As explained in chapter 3, this ensures better punditry placement.

z. I need consulting work: Please hire me, so I can do this again.

aa. I'm mature, but not old.

bb. Put me on your show: Always give plenty of contact information.

cc. But no phone numbers: These releases wind up on the Web. What we don't want is a bunch of crank callers harassing our attractive young intern Veronica.

dd. Send them to the blog: Always give your blog URL.

ee. Remember the number signs and the dashes: No one in journalism remembers what these are for, but it makes it look like a real journalist already copyedited your story, and they should just run it as is.


Jimmy ran with the copy and started e-mailing it out from his Harding Institute account. Unfortunately, the one thing Jimmy doesn't have a clear grasp of is how to get e-mail addresses for most of the big journalists in town. But he did his best. And I had carefully instructed him to steer clear of the Internet media for this story—it would be too easy for them to stumble onto the Brazilian blogger's accusations and nix the story altogether. So instead we tried to focus on traditional print and TV media.

It's hard to know for certain when to put out any given press release. Timing is everything, and while you can control your own news, you can't control other news of the day. As Don Rumsfeld—or perhaps Yogi Berra—might have said, the one thing you can never predict is the unpredictable. Sure enough, July 7 turned out to be a pretty big news day with Senator Jesse Helms dying and rumors spreading of an affair between Madonna and A-Rod.[22]

The end result is that not much happened with the release. Ironically, the biggest news source that picked it up was Scoop—a news service based in, you guessed it, New Zealand. Coincidence? Or maybe there was more to the so-called Air New Zealand flight attendant than met the eye. It's no wonder she was ultimately more interested in a congressman than me. As someone who's been in the intelligence field a long time, I can tell you that it's a statistical fact that one out of every nine international flight attendants doubles as either an intelligence operative or a freelance travel writer. In retrospect, I'm thinking she was both.

Danny was monitoring the Web and noticed that the other place that picked up the story was *Mother Jones* magazine. A cub political reporter named Jonathan Stein—a 2005 graduate of "Harvard" (that should tell you all you need to know)—wrote this typically invective piece of drivel:

> *This is absolutely horrifying. The man speaking, Martin Eisenstadt, has since apologized. He also claimed to be taken out of context. You've seen the video. Judge for yourself. What on earth does the McCain campaign do with this guy now?*[23]

Danny was, of course, horrified, but I assured him that the important part wasn't the spin—it was that he mentioned the apology and didn't mince words in describing me in the context of being a McCain adviser. Mission accomplished! The *Mother Jones* piece got picked up by a few more online sources like Daily

Kos, but unfortunately it didn't get the widespread attention that the Charlie Black apology got. We were back where we started.

## A Billion Nuclear-Armed Musical Fans Can't Be Wrong

"Boys," I said. I heard a throat clear from Poppy's cubicle. "Yes, and of course, Poppy." And then another throat cleared from the reception desk. "And yes, Veronica, the intern." I continued. "Let's focus on the main goal at hand. If we're just trying to push the word 'hoax' out of Google searches for my name, then why are we limiting ourselves to media in the U.S.?" Stunned silence as the thought sunk into the heads of my young charges.

"I mean, if there was interest in this interview from Iraq to Japan, then maybe we should put the apology out on a global basis." Jimmy's brain nearly exploded. He'd had a hard enough time finding e-mail addresses for U.S. press outlets; he would really have no idea how to approach a global PR campaign.

Just then, Marwan poked his well-coifed head up from his cubicle, a curious gleam in his one good eye. "Jimmy, my man, don't freak out," he said in his lilting Pakistani accent (strange for a guy who actually grew up in Cherry Hill, New Jersey). "All you need to do is find a couple of wire services from each region. For example, with South Asia, all you need to do is send it to their two wire services, Press Trust of India and Asian News International."

"But, but," Jimmy stammered. "What does the apology have to do with India?"

Nothing yet, I explained. But remember during the video when the Iraqi interviewer got confused about the "Indian casinos" and didn't understand I was talking about Native Americans at the time? Just because I'm not the one who got confused between the teepee Indians and the 7-Eleven Indians, doesn't mean I can't *take credit* for the confusion.

I let Marwan take the initiative and he altered the press release headline to: "McCain Adviser Apologizes to India for Casino Remarks in Iraq." He changed a couple of other words in the second and third paragraphs, and we sent it out, hoping for the best.

The very next day, Marwan burst in the door of the institute yammering into his cell phone in Urdu. He was very excited, but the rest of the staff couldn't figure out a word he was saying. Thankfully, being an expert on Near East studies, I was able to piece together a few key phrases: ". . . Yes, Uncle Salim, I hear you. Can you hear me? . . ." ". . . What? Did you say *The Times of Indiana* . . . ?" and ". . . Yes, I know he's an imbecile, but I get dental . . ."

Marwan hung up and marched through the office in a grand gesture: "Hey everyone, we did it! Come look." We all followed him to Danny's cubicle. "Danny, check out *The Times of India*." Danny's fingers darted over the keyboard like salmon swimming upstream. In a moment, we saw it. Page 26—front section, above the fold:

### McCain aide apologizes to Indians for 'casino' gaffe

*10 Jul 2008, 0122 hrs IST, PTI*

WASHINGTON: An adviser to White House hopeful John McCain has apologised for confusion over the use of the word 'Indian' while referring to the casino business being carried out by American Indians in the US.

Martin Eisenstadt apologised for remarks made during an interview he had with Al-Iraqiya TV on February 16 at Baghdad's Business 2 Business Expo.

"It's come to my attention that excerpts of my interview at the Business Expo were recently taken out of context and posted on YouTube," said Eisenstadt, an aide to Republican senator McCain.

"I misspoke, and was referring to casinos in the US operated by native Americans. If anyone in India was offended by those remarks, I sincerely apologise," Eisenstadt said. "To be clear, John McCain has the utmost respect for the Indian people, and for all regions of South Asia," noted the expert on near eastern military affairs.[24]

Not too shabby! With 2.3 million copies printed each day, *The Times of India* has the largest circulation of any English-language newspaper in the world. More than *USA Today*. More than *The Wall Street Journal*. Even more than *The New York Times* and *The Washington Post* . . . combined![25] The story got picked up by both wire services we sent it to, and subsequently appeared in every English-language newspaper and website in India. In short, a *billion* nuclear-armed, musical-loving Indians woke up that morning, drank their chai, and read about me in their newspaper.

"Well done, Marwan!" I declared. "Consider yourself first up in the batting rotation in this week's softball game. We're playing the American Enterprise Institute and we'll need your line drives." Marwan jammed his fist in the air: "Yes!" As I explained to the team, it's a global village we're living in. Pundits are just as likely to get interviews on the BBC or Al Jazeera as they are on CNN or MSNBC. Campaign consultants are just as likely to get hired on elections in Argentina, or Taiwan, or South Africa as they are in Washington or Albany. And you can get the same number of Google search hits from an obscure website in Jaipur as you can from a mention in *The New York Times*.

In the end, the apology did its job. We got the word out once and for all: Martin Eisenstadt is alive and well. He does exist. He is an adviser to the John McCain campaign.

## Bobby Jindal and the Voice Mail

Late that night, as I was flossing my teeth, I noticed that my passive-aggressive Sprint clamshell was flashing on the counter.

The thing is conveniently "out of range" whenever a call comes in but is more than happy to tell me a minute later that I have a missed call. (I'll bet real BlackBerrys don't do that.) I checked the voice mail. It was Charlie Black.

"Marty, Marty? Why aren't you answering? Bobby Jindal just took me and Schmidt out for dinner at the Bombay Club on Conn Ave. So here's the thing, Marty: While we're waiting for the table, Jindal buys us a round at the bar and ordered up some appetizers. He's going on and on and on about Katrina this and Bill Jefferson's freezer full of cash that, and while he's talkin', I glanced down at a copy of *The Times of India* sitting on the bar."

Nuts, I thought. This can't be good.

"I showed it to Steve and we laughed so hard, Steve damn near choked on his samosa. Hell, even Bobby got a kick out it, and we all know that Louisiana Punjabis aren't known for their great sense of humor. We loved it, Marty. Ol' Lee would have been proud of you. Let's talk in the next few days about where else we can use you on the campaign."

He burped. Loudly.

"Goddamned vindaloo."

And with that, I was back in business.

# 9

# When Think Tanks Play Softball . . .

## Ahmed Chalabi's Curveball

If you haven't already gathered, it is worth noting that in the world of Washington think tanks, nothing is more competitive, or more important, than the annual summer softball league. Some of you may remember the infamous Brookings–American Enterprise Institute bench-clearer of '98 that sent Irving Kristol to Georgetown University Hospital with a broken nose and a detached retina. To this day, Brookings president Strobe Talbott is afraid to let his team have a rematch with AEI.

I've played on and off for years on different teams, starting with my first foray on the old Heritage C team when I was there in the early nineties. Perhaps most memorably, though, I played center field on the old Committee for the Liberation of Iraq (CLI) team in '02. When Ahmed Chalabi was in town, he'd step onto the mound. Ahmed was more of a cricketer by dint of his years in London, but that made him a surprisingly able pitcher (or "bowler" as he embarrassingly kept referring to himself). As you might suspect, he threw a halfway decent curveball.

Chalabi gave us all nicknames, then paid for our Savile Row monogrammed jerseys out of his exiled Iraqi National Congress "discretionary" fund. We had Bill "the Joker" Kristol at first, Charlie "Big Balls" Black on second, Randy "the Hawk" Scheunemann at short, and of course, in the outfield I was Marty "Slippery Fingers" Eisenstadt (early in the season, Ahmed had noticed my near obsession with Jergens hand lotion, on account of my eczema, and he attributed its use to one particularly inglorious fly-ball fumble). Douglas "Ferret Face" Feith was on waivers from the Pentagon League so he could play on our side of the Potomac at third. As honorary co-chairs of the CLI, John "Blonde Magnet" McCain and Joe "Hebrew National" Lieberman were technically the co-GMs of the team, but we rarely saw them during the regular season.

Sadly, our record was a disappointing 4-8. Perhaps prophetic of the Iraq War itself, we opened strong with three wins in a row, but we just didn't have a strategy for making it to the end of the season and into the playoffs. But we always had a good time, and after most games, we'd head over to one of the most exclusive private happy hours in town, a weekly get-together at the Kenyan Embassy on R Street. And happy it was! By late 2002, longtime Kenyan strongman Daniel Arap Moi had stepped down from power and the new regime was eager to curry favor from Washington power players. From the beautiful Kenyan consular officials who'd greet us with *"Hamjambo, mabwana!"* to their goodbye embraces when we left, this was a place that entertained well-connected American neocons with open arms. It was an ideal postgame venue for our CLI team to chat with Chalabi over bottles of imported Tusker: to discuss the strategies for overthrowing Saddam Hussein as well as the tactics for toppling the Cato Institute's perch atop the regular season rankings.

Since that season, though, it's been tougher for me to stay on a team for any length of time—what with travel to Iraq and working on campaigns. In '05, I played a couple of games with the Heritage B team, until Coach Ed Meese kicked me off for missing too many practices. (Practices! Can you believe that?) Until recently, we've never had enough employees and interns to make up a full Harding Institute squad for the length of the season. But this year would be different! As a relative newcomer to the league, having played only a few exhibition games last year, we felt we were ready to step up to full strength for the 2008 season. I knew that if other think tanks were taking this seriously, then we had to as well.

## Dropping My Towel for Clinton's Ringer

When it was time for me to decide the lineup for this year's team, I knew we didn't quite have enough people in the office to field a full team. We had to bring in a couple of ringers, no matter how distasteful their politics may be. To quote what Malcolm X once famously said about the old Negro League, we would need to win "by any means necessary."

There are some people in Washington who have slept their way to the halls of power. Others have traded on their family fortunes to make it to the top. But my friend Paul Orzulak is one of the few who have succeeded in Washington based on the strength of a fast ball.

Paul, an ace high-school pitcher from Connecticut, leveraged his skills on the mound first to get speechwriting work for Senator Tom Harkin (whose office competes in the Senate Softball League) and then majority whip David Bonior (the House League). Throughout the nineties, Orzulak was traded up the Executive League ranks, first allegedly writing speeches for Andrew Cuomo on the HUD team, then for Vice President Al Gore's team. In the dark days of the Lewinsky scandal, Bill Clinton lost longtime players like Stephanopoulos, Begala, and Carville from his beloved West Wing Warriors team. In a fit of pique that to this day Al Gore refers to as "the Friday Night Massacre," Clinton promoted Orzulak to presidential speechwriter late on a Friday and had him suited up as starting pitcher the next day.[1]

Orzulak was now writing many of Clinton's highly paid "corporate" speeches. But as a softball player, he was largely forgotten. I went to the same gym as Paul, and seeing him in the showers every other Thursday, I knew he was still in reasonable shape (by Washington standards). I appealed to his lost sense of glory and begged him to join our team on an "interim" basis. Knowing my politics full well, he refused. And told me to put on a towel.

So I called the Harding Institute's main benefactor, Clifford Harding III, and begged him to dip into the endowment. If not for me, then for the honor of Warren G. Harding. Clifford was always bitter that Herbert Hoover, the namesake of Stanford's famous Hoover Institute, was to this day better remembered for being president than for serving as Warren G. Harding's secretary of commerce. President Harding reportedly said to Hoover on the eve of his appointment as cabinet secretary, "Herbert, dear boy, you've got a gloriously bulbous head for commerce. Now, don't screw it up." When I explained the situation, Clifford opened up the coffers and I went back to Orzulak. Again, he told me to put on a towel. But this time I was offering him a fat check for "speechwriting" services on behalf of the Harding Institute. He made sure the check cleared, and we had our pitcher!

But we were still one player short. We needed a center fielder. So I hesitated, panicked, and then finally made the call. To my old punditing frenemy, Marnie Vander Helsing.

You see, as a prominent blogger and pundit, Marnie was rare in that she was not affiliated with any of the big think tanks.

And unlike me, she hadn't found any generous descendants of erstwhile presidents with which to start her own institute. (I know she's been talking to the Grover Cleveland folks on and off. It's complicated with them, though. Since he served as president twice, they're looking to start up two different think tanks.) But Marnie's a smart cookie, and she knew that she'd have to make her mark on the softball circuit if she was going to get into the big leagues of the D.C. punditocracy. So I called, and at first she refused. But when I told her we had Orzulak as starting pitcher, she relented (she and Paul had had some sort of romantic entanglement during the '92 Iowa caucuses, and she knew he "had a good arm"). I knew, too, that if Marnie was on the team, it would help ensure that my adjunct fellow Stanley Rubin might show up to games reasonably sober. Stanley's always had a thing for her, but out of respect for my long-delayed dinner date with Marnie, I know he'll never actually make a move on her.

I like to keep a notebook of the season, so at the risk of tipping my hand to next season's opponents, I've allowed my publisher to reprint some of my notes (see next page).

## Postseason Musings

Let's just say that there was a steep learning curve in being the new kid on the think-tank league in '08. Naturally every other team was gunning for us, but I think we held our own. We had a couple of close calls: if Danny hadn't squinted in the sun and dropped the ball in the Carnegie game, or if Stanley had shown up sober to the Eagle game, I think we might have pulled out some wins. But I don't like to live in the past. I live in the future, and the future means we just work a little harder.

I've also instructed Jimmy to focus more on our selection process for the summer interns. While we all agreed that Veron-

## Harding Institute 2008 Season-at-a-Glance

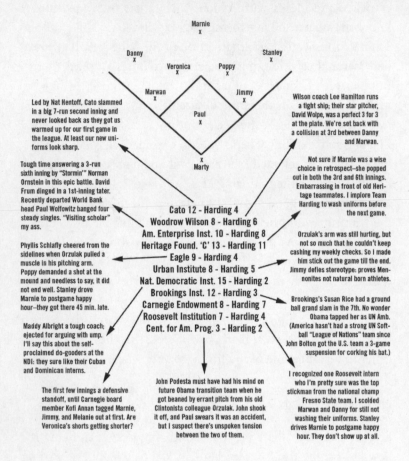

Marnie
X

Danny
X

Stanley
X

Veronica
X

Poppy
X

Marwan
X

Jimmy
X

Paul
X

X
Marty

Led by Nat Hentoff, Cato slammed in a big 7-run second inning and never looked back as they got us warmed up for our first game in the league. At least our new uniforms look sharp.

Tough time answering a 3-run sixth inning by "Stormin'" Norman Ornstein in this epic battle. David Frum dinged in a 1st-inning tater. Recently departed World Bank head Paul Wolfowitz banged four steady singles. "Visiting scholar" my ass.

Phyllis Schlafly cheered from the sidelines when Orzulak pulled a muscle in his pitching arm. Poppy demanded a shot at the mound and needless to say, it did not end well. Stanley drove Marnie to postgame happy hour—they got there 45 min. late.

Maddy Albright a tough coach; ejected for arguing with ump. I'll say this about the self-proclaimed do-gooders at the NDI: they sure like their Cuban and Dominican interns.

The first few innings a defensive standoff, until Carnegie board member Kofi Annan tagged Marnie, Jimmy, and Melanie out at first. Are Veronica's shorts getting shorter?

Wilson coach Lee Hamilton runs a tight ship; their star pitcher, David Wolpe, was a perfect 3 for 3 at the plate. We're set back with a collision at 3rd between Danny and Marwan.

Not sure if Marnie was a wise choice in retrospect—she popped out in both the 3rd and 6th innings. Embarrassing in front of old Heritage teammates. I implore Team Harding to wash uniforms before the next game.

Orzulak's arm was still hurting, but not so much that he couldn't keep cashing my weekly checks. So I made him stick out the game till the end. Jimmy defies stereotype: proves Mennonites not natural born athletes.

Brookings's Susan Rice had a ground ball grand slam in the 7th. No wonder Obama tapped her as UN Amb. (America hasn't had a strong UN Softball "League of Nations" team since John Bolton got the U.S. team a 3-game suspension for corking his bat.)

I recognized one Roosevelt intern who I'm pretty sure was the top stickman from the national champ Fresno State team. I scolded Marwan and Danny for still not washing their uniforms. Stanley drives Marnie to postgame happy hour. They don't show up at all.

John Podesta must have had his mind on future Obama transition team when he got beaned by errant pitch from his old Clintonista colleague Orzulak. John shook it off, and Paul swears it was an accident, but I suspect there's unspoken tension between the two of them.

Cato 12 - Harding 4
Woodrow Wilson 8 - Harding 6
Am. Enterprise Inst. 10 - Harding 8
Heritage Found. 'C' 13 - Harding 11
Eagle 9 - Harding 4
Urban Institute 8 - Harding 5
Nat. Democratic Inst. 15 - Harding 2
Brookings Inst. 12 - Harding 3
Carnegie Endowment 8 - Harding 7
Roosevelt Institution 7 - Harding 4
Cent. for Am. Prog. 3 - Harding 2

ica's short shorts were a cunning distraction for batters on second base who were contemplating a steal to third, her batting average of 0.233 was the third worst on the team. And frankly, while Orzulak proved to be a valuable pitcher, we could have used that money elsewhere. With a little forethought, we might have gotten a college intern from the University of Texas who wouldn't have cost us a dime. Or better yet, now that the Olympics don't have softball anymore, I'm sure we could get one of those muscular young ladies to play for national pride on the Harding Institute team instead.

In short, we'll be back next year, ready to play. Bring it on, Heritage!

# 10

# Paris Hilton and Beyond

### The "Celebrity" Ad

I'll never forget where I was when I first saw the Paris Hilton video. And no, I'm not talking about the sex tape, which if you ask me was overrated. And I've traveled a lot, so I've seen all types of pornography. I even once brought the full, uncensored tape as a gift to a certain UAE Sultan. And you know what he said to me the next time I saw him? "I watched your gift. The Kardashian tape is better. Don't get me wrong. I like that Paris is young and blonde and the daughter of very rich Crusaders, but the actual performance . . . too childlike. Both him and her." (This coming from a man with a fourteen-year-old wife and a sheep out back he practices on.)

But that's not the tape I'm talking about. I'm talking about the brilliant political ad "Celeb," released by the McCain campaign in the waning days of July '08, accusing Barack Obama of being a "celebrity" and comparing him to Britney Spears and Paris Hilton. A stroke of genius that could and should have been the turning point in the campaign. Barack isn't unflappable. He's arrogant. Barack isn't loved. He's "popular," too cool for school. Never underestimate the power of envy. It's like I wrote earlier that spring in my blog.

### McCain is right for our Times

March 7, 2008, by Marty

I don't care how many Harvard degrees Barack has. Try bullshitting a hero who's seen his buddies obliterated, who can't sleep because of nightmares. Try telling him "yes we can" and see how far you get. The last thing a patriot mired in debt wants to hear is the naive optimism of the young, tall and good looking. That's why McCain is a perfect fit for today and tomorrow's zeitgeist and that's why he'll be our next President.[1]

So you can imagine my excitement when I looked up from my happy hour buffalo wings at the Exchange Saloon to the flat-screen TV above the bartender's head and saw images of Barack Obama interspersed with those of Paris Hilton and Britney Spears. If only the campaign had continued with these sorts of attack ads, John McCain would be president and Wednesday, July 30, the day the "Celeb" ad was released, would be etched into history. I especially loved the huge phallic symbol, the Victory Column, a German variation on the Washington Monument, that was cleverly woven into the fabric of the ad. (Because of my history with the Willie Horton ads, I'm very good with symbolism, especially as it pertains to African Americans.)

I was excited. The American people were finally getting the message. Obama has no experience of any kind. He is the choice of the cool crowd. What has Barack ever done? Why is he worshipped? For the same reason Paris and Britney are worshipped. Because the gay, liberal media tells you to.

Finally, somebody at the campaign had listened to me, had

paid attention to my years of experience and lessons learned. Those late-night drinking sessions with Steve Schmidt must have paid off. When Steve puts his mind to something, he is a bulldozer, a magician. I grabbed my cell phone to dial Steve and congratulate him. But then I thought, better not bother the boss on a day like this. I needed to know what was going on, why I was kept out of the loop on such an important shift in tactical strategy. I was starting to worry that I had missed out on important early campaign bonding by coming in late from Giuliani. I hadn't yet been on the plane where Salter and Schmidt had become so close. I needed to get myself back into the loop.

I reached for my phone again and dialed my buddy Randy Scheunemann's cell. Randy was about as inside as you get. He was the senator's top foreign policy adviser, the head of my department over at the campaign. The senator loved Randy. They went back. And Randy and I went back. He was the founder and executive director of the Committee for the Liberation of Iraq, and it was an honor to serve with him. Heck, we drove to Annapolis together. (Ever the gentleman, Randy had put behind us the unfortunate incident involving Denny Hastert's *kisbet* and the Annapolis trip.)

"Randy, my man! Did you see the ad?"

"You think this one's good. Wait for the one coming out in a couple of days. It's called 'The Messiah.'"

"I love it. Who should I call at the campaign to congratulate?"

"I'd hold off on that."

"Why?"

"Because the celebrity ad's been generating some controversy."

"Controversy?"

"Rick Davis got an earful from Barron Hilton today who was none too happy about the campaign sullying the family name and brand. Even Peterson from Blackstone called to complain."

"Blackstone?"

"I think the phrase he used was 'biting the hand that feeds you.' Listen, I'm getting another call."

"We should get together for a drink one of—"

"I got to go. It's the prime minister of Georgia. And he doesn't seem himself. Something's up. I need to take it." CLICK.

I wasn't sure how yet, but I knew I had to get in on this. I was quickly becoming an outsider. I needed to insert myself back into the mix. I had to get off that loser pundit circuit of podcasts and public radio. I needed to get back on the A-list. I dialed my new assistant over at the institute.

"The Harding Institute. How may I direct your call?"

"Give me Danny."

"Who may I say is calling?"

"The boss. Martin Eisenstadt. Who is this?"

"Melanie, the new intern. Veronica quit."

"Welcome aboard. Now please get me Danny. The nerdy guy with glasses."

"Sure thing, Mr. Eisenstadt."

I was becoming agitated. Between the three bourbons under my belt and the standing on the curb, I was starting to crave a cigarette and began to quack like a duck with hiccups. Goddamn hypnotherapy! How long was it taking her to find Danny? I bet he cut out of the office five minutes after I left. Note to self: every once in a while I need to sneak back to the office, so the staff won't be so sure of my schedule.

"Danny Sadler."

"Danny, it's me, Marty."

"Oh hi, Marty, how's it going? I'm almost finished alphabetizing your Rolodex."

"Forget that for now. I have something more important for you to do. I need you to find out how much money the various members of the Hilton family have given to the campaign. And to the party. And do the same for executives at the Blackstone Group."

"Can I do it tomorrow? I need to pay a shiva call. My aunt just passed and I have cousins in Gaithersburg. Actually, do you know if the Metro goes to Gaithersburg?" I was livid.

"This is a priority," I yelled. "You think Lee Atwater left the office at five? This isn't college here, Danny. This is the real deal. And if you're not willing to make sacrifices, well, maybe you're in the wrong business. I made sacrifices to get where I am."

"I know, but it's the last night of the shiva. Maybe I can come in early—"

"You know, Danny, I'm not sure if this arrangement is working out. Maybe I should call Pipes and see if he has something for you in Philly."

"Okay, Marty. Okay. I'll do it. Of course I will. I'm sorry."

When I returned to the office I made a beeline for Danny's cubicle. Marwan was trying to get my attention but I managed to avoid eye contact. Like most South Asians, Marwan has a problem with jealousy. And I could sense that he was becoming insecure about my relationship with Danny. And I was happy about that. Let him feel Danny's breath on the back of his neck. I reached Danny's desk.

"What do you got?"

"You were right. The Hilton family did give a lot of money to the McCain campaign."

"You have the numbers? Show me the numbers."

I retired to my office to write the blog post that I was sure would catapult me back into the big leagues. Nobody ever lost money piggybacking on Paris Hilton, I thought. And even though I had been having difficulty concentrating and finishing sentences of late, this post just flowed right out of me.

### Paris Hilton's family fuming at McCain campaign

July 31, 2008, by Marty

I hate to be the bearer of bad news, but it seems that the new McCain ad criticizing Obama for being a celebrity has ruffled some unintended feathers. I, for one, quite liked the ad, but I hear whispers from the inner campaign staff that the phone was burning off the hook today with calls from Paris Hilton's grandfather, William Barron Hilton (co-chair of the Hilton Hotel empire), furious that the McCain ad drew an unflattering comparison between Obama and his own granddaughter.

It seems that the elder Hilton has donated $18,400 to the McCain campaign, and $35,000 to the National Republican Senatorial Committee in the last couple of years. (Paris's father, Rick Hilton, has given an additional $6,900 to the McCain campaign. Suffice it to say, he's none too pleased either.)

Paris Hilton isn't just a tabloid tart to be tossed around willy-nilly. She's the living brand name of one of America's most successful global corporations. It's no wonder her grandfather's upset: every time Paris is in the news, fewer people stay at their hotels. Try explaining that to The Blackstone Group—the hedge fund firm that bought into Hilton Hotels last year. Blackstone chairman Peter G. Peterson gave $30,800 to the McCain campaign this year. Guess who also called the campaign today?[2]

I looked over what I wrote and felt good. Not only was I breaking an inside political scoop, it involved Paris Hilton. This story was going to get picked up. I just knew it. I would have to be ready to defend myself against those who would claim that I was airing campaign dirty laundry in public. As a loyal McCain adviser, how could I justify doing that? Nobody likes a leaker, especially one who takes credit for it. Were Schmidt and Charlie Black going to go ballistic on me? I mean, these guys, like all great Republicans, have a bit of Nazi in them. Then again, we're all in the same business, and they know the campaign doesn't pay me nearly what I deserve, and that I need to make a living just like everyone else. And that I would be sure to use my new-found exposure to help the campaign, to help them. Who am I kidding? Rick Davis is mean, vindictive. He'll come after me. I have enough enemies as it is. And then it hit me.

I'm not leaking inside dirt for personal benefit. I'm leaking it to help the candidate whom I worship. What did I learn from working with Atwater on the Willie Horton marketing campaign? Generating controversy around an ad gives it extra life. People's calling the Horton ad racist kept the ad in the news and in people's minds for weeks. Creating controversy around an ad turns it into a news story, thus extending the ad's life. Every time the ad is mentioned as news, it's shown again, so in the end, it reaches even those who missed it the first time. After a while, people don't even realize they're watching an ad. They think they're watching the news. And since I believed in this ad, the "Celeb" ad, it was my responsibility to spread it as far as possible, to hammer it into the collective unconscious.

I clicked Send on the e-mail with my post as an attachment. I lifted myself from my swivel leather chair and walked to the door of my office. I opened it, looked to the common space, the bullpen as we like to call it, where my revolving door of interns, assistants, and associate fellows sit.

"Danny, check your e-mail. I just sent you the post. I need you to post it on the blog ASAP. And I need you to spread it across the Internet big-time, the way we did with the YouTube apology."

We were an instant hit. Huffington Post, MSNBC, and the *Los Angeles Times* all ran with the story and quoted me by name. Here's an excerpt from the *Los Angeles Times*'s Top of the Ticket blog column:

### Paris Hilton's rich gramps is reported steamed at John McCain

August 1, 2008, by Andrew Malcolm

As the Ticket noted previously, P.H.'s ma and pa, Kathleen and Richard Hilton, have donated the $2,300 maximum to the McCain operation. But there's a lot more Hiltons apparently, including Gramps Hilton (William B.), who is the vast hotel empire's co-chair. And according to Martin Eisenstadt's blog, he's been quite the generous donor to the tune of more than $50Gs to Republican campaign operations.

Not only that, he reports, but members of the Blackstone Group, the private equity group that bought into Hilton Hotels last year, have also been generous GOP donors. And Marty says they've expressed themselves angrily to McCain representatives in recent hours.[3]

I was ecstatic. The Harding Institute name was all over the press. My name, Martin Eisenstadt, senior McCain adviser, was all over the press. Even *The Daily Show*'s devilishly good-looking Jon Stewart made a joke about our story, although he neglected to credit me as the source. But what can you expect from the tea-sipping liberal elites at Comedy Central?

After a couple of days, Paris's mom, Kathy, essentially confirmed my story by publicly condemning the ad.[4] Even Paris herself entered the fray when she released her own wildly successful rebuttal video. The original ad was getting so much free play, like I had predicted, that no one at the campaign thought to be angry with me. I was a little concerned that Randy might hold a grudge, since one could argue that I betrayed his trust. But I don't think he ever made the connection, as his attention was elsewhere, in the Caucasus, where tensions were escalating between Russia and one of Randy's most important clients, the Republic of Georgia.

And as I had written in my blog about campaign headquarters, it was now the Harding Institute's phones that were "burning off the hook." The press couldn't get enough of this story. The publicity surrounding the ad bounced McCain past Obama in the polls for the first time since the campaign began. The momentum of the race was changing. The field had opened up. John McCain was back in the game. *I* was back in the game.

## Larry King and I

I was in the middle of doing a Google search on my name when I heard the knock.

"Come in." Danny pushed open my door. "Yes, Danny."

He was fidgeting like a schoolgirl about to receive her first pony.

"Guess. I want you to guess."

"Guess what?"

"Guess who's on the phone."

"Just tell me, Danny. I don't have time for this."

"Larry King's office."

"Larry King?"

"Larry King!" Danny jumped up and down.

"Well, put it through. Don't keep them waiting. Hurry up!!" Danny ran (or should I say, skipped) back to his cubicle and patched through the call. I waited for it to ring twice before picking up.

"Hello."

"Is this Martin Eisenstadt?"

"Speaking."

"The Martin Eisenstadt who broke the Paris Hilton story?"

"Yes." I wasn't taking any chances. I learned a long time ago that when things are going your way, say as little as possible.

"This is Marcia Radcliff from Larry King's office and we were hoping we could fly you out . . ." I looked to the ceiling, clenched my eyes and thanked the pro-West, Judeo-Christian God who looks over and protects me. California, here we come.

Because I'm not going to lie to you. The previous few months had been difficult. I wasn't getting the punditing gigs I felt I deserved. And all because of a silly Internet rumor. Being on Larry would dispel once and for all these ridiculous notions that I don't exist while at the same time returning me to the big shows and the A-list rotation. Although I had been on Larry before (via satellite), this would be my first time seated with him at the desk in his Los Angeles studio. In the pundit game, that's status, a rare feat, a game changer.

Still, I would need to navigate the segment carefully. I didn't want to be pigeonholed as a "leaker" or a "celebrity whore." I would be representing the Harding Institute and the Eisenstadt Group. Even if Larry was going to harp on the Paris Hilton aspect of the story, I needed to be prepared to segue myself into weightier topics, to convey that I'm bigger than this one specific leak, that I'm an insider with experience and wisdom.

## Michael Phelps with the Smoking Chinese Gymnasts

At home packing for my trip, I was one day away from escaping the heat, humidity, and stuffiness of Washington for the cool, laid-back sunshine of Southern California. The phone rang. It was Danny. I ignored it. The Olympics were on TV and watching Michael Phelps win another gold medal seemed more important. I was so proud of him and all he was doing for the prestige of our country.

My phone rang again. It was Danny. I ignored it again. I would be spending enough time with him over the next couple of days in California. And then he called again.

"What, Danny? What? This better be good."

"Are you sitting? I have some bad news."

"Who cares if I'm sitting? What difference does it make if I'm sitting? Just tell me. What? What happened?"

"We've been bumped."

"Bumped? Why?" I noticed that the Olympics had been interrupted by a breaking news story. I flipped the channels. On every channel, I saw the same images of war, of carnage, of Russian soldiers fighting in Georgia. "The Russian invasion of Georgia?"

"That's what they said. But they also said not to worry, that this happens all the time and that you would be rescheduled—"

"Bullshit. That's what they always say. Bumped means canceled, Danny. Canceled! Those lying cowards! You cancel on a doctor and he charges you. Who's going to reimburse *me* for my losses?"

"And Marty. There's something else."

"Something else?"

"Yeah. A BBC crew is supposed to meet us at the airport in Los Angeles. Remember. I told you about that."

"No. I don't remember you telling me that."

"The woman's name is Samantha Hensington. She's British but based in L.A. She requested an interview with you but your schedule was too tight, so we agreed that she could meet us at the airport, you know, drive around with us, film you going to your interviews."

"You're sure she's with the BBC? I mean, did you do your due diligence?

"She has an accent, and she seemed very smart."

"You call that due diligence?! Anybody can fake an accent. Anyone can say they're from the BBC." With this crazed golf blogger out there, I was starting to become paranoid. Maybe this Samantha was connected to the golf blogger. Maybe she *was* the golf blogger. My ex-wife Zolzaya's first husband, the oligarch with the KGB past, lived in London. He did swear on a saint's grave that someday he would get me. A sharp pain pierced my toe. Damn you, gout! "How do we know it's not a trap?"

"A trap? But I checked her out on Facebook. And I looked at something called the Internet Movie Database. She was a production assistant on a 2003 BBC sports show about Manchester United. But we're not going to L.A., so I'll need to call and cancel, right?"

I thought for a moment. About the BBC. About my toe. About palm trees. "Don't cancel a thing Danny. The tickets are paid for. We're going to L.A."

NBC was now featuring the scandalously young Chinese gymnastics team on TV. Distracted by Jiang Yuyuan's grace and sensuality on the high bar, I tried to block out what I had just heard. I would worry about tomorrow, tomorrow. I concentrated on the television. What a landing. What firm buttocks. I reminded myself that statutory laws are arbitrary and vary from country to country. And anyhow, the law in this country doesn't forbid lusting after a minor (or, for that matter, a senior citizen). It forbids sexual interaction, and as long as I am in the contiguous United States I respect that law.

And then it hit me. I needed to stop being so negative, so fearful. A BBC crew was expecting me, and I intended to be ready.

I called Danny and instructed him to guilt, beg, and threaten the Larry King people until they agreed to send us a car (so we could at least get around while the BBC filmed us), but Danny resisted that idea. Instead, he blasted a mass e-mail to my blog's database (essentially, anyone who had ever left a comment), letting our fans know that I would be in L.A. and that we were in need of transportation. Miraculously, someone offered the services of a friend, a down-on-his-luck limo driver recently returned from Iraq. I was excited.

If Howard Dean could implement a fifty-state strategy, why couldn't we? I kept screaming to Steve Schmidt and anyone over at the campaign who would listen that sitting in air-conditioned offices in D.C. sending out e-mails and press releases wasn't going to cut it. To fight this war effectively, we would have to get off our butts and target even the most azure of blue states. People like to dismiss California as la-la land, but it's not true. California is 50 percent Hispanic, and Hispanics are natural supporters of John McCain and the Republican message. Plus California is filled with immigrants from repressive regimes—the former Soviet Union, communist Vietnam, jihadist Iran—people who possess that healthy mix of paranoia and cynicism that makes them particularly open to our message.

## Flying Ain't What It Used to Be

"Two dollars?" I couldn't believe my ears. The stewardess push-ing the beverage cart had just asked me to pay two dollars for a minuscule bottle of water. "For water? Water is a medical neces-sity. Flying causes dehydration."

"I'm sorry. Those are the rules. As of August first." I returned the water bottle and cup and napkin to her. Danny, who was sit-ting next to me, removed two dollars from his pocket and handed it to the stewardess.

"It's okay, Marty. I got it."

"You think I don't have two dollars, Danny? It's not about the money. It's the principle. Flying causes dehydration. It's like charging you extra for a seat belt." I was livid. Not so much at U.S. Airways as at the Larry King show. Not only did they put us in coach, they stuck us in the back rows with students and strug-gling rappers. And now this nonsense. I took back the water and cup and napkin from the stewardess.

"Thank you, Danny." Under normal circumstances, I would have stood on principle, but considering my issues with gout, I didn't want to be penny wise, pound foolish. According to the re-search I had Eli do for me online, dehydration is the primary cause of flare-ups. *And flying causes dehydration!* I poured water into my ice cup. The stewardess continued to the next row. I turned.

"Excuse me. Do you have wine?" I asked. The aging glorified waitress looked at me rudely.

"They're seven dollars." Essentially, calling me cheap. It's funny how she's talking to me like I'm a nobody when actually I'm a pretty big deal. If she knew who I was, she'd be a whole nother person.

"Bring me two," I instructed her. You see? I'm not cheap. I just don't like to get hustled. There's a difference. Screw fourteen dol-lars. Of course, the campaign will cover it. What's fourteen dollars to a $500 million operation?

## Marty Does California

After landing at LAX, we were met at the terminal by Samantha, the freelance BBC journalist, and her cameraman, Steve. Our driver, Lance, had served as a Blackwater driver in Iraq, so we had a lot to talk about.

And what a day we shared together. We visited Hispanics at the Olvera Market, African Americans in Baldwin Hills, and Persians in Beverly Hills. I was ecstatic. Our message of attacking Iran and drilling for oil and gas in national parks was resonating with the people. From the barrio to Beverly Hills, the people embraced us. Crowds swarmed to hear our message. And the BBC was there documenting it. We were a genuine hit. It was somewhat new and overwhelming for Danny to be treated like such a rock star. I, of course, was used to it. It was this kind of excitement and enthusiasm that was missing from our campaign. It was this kind of excitement and enthusiasm that was needed to win elections. Trust me. I know. I've worked on plenty of winning Republican campaigns.

People sometimes ask me if I regret allowing Samantha and her cameraman to follow me around like I did. I mean, one could argue that her depiction of me in *The Last Republican* was less than positive. On the other hand, in this game even bad press is good, and the world got a chance to hear our message and see the important work that we do at the Harding Institute. And even though words that I said were misconstrued, cross-edited, and taken out of context, I was able to issue rebuttals that set the record straight. Also, when the allegations that I don't exist started to surface online and in the mainstream press, I was able to point to her documentary as easy proof that I do, in fact, exist.

My only regret is that I wasn't able to speak at the Abundant Life Fellowship, an African American church in Inglewood. I craved the opportunity to chip away at Barack's base. I was looking forward to finding common ground, to pointing to my benefactor's great-uncle, our institute's namesake, Warren G. Harding, as the first African American president. I refer to *The New York Times*, which uncovered a long-lost biography of Harding, published in the early 1920s.

## Our First Black President?

*April 6, 2008, by Beverly Gage*

Will Americans vote for a black president? If the notorious historian William Estabrook Chancellor was right, we already did . . . According to the family tree Chancellor created, Harding was actually the great-grandson of a black woman. Under the one-drop rule of American race relations, Chancellor claimed, the country had inadvertently elected its "first Negro president."[5]

Sadly, at the last second the church canceled, and I didn't get the chance to make my case in front of a large audience. I couldn't help but wonder if Beatrice, the church secretary, had canceled because she did a Google search on my name and saw Wolfrum's postings. Instead, as you saw in *The Last Republican*, I met with an African American community organizer at the Marcus Garvey Community Outreach Program Center, in nearby Baldwin Hills. Rather than being receptive to my message, he tried to hustle money out of me and the Harding Institute. He even implied that I was a racist, which is nonsense because I was behaving especially politically correct that day. You see, I was still traumatized by a recent unfortunate incident with Soledad O'Brien in the CNN greenroom. All I said to her was: "Barack Obama is African American like John Kerry is a Vietnam veteran. When are the blacks in this country going to realize that Barack is playing them for suckers, riding their coattails? That he has no actual African American blood in him, that he was raised by white people in Hawaii. His wife is a real African American. That I'll give you." How was I to know that Soledad's background is Afro-Cuban? Boy, did she hit the roof. She called me an "evil little man." Why did I have it in my head that Soledad was a French Canadian name? If that wasn't uncomfortable enough, Anderson Cooper came running from his changing room and escorted me out of the building (it was hard to be scared of him, though, as he was essentially pantless, wearing only a waist-length silk kimono). So trust me when I tell you, I didn't say anything controversial or inappropriate to that community organizer. He clearly overreacted. I'm glad the viewers of *The Last Republican* got a chance to see a real-life community organizer in action before casting their votes.

Later in the day, we dropped Danny off so that he could spend the night with relatives. Samantha and I then went out for a drink. I definitely had the sense that she had been hitting on me all day, but I took it in stride, as it's not uncommon for journalists to develop crushes on their subjects (it's called the "Walters Syndrome," named after an uncomfortably intimate interview Barbara Walters had with Burt Reynolds in 1978). So I have to admit I was shocked when I saw *The Last Republican* depict me as a randy drunk who sexually propositions reporters and says nasty things about his bosses. She assured me the cameras were off and plied me with alcohol . . . I've said enough. The attorneys at Dickstein Shapiro have counseled me to say no more. It will all be covered in the lawsuit.

After leaving Samantha, Lance and I talked about going out to a club, but in the end, I decided to call it a night. I had been up since very early. Lance drove me to the hotel where the Larry King show had booked us our room. Danny had assured me that the room was paid for, that the Larry King people had agreed to let me use the reservation they had made for us when I was still scheduled to appear on the show. So imagine my surprise when the handsome, lip-enhanced clerk with rock-hard abs and pecs, informed me that there was nothing booked under my name or

## *The Last Republican*: Excerpt 1

*(Courtesy of Samantha Hensington/BBC)*

**COMMUNITY ORGANIZER:** You know how many products have gluten in them?

**MARTY:** I agree with you, and John McCain agrees with you. We are anti-FDA. Like we had a war against drugs and a war against terror, we need a war against the FDA and a war against gluten.

**C.O.:** And with your grant of fifty thousand dollars, you're looking at the site of the Marcus Garvey Harding Institute Gluten-free Awareness Center.

**MARTY:** I think if we were to contribute that amount of money we would probably want our name first.

**C.O.:** So you're going to give us fifty thousand dollars?

**MARTY:** In kind. (*Turning to Danny*) Danny, how much do I get when I speak?

**DANNY:** Ugh . . .

**MARTY:** Twenty-five thousand dollars I get when I speak.

**C.O.:** So you're only going to donate twenty-five thousand dollars.

**MARTY:** I'll do it twice. I'm very inspiring. I'll talk to the kids. I can do couples counseling.

A classic case of Walters Syndrome
*(Courtesy of Samantha Hensington/BBC)*

under the Larry King name and that if I wanted a room, the cheapest one available was $200 a night.

## Rolling with My Blackwater Buddy

Lance invited me to stay with him in Northridge, but I had concerns. Lance was a war veteran going through a divorce and unemployment. If there were to be a misunderstanding between us, if he suddenly insisted that I pay extra money, I would be stranded or worse; he could have some post-traumatic-stress freak-out on me. I learned from my travels to be suspicious of overly friendly drivers. In Iraq, I once had a bad experience staying with a driver who the next morning presented me with a bill for each blanket that I used, for the water that I drank, for the two times that I used the restroom (actually, more like an outhouse).

"Thank you so much, Lance, but I have someone I need to see."

After watching Danny say the wrong thing time after time today, I was suddenly feeling nostalgic for my former assistant and partner in crime, Eli Perle, who was now living in Los Angeles. (My attorneys at Dickstein Shapiro have counseled me to point out that when I use the term "crime," I intend it euphemistically.) I scrolled through my clamshell phone book. There it was.

Stranded at my driver's home in Iraq
(*Courtesy of Abu Moustafa*)

Eli's new number. He had called once looking to use me as a reference, and I may have forgotten to call him back.

"Eli? It's Marty!"

"Marty, how's it going?"

"Great. How are you?"

"Awesome, man. Awesome!" Awesome? I thought *I* was a chameleon! This guy really had no center. Mind you, in Washington Eli wore bow ties. I was just waiting for him to call me "dude." That's where I would draw the line and reassert my boss privileges.

"LA treating you well?"

"The best. I just landed an agent."

"I thought you were an agent."

"No. I'm a manager."

"So what do you need an agent for?"

"Well, remember those Abrad videos we did? I showed them to some people."

"Which people?"

"TV people. Doesn't matter who specifically. What's important is there's been some interest. We're thinking about calling it 'The Bitter Valet.'"

I knew I came to California for a reason. Let Eli do the grunt work. That's what he was good at. Now I'm here to close the deal. What's the point in waging the primary's most successful viral video campaign and have no one know about it? Maybe Hollywood *was* the way to go.

"Okay," I told him. "This is how we're going to do this. I know a guy over at Warner's. I can't remember his name. He wears transitional lenses. He's a putz, but he owes me—"

"Marty, the most I can give you is a co-producer credit." That little pisher. After everything I'd done for him.

"What are you crazy? They're *my* videos. I made them. You were my intern."

"Associate fellow," he snarkily snapped back.

"Well then, I'll have to sue you."

"How? The whole thing was done undercover, with no paper trail. Remember?"

"I got the biggest proof in the world, Eli. Have you forgotten? That's me in the videos!"

"Yeah, about that. My agent sees Michael Rappaport for that role. Listen, Marty, I can't really talk now. I'm in a screening, and it's about to start. If you're ever in L.A., call me. We'll do lunch."

"I'm in L.A. now. That's why I'm . . . Hello. Hello." He was gone. I wasn't worried. I would wait for Eli to get further into his process, to involve bigger entities, and then when the stakes were highest, I would sick Dickstein Shapiro on him. The student may have learned some of his teacher's tricks. But not everything. If there's one thing I know, it's our legal system and how to use it to crush unsuspecting adversaries.

Lance looked at his watch, looked at me. I had one last option. You see, what I neglected to tell you, dear reader, is that my father, Izzy Eisenstadt, lives in Santa Monica, having moved there from Brooklyn soon after 9/11. And that's the story Dad likes to tell. That he was supposed to be at the second tower to renew his cell-phone plan. And he slept late. Something Dad never does. He took it as a sign and decided to change up his life. As I said, that's the story he likes to tell. If you ask me, his zipper business had been crap for a long time (since the button-fly revolution of the late eighties) and abandoning his business, family, and friends was easier than ... Doesn't matter. Anyway, my father lived in Santa Monica, and I could always stay there. It had been a while since I'd seen him, at least a couple of years. I gave him a call.

"Dad. I'm in L.A. and I—"

"What are you waiting for? Come on over!"

He gave me directions from the hotel, which turned out to be walking distance from his apartment. I informed Lance that I would get there by foot as I had only one bag. Lance insisted that I let him drive me. He was real adamant about it too. Danny, you idiot! What were you thinking sending out a mass e-mail to everyone in our database, effectively announcing to the world that I was coming to L.A. and needed a driver?

How could I know that Lance wasn't working for Wolfrum? Come to think of it, Sharif Investments often used ex-Blackwater for jobs. Between Jamie's pride and Nabil's inability to forgive, I clearly had formidable enemies. I couldn't have Lance knowing where my father lived.

"It's better if I walk. I need the exercise."

"It was a pleasure being at your service today, Mr. Eisenstadt."

"God bless America." I responded. I saluted him. He saluted back.

I crossed streets, took alleys, and backtracked a couple of times just in case Lance was following me. I arrived at my father's address.

## Izzy Eisenstadt

I climbed wood stairs to a second-floor bungalow overlooking lemon and avocado trees. Leonard Cohen blasted through open windows. I knocked. No response. I banged harder. What was he doing? He knows I'm here. I just called him two seconds ago.

The door opened, and there stood my dad, Izzy Eisenstadt, sporting a bushy beard and a creepily tight Che Guevara T-shirt. Beads dangled from his neck and wrists. Around his waist he wore a purple cloth, resembling pajamas, which he probably picked up in Thailand on one of his sex tours. I had to hand it to him though. He was tan and trim and seemed genuinely content. I hadn't seen Dad this happy since the late seventies, when he had the Jordache account and was a regular at Studio 54.

"You beautiful spiritual being. I love you. I love you. I love you." He squeezed me tight. Everywhere I looked I saw plastic medicine bottles labeled with names likes Pineapple Frost, Purple Diesel, and AK-47 lining his shelves and coffee table. My father is very proud of his medical-marijuana prescription.

"How come you don't answer my texts?" asked Dad.

"Because I'm busy. Unlike you, I have a job, responsibilities." I kicked off my shoes and made myself comfortable on a beanbag. "Today I was followed around by a BBC crew."

"Washington makes people tense. I always warned your mother about that. And how is dear Connie, still dating the Swedish ambassador?"

"He was the Norwegian chargé d'affaires, and no, she's not."

"Maybe now's a good time to pay a visit."

"I don't recommend it."

"What do you mean?"

"You should have listened to my advice and opened that factory in China, Dad. I could have helped you. I have contacts."

"What contacts? It's one thing to lie to others, son. Just don't lie to yourself. Smoke some medicine. It'll relax you." Dad filled a pipe with marijuana and offered it to me. I inhaled.

Although I have always been a big supporter of the War on Drugs, I am also a movement conservative, which means that I believe in state's rights. And as I understand it, under Governor Arnold Schwarzenegger, smoking marijuana is being encouraged and taxed to help defray California's budget shortfall. Plus, my father had a prescription and I was a gout sufferer. I noticed that Dad was having trouble keeping his eyes open. I myself was starting to feel dizzy. Which is when it struck me.

Sure. People were generally nice to my face, but behind my back, they mocked me. I had become a laughingstock among pundits. I had an anonymous enemy out there, in the shadows, and he was inflicting great shame and trouble on me. That's why we had so many cancellations today.

Suddenly I felt cold. My pulse quickened, and I was having trouble catching my breath. I thought about being in my forties, about not having any children, about still living in the basement of my mother's Georgetown town house, or worse, winding up stoned and all alone in California like my father. I was so cold that I was shivering. What was that noise? I saw a shadow. Could Lance have followed me? I turned off the lights, double locked the door, and huddled into a fetal position until sleep overtook me many hours later.

# 11

# The Sarah Palin Choice

## The Mile High Club

On only day three of the Democratic convention in Denver, it hit me like a brick that I was in the wrong place. Most everybody, especially the media, was high on the drug of Obama, a man among mice, the Übermensch prophesied by Gandhi, the second coming of Martin Luther King (brought to you by AT&T). Wherever I ventured, the supposedly politically correct mocked my flag pin. Most of the time, I didn't even wear it, out of fear. Which is a scary metaphor, I thought at the time, for what this country will be like if Obama becomes president.

I had come to Denver to pundit. As every TV segment requires two sides, what better place for a Republican pundit than a Democratic convention. Unfortunately, the Clinton surrogates pretending to be disgruntled delegates were hogging all the opposition airtime. But that's not why I started getting panic attacks about being in the wrong place. It was because anybody who was a somebody on my side was now in Arizona. They were with John at his ranch as he interviewed contenders and decided on his pick for vice president.

As Denver braced for Bubba Clinton's big speech that night, I loaded my stuff into a rental car and headed due south, to Arizona, where the McCain team, my team, was huddled. I knew in my gut that that was where I needed to be.

## From John Wayne to John McCain

The drive was breathtaking, snowcapped mountains giving way to high desert to red rock formations. It was almost 10:00 p.m. when I approached Flagstaff, population 50,000, elevation 7,000 feet. Only forty miles from Sedona, it was the logical spot to spend the night. I stopped at the hotel where Mark Salter was known to sometimes write, the rustic Monte Vista in downtown Flagstaff. Who knows? Maybe I would get lucky and find him here. And then I could tag along to the ranch. Otherwise, how was I going to get in? Scheunemann wasn't taking my calls. Meghan McCain never seemed to recognize me. And Cindy was known to guard her property with a shotgun.

The eager clerk informed me that years ago John Wayne and Gary Cooper had stayed here. "Yes, but is Mark Salter staying here now?" I inquired.

"Sure," the clerk told me. "He's in the bar."

I checked in and headed for the bar. It was karaoke night at the Monte V in the basement of the hotel, and a long-haul trucker was doing his best rendition of "I Touch Myself" by the Divinyls.

And there they sat—I noticed them right away: Mark Salter, with his trademark goatee, and Steve Schmidt, with his shaved head, chief of day-to-day operations. I wondered why Schmidt was here as well. Had they run out of rooms over at the ranch? That seemed unlikely, as John's fifteen-acre property housed six complexes with abundant available lodging. I approached the bar where Steve and Mark tossed back whiskeys using Budweiser bottles as chasers.

"Hey, guys." I patted Steve on the back since he was sitting closest to me. He turned and looked genuinely surprised.

"Marty Eisenstadt? What the hell are you doing here?"

"I'm coming from the Democratic Convention. Or should I say the AT&T Democratic Convention?" I showed him the AT&T Democratic Convention flashlight I was carrying. He chuckled. I took off my jacket, pulled up a stool, and continued. "I hope we have good sponsors this year. I got a gym membership that I still use out of 2004." I sat down. Salter looked at me. I noticed his cowboy boots.

"You didn't stay for Hussein Osama's Sermon on the Mount?" Mark facetiously asked, referring to Obama's upcoming speech before eighty thousand in Mile High Stadium.

"I know. What a clown. Who does he think he is? The Messiah? We need to stop being so scared of this guy. He's vulnerable just like every other Democrat. It'll be a cinch to poke him full of holes." Before uttering my next remark, I looked both ways to make sure no one was in earshot. "Is the senator any closer to a decision?"

Mark lifted an eyebrow and looked at me condescendingly. Thankfully Steve defended me, piping in, "You'd be surprised. Marty here has been around the block. He worked with Charlie Black back in the Atwater days. We might actually get some good advice out of him."

"You're the general," offered Mark. He respected Steve, the way he respected John. Unlike most cynical pols, Mark had the soul of a thinker, a writer, an artist. Though he went by Mark, his real name was Marshall—like Thurgood, McLuhan, or Mathers. It is in his nature to be drawn to bold, decisive men like Steve and John.

Steve accepted Mark's gesture of respect with a nod, turned to me, put his hand on my shoulder, and looked into my eyes. "Listen, Marty, I know you're always looking for scoops for that little blog of yours. But this leaks to anyone and you're dead, you hear me? We have people, and for this kind of betrayal, we will not hesitate to use them."

"Of course. Who is it?"

"We just came from seeing Sarah Palin."

"Palin? Really?!" I was stunned.

"She's here in Flagstaff. She landed this afternoon. Tomorrow we bring her to the ranch to meet John. It's looking like a distinct possibility. We both like her."

"I'm starting to come around," added Mark. "It'll really shake things up. Plus, we'll be able to peel off disgruntled Hillary supporters."

"There are no disgruntled Hillary supporters. I just came from Denver. That's a myth created by the Clinton machine. Didn't you read my blog about the Jonas Brothers and Miley Cyrus from a couple weeks ago?" From their expressions, I could see that they hadn't. "Girls say they're fans of other girls, but in the end they'd rather swoon over the cute boys."

"So who do you think he should choose?" asked Steve.

"Doesn't matter what we do or don't do, our base will be at the polling booth bright and early voting against the black man. So my advice is pick someone safe, like a Pawlenty, so we can still appeal to the swing voters."

Salter nodded. "I'm inclined to agree with Marty. Maybe Pawlenty is the way to go. John's integrity speaks for itself. Let's win this thing positive."

"I didn't say anything about positive. We need to go hard-core negative to win this one. We need to expose Obama as a faker, as just another salesman for the Democratic machine. That should be our slogan 'He's a politician. Don't be such a sucker.'"

"Haven't seen you around in a while, Eisenstadt," Steve finally interjected.

"I was in California," I reminded him. "Getting off my ass and actually doing some campaigning."

"That's right. You called me from there. You left a message. Something about the BBC. Right?"

"Right."

"Right? Right?!" Steve grabbed my head and rubbed his knuckles against my skull. He released me. "Why do you keep calling me and leaving rambling messages? Come on."

Mark smiled. "What are you drinking, Eisenstadt?" I liked him. He struck me as someone who believed in manhood, in honor, in getting drunk. Mark motioned to the tired bartender. "Another round, barkeep!"

As we awaited our drinks, Mark walked to the karaoke mike and began to sing an old Bob Dylan song. Schmidt leaned over to me. "I'm partial to John Denver, myself."

Mark didn't have a bad voice actually. "Oh, where have you been, my blue-eyed son? Oh, where have you been, my darling young one?" Was this his ode to McCain? I wondered. Steve and I grabbed our drinks and joined him on the prophetic chorus. "And it's a hard, and it's a hard, it's a hard, and it's a haaaard . . ." The three of us hugged onstage. "And it's a hard rain's a-gonna fall!"

## The Neiman Marcus Experience: Shopping for Sarah

The next morning I awoke with a hangover and a mild discomfort in my foot, almost like I had sprained the ankle. The sheet had come off the mattress, and I had a vile taste in my mouth. How did I get so drunk? I didn't even remember drinking that much. Through the hotel window, I saw mountains. Maybe it was the altitude. That's right. I was in Flagstaff, but why? Why was I in Flagstaff?

The clock on the night stand blinked 12:00. I found my pants, my cell phone. There it was, the time, 10:00 a.m., assuming my

Sprint clamshell automatically changed with the time zones. (I'll bet BlackBerrys do.) Memories were coming back to me. Are Denver and Flagstaff in the same time zone? I didn't know. Either way, it was way past 7:30 a.m.—crap!—the time I was supposed to meet up with Mark and Steve to collect Sarah Palin from a wealthy contributor's home and proceed in caravan formation to the ranch. How did I sleep through that? That would have been huge. To be a part of the campaign inner circle during such an important bonding moment. I suddenly felt my foot. I hoped that, in my drunkenness, I had twisted it. Otherwise, I was in the early stages of a gout attack.

I grabbed my phone and dialed Steve Schmidt.

"Go."

"Steve, it's Marty. I can't believe I missed you guys."

"You snooze, you lose."

"You guys still at the ranch?"

"We're Oscar Mike, Marty boy, outta here. On our way to Dayton for tomorrow's announcement. We're just now piling into the Gulf Stream."

"So did he pick Palin?"

"On a cell phone, Marty? Come on. Gotta go."

I studied the map at the front desk. Dayton, the next stop on the McCain traveling circus, was more than 1,700 miles away. They would already be on their way to Minneapolis for the convention by the time I got there.

So I skipped Dayton and drove a day and a half straight to Minneapolis. The convention was officially slated to start Monday, but already Minneapolis felt like it had been taken over by an invading army. The RNC was based at the Hyatt Regency, so I went there, hoping to bump into someone from the gang. I stood around in the lobby for four hours until I finally spotted Nicolle Wallace, a senior adviser to the campaign, standing with some guy who looked vaguely familiar. Nicolle was in the campaign inner circle. I approached her.

"Hey, Nicolle. Good to see you." She smiled, acknowledging me politely, before going back to her BlackBerry. "Have you seen Steve?" I asked. Nicolle and Schmidt were both former Bushies from the '04 campaign.

"He's around here somewhere." She pointed to the man next to her. "You know Jeff Larson?"

"Jeff, of course," I shook his hand. Jeff was a principal in the robocalling firm FLS Connect. Ironic that we'd teamed up together on the 2000 whispering campaign against John McCain in South Carolina, and now we were all here working for him.[1]

I noticed Nicolle checking me out. I've always prided myself on being a fiscal conservative, not a social conservative, but still, I draw the line at married women. Especially since her husband, Mark Wallace, also worked on the campaign and was here at the convention.

"What size are you?"

"Forty-two."

She grabbed me by the shoulders and ran her hand down my back. She glanced at Jeff. "He'll do."

Nicolle and Jeff whisked me into a waiting town car. Next thing I knew I was at the downtown Neiman Marcus trying on everything from Italian suits to silk boxer shorts. Apparently I have the same measurements as Todd Palin. Nicolle was in the next dressing room trying on potential clothes for Sarah. It was obvious she didn't want to be there. She was, after all, a former White House communications director. But she was the only woman in the campaign staff's inner circle and her figure was similar to Sarah's.

While Jeff unsuccessfully badgered the Neiman Marcus manager for a bulk discount, Nicolle got an urgent BlackBerry message.

"Yes!" she shrieked excitedly from behind the dressing-room door. "Hurricane Gustav is about to hit New Orleans!"

"How is that good news?" I asked while trying on a $1,980 Salvatore Ferragamo striped blazer.

"It's the best time to release the word that Bristol's pregnant.

But I've got to head back to the Hyatt to deal with this. Marty, pick out the rest of Sarah's clothes. Just remember, she's partial to red, black, and pale taupe. And she gets hives from rayon. Whatever you do, don't get yellow. That's Cindy's color." And with that, she was gone.

So with all due humility, it was me, Marty Eisenstadt, who chose the Palin family wardrobe that seduced America into falling in love with them. Nicolle was right. With the news of Bristol Palin's pregnancy about to get out, we couldn't have Sarah and her family dressing like a clan of snowmobilers making the meth run from Wasilla to Barrow. So I aimed high. As I'm not the most decisive shopper in the world, it was especially hard for me to choose between the Carolina Herrera beaded dress for $4,690, the Nina Ricci gathered-sleeve bolero for $2,890, and the Valentino origami V-back for $3,750. None of them fit very well on Jeff (he's a little leggy), so I made the executive decision to run his AmEx Black Card up to seventy-five grand, a drop in the bucket compared to the task at hand, dressing the second family. Better safe than sorry, I figured. Anyhow, the RNC would cover it. And if they didn't like something, they could always return it.

Still, for PR purposes, the purchases should never have become public. Unfortunately Jeff was too eager to get reimbursed and jumped the gun in filing the FEC expense reports.[2] Had I filed those expenses, with my three decades of Washington experience, they would have shown up the week after the election as "office supplies" or "postage" or "campaign T-shirts." Because of other people's sloppiness, what should have been a badge of pride for me, being responsible for crafting the Sarah Palin image, turned into something tainted, something I had to keep under wraps. But that's politics.

Nicolle instructed me to drop the bags off at Sarah's hotel suite. It took three big hotel luggage carts to carry everything. I knocked on the door, and out came Sarah wearing nothing but a towel and a smile. She peered into one of the bags.

"Ooh, Neiman Marcus! Come on in!"

As I pushed the clothes into the suite, I began to understand that this was some sort of prep area for all the Palin and McCain women. It was like the giggling bridal party just before a wedding. Meghan, Bristol, and the other assorted daughters were all lined up in chairs, with four hair and makeup artists buzzing around them like agitated bees at a honey convention.

Cindy McCain was in charge. Dressed in a buttercup-yellow Oscar de la Renta couture number with three-carat diamond earrings, she was a woman who took personal grooming very seriously. "Marty," she ordered, "put the clothes over there. Sarah, get back on the table. Bristol, what do we do about the baby bump? Meghan, teach her to accentuate her cleavage."

"Mom!" whined Meghan.

"What?" barked Cindy. "Just do it, they're family now! Marty, did you meet the makeup team from L.A.? Angela, Amy, Heather, and Tifanie."

"Hey, Marty!" the beautiful California makeup girls cooed in unison. If there's one lesson I learned from John Ehrlichman and his experience with Nixon and the JFK debate, makeup matters.

"Girls," I said. "You're an essential part of this campaign. I mean that. If there's anything you need, I'm in room 451 all week."

Meghan couldn't contain herself. "Amy, tell Marty 'bout the Emmy you guys won for *So You Think You Can Dance*. That is *so* wicked!"

"Hush, Meghan!" scolded Cindy. She walked over to Sarah and grabbed her limp wet hair. "Sarah, honey, you can't hide that mop under a ski hat forever. I'm going to give you Angela for the convention. Maybe for the full campaign, we'll see. She's a genius."

As Sarah lay flat on a portable tanning table, her towel dropped to the sides. Her back was as white as the Alaska tundra, with the top of her buttocks rising like the foothills of Mount McKinley. A very attractive woman began to spray on a smooth golden mist. "Cindy told me to get rid of my Eskimo tan before going on TV

## So You Think You Can Dance . . . with Cindy?

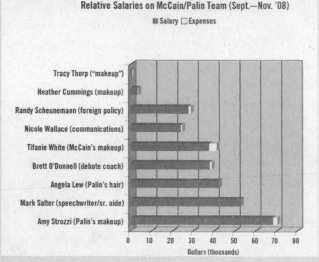

Relative Salaries on McCain/Palin Team (Sept.—Nov. '08)

■ Salary □ Expenses

(Source: FEC)[3]

What Cindy did *not* count on was that Sarah was going to monopolize the hair-and-makeup team. The convention was all smiles, but once everyone left St. Paul and went their separate ways, Sarah commandeered Angela and Amy as her traveling retinue. Cindy was none too pleased. For the rest of the campaign, all John and Cindy got was Tifanie (Amy's *assistant*) for both makeup *and* hair. And forget about poor Meghan McCain—she was stuck doing her own hair and makeup on the surrogate campaign bus.

For Cindy—an heiress in her own right, who once stole John away from his first wife—the Palin phenomenon was a personal affront. The second-string makeup girl for the presumptive first family? Not without consequences. And don't think the rest of the campaign staff didn't notice either. As the FEC reports started trickling in, it was clear that the members of Sarah's grooming team were some of the highest-paid staffers.[4]

tonight. John's funny about the melanomas, so they flew in Tracy here to spray me up good." I noticed Randy Scheunemann kneeling on the floor, pumicing Sarah's feet. "Ooh, Randy, that tickles!"

The rest of the convention went as planned. I proudly looked on as the newly dressed Palin family wowed America, and McCain surged in the polls. Sarah looked regal, yet accessible. And Todd filled out his suits and silk shorts almost as well as I had. As anticipated, it was harder to get punditing gigs here than in Denver, but I was satisfied I'd played at least a small part in the coronation of Sarah Palin.

## The So-called Financial Meltdown

When I got back to Washington, I busied myself with the blog, with the institute, with looking for apartments on Craigslist. I couldn't stay in Mom's basement forever. Plus, it looked like I would be coming into some money. Danny had just finished preparing my campaign invoice, and I was pretty sure that this time it would be approved. In true Ehrlichman fashion (what you learn during the formative years really does stick with you), I had been using the blog to funnel information from the campaign to the mainstream media. The campaign would surely sign off on my fees and expenses.

It was autumn in D.C. and barely two weeks since John McCain told a campaign crowd in Florida that the "fundamentals of the economy are sound," the day after Lehman Brothers filed for bankruptcy and the day before Mom's old friend, Secretary Paulson, announced the government's intention to bail out AIG. The campaign tried to explain that when John was talking about fundamentals, he was referring to the American workers, who are the best in the world. APPLAUSE! And as a former fighter pilot, John isn't afraid to change course, to bob and weave, to get shot down.

So when, after being briefed by the experts, John recognized how dire the crisis was, he announced that he was suspending the campaign so he could return to Washington to fix the mess. In the name of "Country First," McCain even called for a postponement of the first presidential debate scheduled for that Friday. Obama pointed out that a president should be able to do two things at the same time. But that's because he's young and brash. He's from a different generation. He doesn't understand "Country First."

After talking with Steve Schmidt, I wrote a blog post predicting that John was returning to Washington to stand tough against the bailouts.[5] Unfortunately, my "scoop" did not come to pass. In the end, McCain called for bipartisanship and sided with the Washington establishment in support of rescuing the banks. If only the campaign had followed my trial balloon, John McCain would be president today. But what do I know? I've only worked on five winning presidential campaigns.

## Drinks with Steve Schmidt

"So what gives, Steve?" It was Sunday, September 28, three days after John's visit to Washington and two days after the first presidential debate in Mississippi. I was having lunch and a drink with Steve Schmidt at the Capital Grille. (One look at the menu made me miss the comped Kobe short ribs I used to enjoy at Signatures, Jack Abramoff's old restaurant that was just down the block on Pennsylvania Avenue.)

Strangely enough, it was Steve who had called me. I guess he had more misinformation to feed me. He had only just showed up, but I really wanted to know, so I pressed him further. "Why didn't you implement what you told me to spread? It was a brilliant plan. And it would have worked. The headline should be reading, 'John McCain stands up for the little guy against Ivy Leaguer Barack Obama and his fat-cat buddies in Washington and New York.' Instead it's reading, 'John McCain can't make up his mind.'"

"Like Rumsfeld said, 'You go to the election with the candidate you have.' What can I tell you? Ever since he jumped out of a burning plane over Vietnam, he's had a hard time resisting bailouts."

"Whatever Obama is for, we have to be against. Doesn't he understand that? This was our chance!"

"Are you finished?" Steve interjected.

"Yes."

"We have other problems. Did you catch any of the Couric interview?" While John was suspending the campaign and flying into and out of Washington, CBS was airing (piecemeal, for maximum effect) the train-wreck interview that Sarah Palin had given to Katie Couric. I commiserated with a sigh. I had seen the poll numbers. They were in a free fall.

"But all's not lost," continued Steve. "She has Thursday's debate to redeem herself." I couldn't tell if he was being serious or facetious. Steve continued: "No, really. Tomorrow we're sending Sarah to Sedona for two and a half days of intensive debate preparation. It's going to be all hands on deck. You coming? We'll fly you out." Did Steve just invite me to Sedona to be on the Sarah Palin debate-preparation team?

"And feel free to write about it on your blog," continued Steve. "It would be good to have some 'unofficial' coverage from the ranch. And remember, low expectations work to our favor."

"Got it."

"And another thing." Steve double-checked that no one was in earshot. "We're worried about Scheunemann. John's insisting that he be in charge of the prep. You guys go back, right?"

"We served on the Committee for the Liberation of Iraq together. Why? What's the problem?"

"Don't get me wrong, Marty, we like Scheunemann. He knows his stuff, and Sarah likes him too. But Sarah . . . how should I say? Well, you know, you were there in Minneapolis. She can be quite the vixen. We think Scheunemann might be unhealthily smitten with her. There have been reports that he acts like a teenage boy when she's around. So you understand why I think it best to have someone I trust keeping an eye on him. You'll do that for me, Marty?"

I was Steve Schmidt's bitch. And I liked it! I was going to Sedona.

## Debate Prep in Sedona

John was right in insisting that Sarah hone her debating skills at the family compound in Arizona. The air was fresh. The sky was big. The terrain rough and earnest, like McCain himself. Sarah and Randy stood ten feet apart, each behind a regulation-size podium. Randy played Joe Biden. If I were in charge, I would have made him shave the beard. He looked nothing like Joe Biden. To their backs, a creek flowed.

Brett O'Donnell of Jerry Falwell's Liberty University, John's personal debate coach, sat in the moderator position as if he were Gwen Ifill. I would have made Brett wear blackface and a skirt to look more like Ifill. Proper visualization is important in these kinds of prep situations. But again, it wasn't my call.

Behind O'Donnell, scattered rows of plastic folding chairs were set up on the grass where various staffers and family could observe and take notes. At the prep, I cleverly positioned myself off to the side at the picnic table where the food was laid out. It was mostly leftovers: John's pork ribs, Cindy's chicken wings, Mexican dishes cooked by one of the servants. There was soda and juice and snacks as well. I munched on a tamale while watching Randy and Sarah spar. After paying so many dues over the years, it felt good to be at the candidate's ranch with the campaign heavy hitters.

Debate prep in Sedona: inspiring the team after morning calisthenics. Randy Scheunemann at left; Nicolle Wallace at right *(Courtesy of Todd Palin)*

I added a chicken wing to my plate. Nicolle Wallace stood to my right chomping on pretzels. To Nicolle, Sarah was a concept to be managed. A reformer. A hunter. A hot woman who dug hockey players. All she had to do was follow directions and do what she was told. As Nicolle came from the Bush camp, she believed that politicians didn't need to understand nuance and the nitty-gritty of policy detail. They needed to know how to stay on message and when in doubt revert to tried-and-tested patriotic slogans.

I glanced back to the debate prep. Sarah was repeating after Randy. "When Barack Obama says that all we're doing in Afghanistan is air-raiding villages and killing civilians, that hurts our cause. We're fighting terrorists, securing democracy, building schools for children so there's opportunity."

Brett O'Donnell leapt to his feet. "Okay, Sarah, now *that's* a great place for a wink!"

"Nicolle," I whispered, "I thought you did a great job prepping her for the Charlie Gibson interview. Apart from the Bush Doctrine ambush, she did great."

"That's nice of you to say, Marty." She continued munching snack food in frustration. "I begged her to let me coach her for the Couric interview too, but she was against being 'overhandled.' She wanted America to see the real her. Well, they saw the real her all right."

Back at debate prep, Sarah was becoming distracted. She fished around in her purse. "Nicolle! Nicolle! Where's Nicolle?" demanded Sarah, to nobody in particular. "Has anyone seen Nicolle?"

"What does she want now?" fumed Nicolle. We were behind bushes and not easily seen by the debaters. "Who does that hillbilly from Wasilla think she is? I am a communications director, not a wardrobe assistant. I don't think she quite grasps who is working for whom here. I was Jeb Bush's press secretary during the Florida recount. With all due humility, I'm one of the top media experts in this country. I don't deserve to be treated like this."

Sarah spotted her young daughter playing with frogs. "Piper, go look for Miss Nicolle. Tell her I need my other sunglasses, the Barton Perreiras we picked up in New York."

"That woman!" Nicolle abandoned the protection of the bushes and entered the open space where the chairs and podiums were arranged. "Coming!"

Back at the podium beside the creek, Brett (as Ifill) posed this next question: "Governor Palin, isn't it true you disagree with Senator McCain about drilling for oil in ANWR?"

Palin seemed confused. "What do you mean? Doesn't he want to drill there, too? We've got heaps of oil up there, ya know."

Randy chimed in. "Sarah, if Ifill catches you on a conflict like that, you can always say that you're a team of mavericks, and by definition, mavericks can't agree on everything a hundred percent of the time."

"You betcha." She winked.

Steve Schmidt was now at the snack table eagerly looking for the ribs. After watching a bit of the prep, he shook his head and sighed. "She really is crazy, this one. She honestly believes that because there's oil in Alaska that she's an expert on energy. And she really thinks that we can win this by getting people to chant 'Drill, baby, drill' the way they chanted 'USA, USA' after 9/11."

"Isn't that a bit racy? We don't want to turn off the evangelicals."

"Racy?" Steve asked.

"Yeah. Racy. Sexual. Drill, baby, drill." I motioned with my lips and hips. "You get it?"

Steve looked at me strangely and continued with his thought. "Don't get me wrong. I supported choosing Sarah. On paper, she's perfect. If only she didn't need to be the queen bee all the time. You think Obama has a Messianic complex? Spend some time with the rogue diva." Rogue diva? I made a mental note of his phraseology. "And look at Scheunemann fawning all over her," continued Steve. "It's a bit pathetic, if you ask me."

"It can't just be that. Randy is a shrewd operator. He must see something in her," I countered.

"He sees a smooth round ass to kiss, a future big shot, but he's wrong. After this campaign, we're going to drop her off just where we found her, at the Wasilla Wal-Mart right outside the oblivion department. 'Dan Quayle, cleanup in aisle 8!' We did this lady a favor. She was a nobody. And now she thinks it's all about her, like people actually want to hear what she has to say. And Scheunemann just encourages her, eggs her on. What a putz. Have you talked to him at all?"

"Not yet."

"Yeah. Have a conversation with him. And then you and I, we'll touch base again."

My attention fell back to the debate prep.

O'Donnell was starting a new question. "Governor Palin, Barack Obama has said that he'll consider renegotiating NAFTA with Canada and Mexico—"

"Let me stop you there, Gwen," Sarah interrupted, "and say we can agree to disagree all we want about which countries are in NAFTA now. But I'll tell you the three that *ought* to be in there are Alaska, Canada, and you all down in the U.S."

Did she just refer to the United States as "you all"? I'd heard her husband was a secessionist; maybe she was, too.

"I'm just kiddin' ya, Joe, everyone knows Canadians are just Mexicans in sweaters." Sarah looked straight at Randy. "Do ya mind if I call ya Joe?"

Randy grinned. "Brilliant, Sarah! Beautiful way to disarm me. Makes you an equal. Sure, I might have gone with the 'of course I know which three countries are in NAFTA' line, but the Joe thing works well, too. Speaks to the real America, I love it!"

"Okay, guys," said Brett. "Let's take a little break. Sarah, I think one of your kids needs a diaper change."

"Nicolle!" shouted Sarah.


## Randy, Sarah, and Africa: Oh My

While Sarah directed Nicolle in the intricacies of her domestic fecal-stabilization plan (as we might call it in Washington), Randy sauntered over to the picnic table.

"Hey, Randy, how goes it?"

"Eisenstadt." He grimaced. "Who invited you?"

"Steve Schmidt."

"What's with your eye?"

"My eye?" I knew I'd been feeling something.

"So I was right. It was the herpes," continued Randy. Sarah walked up in front of us.

"Randy, can you be a dear and go fetch Nicolle a wet wipe? She's got a horrible mess on her hands."

"Yes, Sarah, of course." I could have sworn he bowed his head before walking to the house.

Sarah grabbed a plate and piled it with ribs and wings and potato salad. "Have I seen you somewhere before?"

"I'm Marty Eisenstadt."

"I know you! You're the guy who bought me my clothes!"

"I'm also an adviser for foreign policy and a liaison with the Jewish community."

"Would you be a dear and pass me the ketchup?"

"Absolutely, Governor."

She poured ketchup on her potato salad. "These are important times we're living in, Marty. This Obama character, I'm not saying he's Muslim, but he sure did descend from them and grow up with them and, you know, study in their madrassas over there."

"I agree. The choice is clear." She wore a silk Dolce & Gabbana blouse with a plunging neckline. It looked better on her than it did on Jeff.

"So I can count on you?" She leaned in close. I was mesmerized by her bronzed cleavage. Huh, that spray-on tan really works.

"Of course," I said blankly, trying hard to resist her undeniable charms.

"Because I'm hearing chatter."

"What kind of chatter?"

"Well, that John doesn't really want to win this. That he's kind of like agreed to take a dive. Now I know John's been through a lot in his life there. God bless his soul. And he genuinely loves this country. But he's wrong about Obama. Barack Hussein Osama is not just another Democrat. He's a socialist."

"I couldn't agree more. That's exactly what I've been saying!" I could see how Randy was seduced by this woman. She was spunky. "We have to go negative," I continued. "That's the only way campaigns are won. Even Hillary's campaign brought up Obama's connection to William Ayers."

"Who?"

"Hillary Clinton."

"No, the other one."

"William Ayers. Founder of the Weather Underground in the sixties. They planted bombs in the Capitol and the Pentagon. Years later, he was Obama's neighbor in Chicago."

"No way! And these guys were buddies?" Sarah asked.

"You could even say they palled around together."

"Wow! This is important information. You and I need to keep this dialogue going. I like the way you think." Sarah smiled. I smiled. "Where did you say you're from?"

"I'm a senior fellow at the Harding Institute and an expert on Near East policy."

"The Near East—is that Delaware or Maryland? I always forget."

"Either way."

"I've got to admit, I'm not too good with geography. Up there in Alaska, all our maps are different. Everything south of Canada gets a little squished together 'round the edges. But Marty, did you know that Alaska is actually bigger than Texas, California, and Montana combined? True story!"

"Yes, but not as big as Africa." I laughed.

"Well, right, but then again, we're just a state now, not a whole big country there."

Sarah was right. She's not good with geography. So I changed the subject back to her. "You look great."

"Thank you," she said, flipping back her newly frosted bangs. Sarah squeezed my shoulder, rubbed my back. "You have a wonderful frame. Let me guess, you were the forty-two?"

"Why yes, that was me."

"Nice call on the silk boxers. Todd's hung like a walrus, and he needed that extra wiggle room."

"Glad I could help."

Sarah then looked to nowhere in particular and yelled, "Nicolle!" I was again alone at the food table. I helped myself to another tamale.

## Joe. The. Plumber.

**12**

### The Third Debate and the First Rule of Spin Room

It was three weeks out from the election. The economy had collapsed, McCain was down ten points in the polls, and David Letterman was making withering attacks on a nightly basis because the senator had blown off an interview. There was one more chance to turn things around: the third and final presidential debate at Hofstra University in Hempstead, Long Island.

The campaign needed all hands on deck, so when Mark Salter called me the day before and asked if I could come up to help spin, I jumped at the chance. Mark did mention that they were running low on local volunteers (Hofstra's not exactly a hotbed of student volunteerism), so if I wanted a sign holder, I had to bring my own.

"Danny!"

"Yes, Marty?"

"Want to be a sign holder at the debate tomorrow?"

"Sure. What's that?"

"In the spin room. While all the surrogates and pundits are

walking around, they each have someone with them holding a big sign with their name."

"That's it? I just hold a sign? Can't you hold your own?"

"That's absurd, Danny. I'd look like an idiot. You think Charlie Black or Rick Davis or Steve Schmidt hold their own signs?"

"But don't the press know who they are anyway?"

"Everyone gets a sign. That's the rule of the spin room."

"I'll bet if Bill Clinton's there, he won't need a sign."

"Trust me, Danny, everyone. But it's a very important job. Any idiot can have a passive sign holder, but I want you to do more."

"What?"

"I need you to be proactive. While I'm talking to one news crew, I need you to be scouting for others. Hold your sign higher than everybody else's. Maybe twirl it around a little to get us some attention."

"Like those guys on the street corners with the Quiznos signs?"

"Danny, I'm not a sandwich."

"But something like that?"

"Yes."

"How are we getting there?"

"First class all the way, Danny. This is important to us, and it's important to the campaign. Grab my ThinkPad, book the Acela, and send receipts to campaign headquarters. We're headed to Long Island!"

## Joe the Who?

The next night, we were at Hofstra. While the debate itself would be in the David S. Mack Sports and Exhibition Complex, the real action for the press and spinners was in the adjacent Physical Fitness Center. Thirty-one hundred press and media were there to cover the dramatic event. It was like a pundit's wet dream.

But before the debate got started, and before all the post-debate spinning, we retreated with the rest of the McCain spinners to the Hofstra home-team men's locker room, between the stadium and the fitness center. There had been a coin flip the day before and Obama's campaign got the smaller visitor's locker room as their base. (Yes! A small victory.) We were huddled in a clump around TV monitors set up in front of the lockers. Much of McCain's inner circle was there: Mark Salter, Steve Schmidt, Nicolle Wallace, and Brett O'Donnell. Additionally, we had an impressive array of key surrogates and spinners, including Mitt Romney, Lindsey Graham, Joe Lieberman, and Peter King.

In any debate situation it's imperative to watch the debate in isolation from both your opponent and the media. Never let them see your reactions and give them time to coordinate a counter-spin. As the debate moves forward, establish a single unifying spin for everyone to use.

McCain caught a lucky break. The host of the debate was genteel old Bob Schieffer of CBS—the only national press figure who could make John McCain look like a spring chicken. And sure enough, John did have a spring in his step that night.

When Obama made the predictable comparison between McCain and George Bush, John just glared at Obama, sitting not three feet away from him. "If you want to run against President Bush, you should have run four years ago." Damn! We cheered. That locker room hadn't seen towel-snapping and ass-slapping like this since halftime at the infamous Hofstra/George Mason game of February '06.

But it quickly became obvious that the real star of the debate was going to be Joe "the Plumber." He was mentioned twenty-eight times in the debate. Joe the *who*?

When Obama had used the coded phrase "spread the wealth" to an obscure Ohio plumber a couple of days earlier, America instantly thought of images of Karl Marx, Nikita Khrushchev, and the East German women's weightlifting team (circa 1972). Under normal political circumstances, that might have been the end of any Democratic candidate. But Congress (including McCain) had just passed a $700 billion plan to nationalize the financial industry. It was a lot harder to paint Obama as a commie bastard when George Bush and John McCain were behaving like Hugo Chávez and Fidel Castro at a May Day parade.

But with every repeated mention of Joe in the debate, I could see Steve Schmidt and Mark Salter squirming more and more.

"Guys, what is it? He's doing great, no?" McCain's debate coach, Brett O'Donnell, huddled next to them.

Schmidt glared at Brett and shook him by the lapels. "What kind of *idiot* told John to bring up Joe the Plumber!"

"Don't look at me." O'Donnell cowered. "I'd never heard of the guy."

"Then who was it?" Steve demanded.

"Uh, Steve, can you and I take a pee break for a second?" whispered South Carolina's Lindsey Graham, McCain's best friend in the Senate and national co-chairman of the campaign. He pulled Steve aside and the two of them stepped over to the urinal trough, while everyone else resumed watching the debate in the changing area of the locker room.

I may have mentioned that because of my gout, I'm inclined to drink a lot of water. Consequently, I often find myself urinating more frequently than a normal man my age. And that evening was no exception. I had just started to unzip when Steve and Lindsey stepped up to the solid porcelain wall next to me. I couldn't help but overhear.

"Steve," Senator Graham said in his soft voice, "you know how I stayed in the same hotel as John last night? At around 4:30 this morning, I got a call from him. He said, 'I can't sleep.' I said, 'Well, now neither can I.' So I staggered down to his room. John was already pacing around the room like a tiger in a cage practicing lines for the debate. Cindy, of course, was there, too. It was a little awkward since she hadn't yet put on her morning face—and also because she traditionally sleeps in the buff. But you know, me, Steve. Since I'm a confirmed bachelor, they think of me as practically part of the family."[1]

"Of course, Senator." Steve grimaced. "Go on."

"So I hopped onto the bed with Cindy and we watched John rehearse for the debate. At one point, he ad-libbed the line: 'Obama will raise taxes, raise taxes on ordinary folks like Joe the Plumber.' Well, Cindy perked right up out of the bedsheets and said, 'What was that you just said, honey? About the plumber. Now *that's* what you need to hone in on tonight.' Now, me, I was just tryin' mighty hard not to notice her left nipple pokin' out, so I said to John, 'I think Cindy's onto something there.' And from then on, John was full steam ahead talking about using this guy Joe in the debate."[2]

"Thanks, Senator." Steve zipped up.

"But Steve, why are you so concerned about the plumber?"

"Two words, Lindsey," Steve gravely intoned. "Charles Keating."

Senator Graham shuddered at the mention of the man at the center of the Keating Five scandal, which had tarnished John McCain's reputation back in 1989. Steve added, "Let's just say there's a family connection between Joe the Plumber and Keating."

The South Carolina senator looked ten shades of white. "Oops."

"When the YouTube video of Obama and the plumber came out Mark and I vetted him right away. Apparently his name's not Joe and he's not a licensed plumber. But, Senator, don't worry. Go watch the rest of the debate, and I'll take care of it."

Then Steve turned to me at the other end of the urinal. "Marty, I gather you heard all that?"

"Not necessarily."

Steve sighed. "You may as well do something for me now. I know this plumber's going to backfire on us. One way or another, it's inevitable. So I want you to post something on your blog. People still read that, right?"

"Of course they do, Steve."

He continued in a hushed voice. "We can't let anybody know this was Cindy's idea. Or even Graham's. It would crush the old man. As soon as we're done with the spin room tonight, I want you to write something in your own inimitable way. Anything. Just get ahead of the story and own it."

"Got it."

"And Marty"—he glanced around to make sure no one was listening—"we never had this conversation."

"Right."

The debate was coming to an end. Schmidt turned his attention to the spin team.

"Guys!" he announced. "For now, we're going the full dizzy on William Ayers! If anyone asks about Joe the Plumber, just smile and nod. Let's roll!"

## A Run-in with Rahm Emanuel

"Danny, this is the big time. You got your sign?"

Danny was carrying a stick with a yellow sign on top. "Mc-Cain/Palin" in big letters and "Eizenstadt" in small letters.

"Danny, my name's spelled wrong."

"Marty, I told them, but they said there wasn't time to get it right." I sighed. Though my instincts were to yell at someone, my wiser conscience advised me otherwise.

I was decked out in my pundit-blue blazer and flag lapel pin. Okay, it only had twenty stars and six stripes, but times were tough and it was made in China. Danny, on the other hand, looked ridiculous in his campaign-mandated red shirt and bright-red baseball cap (the Obama sign holders were in blue).

Before the debate was even over, we hit the floor running from our corner of the hall. From the other corner, the Obama team ran out. And in the middle were the media. What at first looked like an orderly game of red rover quickly turned into a rugby scrum. There was Chris Wallace! There was Dana Bash! There was Greta Van Susteren! And who is Triumph the Insult Comic Dog covering this for?

Danny charged ahead, beating out the other McCain sign holders, yelling, "Marty Eisenstadt for McCain, Eisenstadt for McCain!" But all the big guns passed him by. I saw CNN jump on Graham. MSNBC had a crew on David Axelrod. And Van Susteren (dear sweet Greta) had her mike pointed at Congressman King. I felt like the kid at the birthday party who always gets shut out of musical chairs.

Finally, "Marty, Marty, I got ABC!" Great! I didn't recognize the reporter, but that's okay. She seemed bubbly enough. I introduced myself and did a perfunctory interview. "Senator McCain did great! He was vibrant, he was eloquent, and he's never met William Ayers!" Then the young reporter turned to the camera and said, "And this is Nicol Lally, reporting live from Hofstra University, for WTEN Albany."

Albany? "Danny, they were an affiliate! An ABC *affiliate*! Your job is to get me on the networks."

"Sorry, Marty, the camera had an ABC sticker on it."

"All right, let's try again." Just then I spotted David Shuster trying to cut off Bill Richardson. The New Mexico governor was kissing Obama's ass so much, his sign should have read, "Please, Please, Please Pick Me for Secretary of State!"

I could see Shuster was darting his eyes to find an available McCain surrogate. "Danny! MSNBC, over there!" I twisted through the crowd, aiming for Shuster. "David, David! I'm available!" Danny was right behind me with the sign. I could see Shuster shaking Richardson's hand and looking toward me, when—*THUMP!*—I heard a loud sound behind me.

"Mother *fucker*!" I turned around. It was Rahm Emanuel, with a hand on his head. "You FUCKING IDIOT!"

Picking up his sign, Danny started to apologize. "Oh, I am *sooo* sorry, sir."

Emanuel, not a man known for his nuanced approach to conflict resolution, grabbed Danny's hat and threw it on the ground.

"Goddamned, punk-ass little nuts-for-brains! Watch where you're going with that thing! Who do you work for?" He read the sign. "Eisenstadt? No wonder!"

Emanuel's own college-aged sign holder started batting Danny's sign down with his blue Obama sign and sniveled, "Yeah! What *Rahm* said!" Then Rahm and his toady brushed past me and beelined it straight toward Shuster and his crew. Rats!

"Danny, you okay?"

He'd picked up his hat by then and dusted himself off. "Marty, I'm so sorry."

"Don't be. If anyone filmed that and puts it on YouTube, then we just won McCain the election." Sadly, amid the turmoil no one had.

## Start Spreading the News: Charles Keating!

The spin room was already starting to thin out, and the major networks were throwing their coverage back to their respective studios in Washington. We were finally able to secure me one last interview. It was some random Sirius radio show, but it was better than nothing. I gave my same routine spin on the election, but then the interviewer asked me, "So what did you think of all the references to Joe 'the Plumber'?"

"Well other than him being related to Charles Keating, I thought it went great."

The reporter's eyes just about popped out of his skull. Not exactly the sort of response he was used to getting that night.

"Excuse me," I said distractedly. "I have to go write something on my blog."

So while the thought was still fresh in my head, I grabbed my old ThinkPad 600, sat in a corner, and wrote . . .

### Joe "the Plumber" Wurzelbacher related to Charles "the Crook" Keating. Oops.

October 15, 2008, by Marty

The debate prep team thought they had a real live Joe Six-Pack who's spurned Barack Obama's tax plan. But what they forgot to do was check on Joe Wurzelbacher's background.

Turns out that Joe is a close relative of Robert Wurzelbacher of Milford, Ohio. Who's Robert Wurzelbacher? Only Charles Keating's son-in-law and the former senior vice president of American Continental, the parent company of the infamous Lincoln Savings and Loan. He was convicted to 40 months in jail.[3]

It was a bit of a Hail Mary pass, but at the very least it would protect John and Cindy if, as we expected, Joe the Plumber turned into a fiasco. My blog post would squarely put the blame on the debate-prep team. On the other hand, if Joe somehow turned out to be the savior of the campaign, then the new first couple could still bask in the glory.

I almost felt bad for poor Joe Wurzelbacher. Did his alleged connection to the Keating scandal make him a bad guy? Of course not. In fact, after that ill-fated night at the Watergate, he finally had a chance to give plumbers a good name. But in a media war, there is collateral damage. And if Joe's privacy and reputation suffered from the cluster bomb of a simple blog entry, then it was all for the greater good.

Danny and I took the red eye train back to D.C. and showed up at the institute groggy but satisfied. By the time we stumbled back into the office the Joe the Plumber story was all anyone in the media could talk about.

It's gratifying to me on a personal level that everyone from CBS

News[4] to Michelle Malkin[5] quoted me on the issue and gave me credit for starting the story. And while I'm certainly no fan of MSNBC's Keith Olbermann,[6] even he talked about it on his show.

With all the added interview requests and references to my blog, there was a nice added bonus. The whole story had reinvigorated my bona fides as a legitimate McCain insider and stemmed the tide of people who doubted my provenance. Even our crazed stalker, Wolfrum, the golf blogger in Brazil, couldn't stop the tsunami of links to my blog. In a pique of frustration that no one was noticing his prior attempts to discredit me, he wrote: "Why is it so hard to Google the name 'Martin Eisenstadt' before going on a Plumber Joe freakfest?"[7]

As predicted, Joe the Plumber became an overnight celebrity. There was never even a hint that it was John's own doing—and certainly not that Cindy ever had anything to do with it. It proves the number-one lesson for all political consultants: Your first job is to protect the candidate from himself. Even if it means losing the election. A week later, I got a text from Schmidt: "Grt wrk Mrty. Rmbr: We nvr sp0ke."

## The Chinatown Bus from Hell

The last few weeks of the campaign were nuts. Between the paparazzi-like coverage of Joe the Plumber and Sarah Palin, people were starting to forget that John McCain was at the top of the ticket. So I put my thinking cap on. My unique expertise in influencing public opinion and national media led me straight to *Saturday Night Live*. I knew the Tina Fey–Sarah Palin comparison wasn't going well for us, especially after Sarah appeared on the show on October 18 (ironically, as her celebrity status increased, our poll numbers dwindled). So before November 4, I made it my mission to do two things: make sure Barack Obama didn't guest-star on the show, and guarantee that John McCain did.

The first job was easy. I'd use my blog to spread the rumor

that Obama would appear on *SNL* the Saturday before the election. You're thinking, "That's crazy, Marty—how does that guarantee that he *won't* appear, especially when everyone from the *Los Angeles Times* to *The Weekly Standard* to *Extra* ran with your rumor?"[8] Simple. I also added the fact that Lorne Michaels had contributed $4,600 to the Obama campaign. Once his bosses at GE (who are, of course, all very reliable Republican contributors) found out, I knew they'd make Michaels rethink whom he was inviting for the November 1 show.[9]

So on the morning of that first Saturday in November, I awoke at 10:00 a.m. to campaign honcho Charlie Black calling me at home. "Marty, are you up?"

"Yes, of course. I've been up for three hours. Working. What is it?"

"We owe you big-time, Marty. Your little blogging merry-go-round with *SNL* and Obama just got McCain booked on the show tonight. We've got an extra floor seat for you with part of the advance team. You in?"

"I'm on my way to Union Station as we speak. I'll hop on the Acela and be there in a few hours. Thanks, Charlie." Click.

Wait. The last time the campaign told me to go somewhere at the drop of a hat, it was for the debate, and they still hadn't reimbursed me. With the election just three days away, and McCain's chances—quite honestly—not looking great, I wasn't going to be the sap consultant who doesn't get paid at the end of a losing election. As much as I wanted to go, I'd be damned if was going to pay $177 for the fast train which usually gets delayed a couple of hours anyway.

So I threw on some pants, grabbed my trusty ThinkPad, and took the Orange Line to Metro Center, switched to the Red Line, and got off at Gallery Place. I still had to hike four blocks through D.C.'s small but cramped Chinatown.

While I was walking, I remembered a new initiative we had just started at the Harding Institute. With the economic crisis at hand, we were bidding on foreclosure properties and leveraging the Harding estate to get new low-interest loans. We'd ride out the crisis and make a fortune with the inevitable upturn. So I pulled out my Sprint and speed-dialed Danny. "I'm heading to New York. Can you text me the address of that place we just got in Manhattan? One person's subprime loss is my pied-a-terre."

Then I saw them. Two rival signs in English and Chinese that said the same thing: "Bus to New York: $20. First come, first served." I picked the one on the right.

I bought my ticket and asked the small Asian woman at the counter, "Do I have time to get some food?"

"No food."

"I can't have food on the bus?"

"No sell food on the bus."

"But is there time to get food?"

"Time to New York is four and a half hours."

"So I *do* have time to get food?"

"Bus start loading in five minutes."

"So it's four and a half hours without a pit stop?"

"No. Eight hours, with traffic."

I looked around the neighborhood, ducked into a Chinese restaurant, and ordered a box of dim sum to go. I had no idea what the dumplings were stuffed with, and I was a little afraid to ask. They started to pack it up. I saw the bus rev its engine. C'mon, c'mon, let's go! The bus started to pull away from the curb. They handed me the bag and I raced to the bus. I banged on the window, yelling, "Wait, wait!" but the driver appeared not to speak English. He speeded up. Thankfully, I remembered the traditional S&M "safe word" I learned from the Chinese ambassador's scheduler after an embassy party last year: "Mao Zhuxi wan sui!" It was the only thing I could say in Mandarin, and I hoped to God it was a relevant phrase even *if* chopsticks and testicles were not involved. "Mao Zhuxi wan sui!" I shouted again.

The driver screeched on the air brakes, winked at me knowingly, and finally opened the door.

The first thing that struck me was the overwhelming stench of urine and Ben-Gay. Though not a great combination, it's surprisingly better than either one by itself. The bus was packed. I walked down the aisle, as the bus jolted to a start. Past the old Chinese couples going to visit grandkids. Past the nose-ringed anarchists heading to an Obama rally in Brooklyn. And past the Capitol Hill interns going for weekend booty calls with their college sweethearts at NYU. I grabbed the last empty seat—in the back. The bathroom door didn't lock, so it kept banging into my knees—wafting a fresh stench of vomit and feces with each swing.

I sat next to a grizzled old Vietnam vet named Wally who reeked of menthols and sweat. It's always an honor to get a chance to speak with America's heroes, but Wally seemed a little out of it. I told him I worked for the John McCain campaign. "Is that the brotha or the motha?" For a guy living on the streets of Washington, he seemed a little underinformed about the upcoming election. But I can't really blame him. His on-bus reading material consisted mainly of a braille copy of *Playboy*. Odd for a guy with perfect vision, but at least he let me cop a feel. I finally explained to Wally that John McCain was the candidate who served with him in Vietnam.

"The Swift Boat guy?"

"No, the POW."

"You mean the dumb-ass admiral's son who got himself shot down?"

"Yes, that one."

The bus stopped near—not at but near—a rest stop in Delaware. A rival Chinatown company's bus pulled up right behind us, gently nudging our rear fender. The two drivers got out into the tall grass and started fighting—Hong Kong kickboxing style. We leaned out the windows and cheered for our guy. The other bus cheered for theirs. Our driver finally prevailed with a combination cross jab to the face and a roundhouse kick to the gut, leaving the other driver facedown in the mud. Our man got back in his driver's seat, the bus erupted in applause, and the journey continued. I gave Wally one of my dumplings, and he gave me a bite of his Lunchables sandwich.

Somewhere in New Jersey, I thought I heard banging and muffled screams from below. "Don't worry none 'bout that," said Wally. "They're bringing up a fresh batch of Shanghai girls to work in Queens." Note to self: Next time, spring for the Acela.

## The Real 30 Rock

"Live from New York, it's . . . Saturday Night!" Just hearing those magical words sends shivers up the spine of any red-blooded American born within the last fifty years. But being in the Studio 8H audience at 30 Rockefeller Center and hearing your boss, the man you admire most in the world and the man who in three days will be elected the next president of the United States, say them, it makes it all seem worthwhile.

John McCain had just finished a brilliant sketch with Tina Fey at the apex of her Sarah Palin impersonation. They were making fun of Barack Obama's half-hour infomercial that aired on all the major networks just a few days earlier. But as McCain said in the skit: "We can only afford QVC." There was McCain pitching blank commemorative plates depicting the ten town hall meetings to which Obama never agreed. There was Fey-as-Palin selling "Palin in 2012" T-shirts behind John's back. And there was even Cindy McCain gamely displaying "McCain Fine Gold" jewelry. It was just the right tone and venue for McCain to end the campaign: he was honest, he was self-deprecating, he was a maverick to the end. *This* was the John McCain that America was going to vote for on Tuesday.

Out came Ben Affleck, the host. He gave an uncomfortable monologue about always supporting Democratic losers. Mondale, Dukakis, Gore, and Kerry. I couldn't help but wonder that if Republicans had more celebrity endorsements, would it actually help or harm our cause? Finally, a commercial break.

While the stagehands whirled around us in a flurry, setting everything up for the next sketch, I turned to the person on my left. "Joe, what do you think of the show?"

"Marty, this is awesome. If you'd asked me a month ago if I'd be here, I'd have socked you upside the face with a toilet plunger. Meghan, what about you?" He leaned in close to the attractive young blonde sitting on his left.

"Oh my God, Joe, this is, like, so totally wicked awesome. It is *so* much cooler than when I interned here last year. Lorne actually looked me in the *eyes* when we came in tonight." (Glancing at her cleavage, I understood her point.) "I think that's 'cause Dad was with me this time. Can you believe it? And can you believe Dad in that opening bit?"

"He rocked," said Joe.

"Totally! And Mom. Dork alert, but I love her."

"Wait." Joe seemed confused. "You used to work here?"

"Oh, sure. During my last year at Columbia, I'd come help out on weekends. Dad's known Lorne for years, so it was an easy phone call. See those cue cards?"

One of the young production assistants was holding a massive pile of three-foot-wide white poster boards with black felt marker handwriting on them. Affleck was squinting, trying to read them.

"Christopher Walken was the worst. He yelled at me for dotting my i's like lollipops. What . . . ever!"

She glanced down at her BlackBerry. "Oh, come ON!" she exclaimed to no one in particular.

"What is it?" I leaned over Joe to ask Meghan.

"It's the stupid Straight Talk Express. They can't find a place to park, and they're just driving around in circles. I can't believe Heather and Shannon are still in there."

"They're not coming?" said Joe.

Meghan started pecking at her BlackBerry like a chicken with Tourette's. "We'll meet @ d'AFTRprty. Ill snd 411 and get p-wrd." She turned to us. "You guys know about the after party, right?"

"Of course. Scheunemann told me all about it after Sarah was on a couple weeks ago," I said loudly as the band started playing again.

Here we were: Meghan McCain, Joe "the Plumber" Wurzelbacher, and me, Martin Eisenstadt, sitting third row, center section, the hottest ticket in America. Twelve million people were watching at home on TV. Okay, maybe that was three million less than watched when Sarah Palin was on, but John was funnier. Added together, it came out to about the same number that had tuned in to Obama's multimillion-dollar infosnooze a couple of days ago. This was unreal. This was intense. This was the essence of the McCain campaign.

## Sharpie McCain

Ninety minutes after it all started, we clapped along in time to the beat as the band played the closing tune. When the *SNL* credits rolled, Meghan, Joe, and I headed for the stage to congratulate the senator and his wife. But the crush of cast, crew, cameras, and Secret Service agents made it impossible. We could just barely see Steve Schmidt and Mark Salter come in from the wings and whisk John and Cindy away. *SNL* is great exposure, but at ninety minutes, plus rehearsal, it's also a huge time suck with only seventy-two hours left until E-Day.

But that didn't mean *we* couldn't go to the after party. Meghan knew most of the crew and some of the cast from when she worked here. People called out, "Hey, everyone, it's Sharpie McCain!" "Yo, Sharps!" "Your dad was great!" "You still put out?" Meghan's a great sport and was happy to get a break from the campaign trail.

"For you, Samberg, yes. Now what's the haps tonight?" She borrowed one of her old pens and wrote down an address and password. A private club in Times Square—we could walk there. Meghan texted her bus posse to meet us and we hightailed it over.

We got to the club, and it was surrounded by paparazzi and autograph hounds. I'm not sure if anyone even noticed Meghan or me; Joe was the center of attention. He posed for pictures, he kissed a baby, he signed a woman's bosom.

You see, Meghan had been on the campaign trail for months doing a series of video blogs with her pals Heather and Shannon. They'd shoot and edit the videos on the bus, then post them on McCainBlogette.com. It was known as the B-team bus, since that's where most of the campaign surrogates would go when the senator and the A team flew ahead in the jet. For much of that last week or so, Joe had spent a lot of time on the bus with the girls and their crew. In the short time since the third debate, Joe had become a rock star. As much as the girls loved their new-found traveling companion (Meghan especially liked curling up with Joe for naps on the back bunk), I couldn't help but think that there was a tinge of resentment. For close to a year, Meghan had always been the "hot" surrogate and warm-up act that all the crowds cheered for. She may be young and spunky, but she'd done her time at greasy diners, Moose lodges, old-age homes, and AM radio stations. And then in these last few weeks of the campaign, first Sarah Palin and now Joe the Plumber became the hot tickets at all the rallies and events.

But Meghan was the one with the *SNL* hookup, and Joe knew it. We met up with Heather and Shannon, and Meghan gave the bouncer the password: "Metamucil." We were in.

Now this, fair readers, brings us more or less to where we started the book. Joe and I with the Maker's Mark. Ben Affleck's agent. And later, Joe giving plumbing lessons to the cast.

## From New York to Paris

No sooner had I downed my third drink when I heard a familiar-sounding monotone behind me say, "You Eisenstadt?" I'd hoped it was my old babysitter from the Nixon White House, former speechwriter Ben Stein.

I whirled around. "Ben, is that you?" No, it was Lorne Michaels, inexplicably wearing a white captain's hat. Uh-oh.

"I just wanted to thank you."

"Really?"

"Those rumors you started about Obama coming on the show increased our ratings by 46 percent this fall. I just bought my own cruise ship. The least I can do is offer you a drink."

"Naturally." I graciously accepted and ordered off the back shelf.

When I turned away from the bar, I bumped into a huge tress of wonderful-smelling blonde hair.

"Paris!"

She stared at me for a split second—a blank look on her face that could just as easily have meant "I snuck in a taser, and I'm not afraid to use it" or "the square root of 289 is—think, think, think—17." But when she broke her stare, she said simply, "Do I know you?"

"I don't know. I'm Martin Eisenstadt. I work for the McCain campaign."

"*You're* Marty Eisenstadt!?" From her deadpan inflection it was hard to tell whether the exclamation mark came before the question mark or after. Then she added: "It is *sooo* hot to finally meet you!"

"It is hot, isn't it?"

"Can I just tell you that my career has completely turned around since you told everyone about my Republican family and that whole celebrity-ad thing. I never would have shot my own campaign ads if you hadn't stirred the pot. I got, like, seven zillion hits on YouTube. And all of a sudden, people started saying things like 'Wow, maybe Paris isn't such an airhead' and 'Oh, I guess Paris really can act' and like 'Maybe Paris *does* know her Keynesian macroeconomic theory after all.' I was invited onto all these like political-punditing shows after that. Those are fun! Even Larry King had me on for a whole hour one night!"

"Larry King?"

"Yeah, they were supposed to be covering some war in Atlanta or something."

"Georgia?"

"That's the one. But they broke into their coverage so Larry could talk to me. He is *such* a sweetie. I gave him a hummer after the show. Anyway, thanks, Marty!"

She gave me a hug and an air kiss, and with that, she disappeared into the crowd. Hmmm, all my blogging was coming home to roost. I half expected the Jonas Brothers to show up and sing with me.

## Canoodling with the Stars

Eventually I circled back around with Joe (after his encounter with Jennifer Garner and the Hollywood agent). We grabbed another round of drinks and headed over to a leopard-skin booth, eager to sip our bourbons in a moment of relative quiet. No sooner had we sat down than two *SNL* cast members slithered into the booth with us. As I mentioned in chapter one, and in fact had blogged about the next day, I'm not familiar enough with the show to remember their names very well, but they were both brunettes or at least they said they were.

(Despite an angry letter of denial I got from an NBC publicist after my blog appeared, I now think they might have been Kristen Wiig and Casey Wilson. However, my publisher's lawyer has advised me not to be too specific with their names.)

Damn, that Joe's a smooth one. In just a matter of moments,

he was canoodling with the skinny one (my British editor Mitzi prefers the term "snogging," but I find that crass). Meanwhile, the pleasantly busty one made small talk with me. The after party was getting late, and I realized that I had an empty apartment waiting for me. So in the course of turning on the Eisenstadt charm, I reminded her I was a big-time presidential campaign consultant.

"Holy cow!" She just about burst out of her dress. (Hmmm, that's a good sign, I thought.)

"So you must know my dad, Paul Wilson? He was a senior adviser to Sam Brownback's presidential campaign."

"Paul? Sure, I know him." Paul's a brilliant campaign strategist and the doomed Brownback job was his first big break beyond parochial congressional races.[10]

"You are *just* like him!" She scratched my beard and giggled effervescently.

As you may have gathered, I'm not a man with strong ethical compulsions, but there is an unspoken rule in the political operative's game book. Never sleep with a fellow consultant's daughter. Especially if she goes all Freudian on you. I had enough unresolved Oedipal issues with my own mother. I didn't need any other baggage in my love life.

Pounding shots with Joe the Plumber at *SNL* after party
*(Courtesy of Lorne Michaels)*

Thankfully, the girls spotted Tina Fey at the bar and needed to go suck up to her to get a guest spot on *30 Rock* They excused themselves for a moment.

"So, Marty." Joe put his massive arm around me.

"Yeah, Joe."

"I understand you're the one who spread the rumor that I'm related to Charles Keating." Suddenly I knew what Fred Armisen must have felt like when we first came in. My knee started shaking with restless leg syndrome. But I didn't panic.

"Damn straight that was me. And it was the best goddamned thing that could have happened to you."

"How you figure it?"

I explained that all the left-wing nut jobs, the mainstream media, and the Obama campaign were inevitably going to unearth all sorts of unflattering things about him within twelve hours after that third debate: That his name was Samuel, not Joe. That he never got his plumber's license. That he had a lien on his house. His voting record, his divorce record, his elementary-school attendance record, even.

"You got that right, brother." He sipped his Maker's Mark. "It was like getting a colonic with a fire hose."

So I told him that when I threw out the red meat about his connection to Keating, it was really a tactical ploy. A red herring. Dare we say, a pipe wrench in the works.

"How so?" he asked.

For the better part of a twenty-four-hour news cycle, people were trying to prove if and to what extent Joe was related to Keating. Had Keating been his father, his uncle, his third cousin twice removed? And if so, what did it mean? That Joe was a plant, a mole, a McCain operative sent to set up Obama on that rope line? Conspiracy theories were wild. Joe's old air force records showed he was based in Alaska. Alaska! Aha, did he know Sarah Palin? Was he the one who really knocked up Bristol? Had he ever wrestled a polar bear? None of it was true (or at least credible or relevant), but it all got mixed up with the *real* stories about Joe's "less than stellar" record as a model citizen. Therefore all of Joe's dubious past got dismissed as left-wing kookery.

And in the meantime, Joe was the story. And America soon forgot how McCain had fumbled the ball on the economy. "Economic crisis?" America said. "What's that? We want to see more of the Adonis-like man in the tight shirt! Hey, Joe, turn around and show us the crack!"

Once Joe actively endorsed McCain and hit the campaign trail with him, his reflected glow cast a glorious halo around the candidate. Suddenly Joe wasn't just a plumber, or even a celebrity. He was a symbol, an icon. He *was* America.

Hell, Joe didn't even *need* to show up. Just two days before, the advance team forgot to bring him to a Defiance, Ohio, rally and McCain called out: "Joe, where are you?" But then realizing the power of Joe, quickly ad-libbed to the crowd, "You're all Joe the Plumber today!" Joe's significance in the election had finally transcended both space and time.

Joe took another sip. He squished up his face and thought for a second. "You're a smart guy, Marty Eisenstadt. But of course you are. Eisenstadt's a Jewish name, right?"

"Thanks, Joe."

"But you know, I really did wrestle a polar bear once."

"I'll keep it a secret."

The two girls came back to the table, and I stood up to let them in. I could see they were both oozing all over Joe's muscular arms. Let the man enjoy his fifteen minutes to the fullest. I reluctantly stepped away. "Joe"—I winked—"they're all yours. Have a blast!" (Sometimes I forget. Is the term "three-way" or "threesome"?)

As for me, I glanced around the room as I walked toward the exit. Past Michael Bloomberg arm wrestling Ben Affleck. Past Paris Hilton fervently debating trickle-down fiscal policy with Meghan McCain. And past what might well have been the high point of my professional and personal life.

# 13

# If Africa Doesn't Exist, Do I?

## The Last Republican

In the week or so leading up to the election, I was also dealing with another personal crisis of sorts. Remember that BBC documentary that I participated in back in August? I barely did. But then in mid-October I got word from Samantha Hensington, the filmmaker, that excerpts from *The Last Republican* would start appearing on YouTube.

I took a look at the first couple of episodes. All documentaries occasionally mock their subjects (what can you expect from the same British media that brought us the Spice Girls and Neville Chamberlain), but I think, all in all, the film showed that I was doing important work on behalf of both the McCain campaign and the Harding Institute. I remember how James Carville's and George Stephanopoulos's careers soared after they were featured in *The War Room*. Better to be seen warts and all, than *not* at all, I always say.

In the world of political consulting, name recognition means a lot more than actual electoral success. For example, Joe Trippi's potential Democratic clients remember him from glowing profiles in *The New Republic*, *GQ*, and *The New York Times Magazine*, all hailing him as the man who "reinvented campaigning." What they forget is that Joe's clients have included the presidential campaigns of Ted Kennedy, Walter Mondale, Gary Hart, Dick Gephardt, Howard Dean, and John Edwards. That's a staggering 0-6 record of achievement, and yet Joe keeps getting hired. I should be so lucky.[1]

But as the election drew nearer, the episodes of *The Last Republican* were looking increasingly less flattering. This Hensington woman had consistently taken my words out of context and cross-edited me to look ridiculous at best, incompetent at worst. (I've included a few transcript excerpts just so you can see what I mean.)

## *The Last Republican*: Excerpt 2

*(Courtesy of Samantha Hensington/BBC)*

**MARTY:** McCain is about winning wars. Based on his Vietnam experience, he feels better than anybody that he can win all the wars we're engaged in and also be able to win the wars we haven't even started yet . . .

You know, you talk to the consultants, the politicians and they'll tell you one thing, they'll tell you, "Oh, there's no jobs!" Why don't we talk to some hardworking Mexicans? They have jobs! Maybe it's the

*(Courtesy of Samantha Hensington/BBC)*

lazy ones who wanna get paid twice what they're worth for half the effort! Maybe they're the ones who don't have jobs. But people with good work ethics, and religious and family values, they got jobs!

I called my old friend Denny Hastert at Dickstein Shapiro about suing the BBC for libel. Denny reminded me that even though he's *at* a law firm, he's not really a practicing lawyer. He's more in the "issue advocacy" side of the firm. But from what he recalled about the Treaty of Ghent, which ended the War of 1812 between the United States and Great Britain, he didn't think I had standing to sue the BBC. So much for legal recourse.

In the fast-paced world of the Internet, where reputations are as fleeting as the mouse click of a blogger, it was essential that I issue my own rebuttals to the spurious accusations raised in the documentary. So Danny grabbed the institute's trusty camcorder and we knocked out a couple of videos between my meetings on the Hill, press interviews, and sessions at campaign headquarters. Danny put these videos on both our website and on a new Harding Institute YouTube channel as video "responses" to episodes of *The Last Republican*.

## A Response to *The Last Republican*

(Courtesy of Harding Institute)

Innocent comments I made about our Mexican brothers and sisters, I believe, were taken out of context, and it is patently false that John McCain asked me to get young prostitutes for him. A man works his whole life to build a reputation. I don't know how you put a price tag on shame. The lawyers at Dickstein Shapiro have been talking about a price tag and it's high and it's steep. This is a professional? She gets me drunk, and then she cross edits to make me look like a fool  I am not a fool! I scored a 1060 on my SAT! And this is the thanks I get. It reminds me of the old adage, you do somebody a favor and they step on your foot. And when John McCain is president, we'll see who has the last laugh, the Harding Institute or the BBC.

There were also things in the documentary that at the time I couldn't refute because I might have endangered the campaign. For example, in part two of the series when we go to McCain's Southern California campaign headquarters, I explain that the reason we don't see any volunteers working phone banks is because the campaign had outsourced to call centers in India. Now

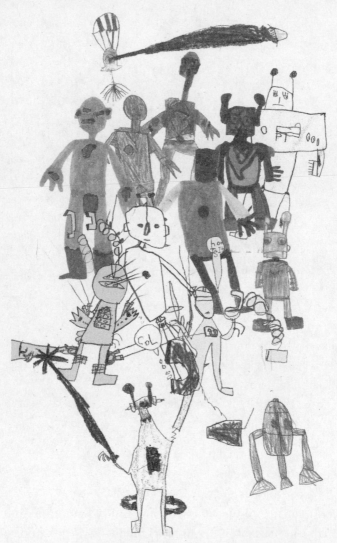

An artist's depiction of a RoboCall center *(Illustration by Jonathan Mirvish)*

that the election is over, I can tell you that I made this comment to divert attention away from the truth.

In reality, most of our calling was being done automatically by robots (they work for even less than Indians and don't eat as much pizza as real volunteers). This so-called robocalling (by the likes of my shopping pal Jeff Larson) ultimately got the campaign into some hot water when the robots kept saying, "Barack Obama has worked closely with domestic terrorist Bill Ayers, whose organization bombed the U.S. Capitol and the Pentagon."[2]

(Frankly, I thought it was an effective message. I like that the possessive "whose" just as easily could refer to the antecedent "Bill Ayers" *or* "Barack Obama." Was it Ayers's terrorist organization or Obama's campaign organization that bombed the U.S. Capitol? Hard to say. Either way, it's best to be on the safe side and vote for McCain—the guy who's probably not a terrorist!)

These were the kind of hardball tactics the campaign had to engage in leading up to the election. One of the reasons the McCain camp was so frustrated that Sarah Palin had started mentioning William Ayers at campaign rallies wasn't the content of her attacks, it was the timing. We were counting on these stealthy October robocalls to go negative on Obama, but Palin chomped at the bit too early. By the time the calls hit, the backlash to her Ayers comparisons had already diminished their effectiveness.

In the last week or two before the election, it was clear that it was an uphill climb and we needed more than just a Hail Mary pass. We needed a fleaflicker, a fumblerooskie, and any other trick plays up our sleeves. Palin's star had faded, and we were doing all we could to exploit Joe the Plumber, but we needed more. One ad I pitched to the campaign team would have had a stark black-and-white picture of Barack Obama, ominous 1950s Soviet music in the background, and a big graphic of the phrase "Community Activist." As the music got louder and the faint sound of marching boots faded in, the letters would slowly rearrange themselves to now spell the phrase "Communist Activity."

This ad was rejected for being too "inflammatory." *(Courtesy of the Eisenstadt Group)*

The audio track would have a Russian countdown and the screen would end in a mushroom cloud.

Rick Davis and Charlie Black liked it (Charlie said Lee Atwater would have been proud of me), but Mark Salter and Steve Schmidt thought it was too much. They had also vetoed ads—per McCain's instructions—that brought up Jeremiah Wright, questioned Michelle Obama's pride in her country, or attacked Obama for not serving in the military. Apparently all Willie Horton–style ads were deemed off limits. At this point, the campaign was just trying to keep McCain's dignity intact.

## My Date with Carl Cameron

It's inevitable: after every election, the losing candidate's campaign staff turn into a circular firing squad of accusations, excuses, and recriminations. But now that defeat seemed all but inevitable, there was no reason to wait for the actual election results. Why put off until tomorrow what you can whine about today?

At least with the core McCain staff, we all had a common target: Sarah Palin. The consensus (or at least rationalization) among the senior staff had been that choosing Palin as VP wasn't the problem. (To admit that would have been to admit that defeat was of our own doing, and worse, of McCain's own doing.) No. Rather, the fault of defeat lay with *how* Palin had conducted herself after her selection. Even in the week or two before the election, some of us had started to sow the seeds of blame: her profligate spending spree and spray-tanning hubris, her refusals to talk to RNC campaign donors, or her husband's not-so-veiled attempts to turn her VP campaign into a launching pad for a national run in 2012.

So when reporters started to put together their inevitable wrap-ups and postmortems on the campaign, we all had a fairly unified message. Blame the closest thing to a Canadian: Sarah Palin.

I pride myself on being a reliable confidential source for political journalists. It's a wonderful two-way street in Washington: political insiders trade information to reporters, and in exchange, they give us an opportunity to vent our frustrations publicly and anonymously. If that was the only reason, it would simply be called "rumormongering." But those of us in the punditing classes know that for every anonymous leak we give to a reporter, he or she will be twice as likely to give us a credited quote—or in the case of TV, an on-camera interview—when we really need the exposure. If leaks are the oil that keep the punditocracy machine running smoothly, then there was no shame in being a little slippery.

So when Carl Cameron at Fox News asked me out for drinks at JR.'s Bar & Grill in Dupont Circle the day before the election, I knew it wasn't for a gay date (not that Carl isn't a handsome man, and not that Dupont Circle isn't called "the Fruit Loop" for nothing). I'd just come back from New York and was one of the few campaign insiders who wasn't either traveling with the candidate or stuck at campaign headquarters. It would be a perfect opportunity to spin the campaign in my own voice.

"Marty, I hear you were the one who leaked the 'rogue diva' line to Politico and *Newsweek* a couple of weeks ago."

"Carl, you know I can neither confirm nor deny such a spurious accusation."

"If it's so spurious, then why can't you deny it?"

"Because what if it's true?"

We both winked and laughed, and Carl bought another round of bourbon for us.

"Marty, tell me about Palin's debate prep. I heard you were there."

"Of course I was there. They needed someone reliable to help her with foreign-policy briefings."

"That must have been a challenge, no?" He ordered me another drink.

"Look, Carl, am I on background here?" I looked around the bar conspiratorially. It was crowded, but loud. Mondays are Show-tunes Sing-a-long night at JR.'s, and a group of Heritage Foundation interns were doing a medley from *RENT*.

"Of course, Marty. This story won't even run until after the election."

"Completely off the record, right?" I leaned in close.

"I give you my word." Carl leaned in close, too.

"Wait, I don't know." I scratched my beard inscrutably. "Maybe I shouldn't."

When you're giving an interview to the press—especially to TV reporters—it's safe to say that 98 percent of what you say won't wind up in the eventual piece they run. The only way to increase those odds is to give the impression that what you're saying is juicy, exclusive, and very, very confidential.

"Marty, come on," Carl begged. "You can trust me. I'm with Fox."

I shifted my eyes a couple of times and leaned in close again. "Okay, I'll tell you." Real close. If this *had* been a gay date, we would have kissed by now. "Sarah's not too good with geography."

"She knows that Russia's right outside her kitchen window, right?"

"True," I said. "But if she looked out her back-door window, she'd be hard-pressed to tell you it was Canada."

"What do you mean?"

"She didn't know what countries were in NAFTA."

"The North American Free Trade Agreement? Maybe she thought you said NASCAR."

"It was NAFTA."

"Was she confused about Belize? To this day, I'd still be hard-pressed to say if it's really in Central America."

"It is, Carl."

"Okay, Marty, I'm sure it was just a slip of the tongue. She must have been a bundle of nerves leading up to the debate. Also, I hear she's still lactating. I don't know much about women, but that could have had something to do with it."

"Carl, she also didn't know that Africa was a continent."

"What'd she think it was?"

"A country."

"You mean like North Africa?" inquired Carl.

"North Africa isn't a country."

"But South Africa is?"

"Correct."

"So she was half right," Carl said proudly. "I'll bet if you asked a hundred of our Fox News viewers where Africa is on the globe, ninety-five and a half percent of them also wouldn't know where it is."

"But Carl, they're not trying to be a heartbeat away from the Oval Office. And with all due respect to Senator McCain, I don't know if his heart has a strong eight years left in it."

" 'Cause he was tortured in Vietnam?"

"That, and because he's old."

"Right." Carl took a slow sip of his bourbon, while I slammed down a shot of mine. I could tell I'd finally gotten through to him.

"Marty, you sure about this?"

"Of course I'm sure. And remember, Carl, I want my name kept out of this."

## The Election

Despite dire warnings that Ohio or Virginia would be the Florida of 2008, Election Day itself went surprisingly smoothly. For the Democrats, that is. As for those of us on the McCain team? Not so much.

John lost. Sarah lost. And in my humble opinion, America lost.

As a professional political operative, I've trained myself not to take losses or victories too personally. But everyone wants to be on the winning team—whether it's softball or politics—that's just human nature. And I truly felt that this was the time in American history where we needed a patriot and soldier like John McCain to lead us into the breach of the abyss. I'd worked too hard—first in the primaries for Rudy Giuliani, and then for McCain—not to feel an emotional loss. Did I cry? I'd be lying if I said that my pal Glenn Beck and I didn't share a few tears and a hug. I mean, come on: Barack Obama? A minor-league Illinois state senator at best. If it weren't for the fact that his father was from there, I doubt he'd know where Africa was, either. But "Country First" is more than a slogan. And barring any pending legal challenges to ACORN or other alleged Democratic voter fraud, I must respect the will of the people and find a way to celebrate our country's finest tradition of democracy.

And among those traditions, it's safe to say that if a campaign is like extended foreplay, then it's axiomatic that there are two ways to get laid on election night.

At a victory party there are countless young champagne-infused volunteers looking to celebrate with any red-blooded man in the room. (Case in point? The 2004 George Bush victory rally in D.C. My semiregular doses of Zithromax are a reminder of that glorious night with a deputy press secretary from the vice president's office.)

Less well known, but equally true, is that you can just as easily get lucky at a concession party when drunk campaign staff need someone to commiserate with. Ah yes, the infamous Dole-Kemp defeat of '96. I remember the blonde "Twin Towers" of Laura Ingraham and Ann Coulter (both of whom were former paramours of my pal, pundit Dinesh D'Souza). Laura and Ann were just starting to make their own marks as conservative pundits, and it was a tough night on all of us. Quite honestly I don't remember which one I went home with . . . but perhaps it's just as well. This way, I'm equally polite whenever I run into either one.

The only time where no one gets laid? An undecided election, like the Florida mess in 2000. For more than a month, no one in the political classes got any action. But remember the night of the Supreme Court decision? People were confused by the pictures of Al Gore smiling ear to ear at his concession party that night. Now you know why: Tipper finally let him "commiserate" with her.

John McCain's concession speech was at the Arizona Biltmore Hotel in Phoenix. There was an open call to all the D.C. campaign staff to attend, but given the situation with reimbursements I decided it was best to stay in Washington and attend a local rally at RNC headquarters on the Hill. At least there would be some despondent Capitol Hill staffers there in need of consoling. (And to the certain unnamed legislative correspondent for Lindsey Graham I met that night, I would still appreciate it if you sent me back my left shoe. It's a favorite.)

But the real fireworks were going on in Arizona. Mark Salter had written a stirring speech for McCain that was equal parts contrition, humility, and pride. Meanwhile, Sarah Palin's husband, Todd, had slapped together a speech for Sarah to deliver. The only trouble was that McCain didn't want Palin to speak— he didn't want the event to be a kickoff for Palin's 2012 campaign. Steve Schmidt was the one who gave her the news: VP contenders don't do concession speeches.

Thankfully for Schmidt, Palin is not an A student of American history. If she was, she might have mentioned that John Edwards did a concession speech in 2004, Jack Kemp did one in 1996, and Dan Quayle did one in 1992. Even Joe "Hebrew National" Lieberman was scheduled to do a concession speech in 2000 had the election gone decisively for Bush that night (my old softball ringer Paul Orzulak wrote the speech and has the text of it on his office wall, next to his framed Harding Institute team jersey).[3]

## The Day After

I woke up late the day after the election, hungover, hungry, and partially shoeless. I stole a Hot Pockets Chicken and Cheddar from Mom's freezer and popped it in the microwave. Mom, still in her bathrobe and slippers, caught me red-handed. "What did I buy you that mini fridge for, if you're just going to keep coming up here and take my food?"

"I'm the one who bought these Hot Pockets," I retorted.

"With my money. And I'm still waiting for the change."

Just then, a voice bellowed down from the top floor. "Connie, I need your help finding my gavel. I can't seem to find it after last night's session." Whether that voice belonged to Justice Souter or Justice Thomas, I couldn't tell. But I thought it best not to stick around and find out.

I retreated to my basement apartment and flipped on Fox News. There was Carl Cameron giving Shepard Smith his postmortem of the election. I got a twinge of pain in my big toe when Carl recounted my stories of Palin's lapses in geographic knowledge, but was relieved that he didn't identify me as a source. Carl's a pro, that's for sure.

In the end, this would be good for McCain's long-term image, and also good for my own reputation as a McCain insider and political consultant. This would also be a plus for Steve Schmidt (that's a guy who'll be hiring again, and I needed to stay in his good favor). Candidates come and go. Operatives stick around for decades. And thanks to me, the narrative being expressed by Carl was clear. It was the Palin camp who lost the election, not the McCain team. Mission accomplished.

In the days after the election I was trying to refocus my attention on the Harding Institute, to take care of matters that I'd neglected during the rush of the campaign. We needed a new fax machine, we'd run out of parking validation stickers, and there was some sort of paternity subpoena from one of our former interns for all the men in the office to take DNA swabs. In other words, things were returning to normal.

It turns out that while I was cavorting with the big boys at the RNC on election night, my staff had their own little party at the office. There were McCain posters and sagging balloons everywhere. I picked up a deflated off-white balloon from my office couch.

"Jimmy! I know it was a rough night for all of us, but clean these balloons up!"

Danny poked his head into my office. "Jimmy's not here."

"Where is he?"

"A long lunch with Poppy."

"What do you mean?"

"On election night, Poppy was really bummed out about the loss. In the spirit of a new post-racial America, Jimmy consoled her. Repeatedly."

I raised an eyebrow. "How 'bout that."

The Mennonite virgin and the Condi Rice disciple. Good for them. It was nice to know that the institute had a lasting impression on the people who worked here. I stirred with pride and felt a bit like Cupid.

I was also keeping an eye on Obama's transition team, spearheaded by my old friend John Podesta. There had been a lot of chatter about Obama reaching out to Republicans for slots in the new administration, and I wanted to make sure I was in the mix. (You'll see now that it wasn't just coincidence that I let Podesta's Center for American Progress beat the Harding Institute in softball last summer.) If Bob Gates stayed at Defense or if they brought in Senator Chuck Hagel, I wanted to be in consideration to be the Pentagon's new Paul Wolfowitz or Douglas Feith. Every administration needs a neocon to start planning the next war. And I was as qualified as anyone to play that role.

Meanwhile, the news of Palin's geographic foibles grew wider by the hour. Every network in America, and indeed the world, was running clips of Cameron's Fox piece. Carl was getting great face time on every network, and for his sake, I hoped he was using the opportunity to renegotiate his contract with Fox. This was the most credible story the network had run in years.

The inevitable naysayers then started to question Carl's reporting and wonder who his sources were. Was it *really* possible that Palin didn't know Africa was a continent? If a story seemed too good to be true, maybe it wasn't? But Carl's a pro: he stuck to his story, didn't reveal his sources, and Fox backed him up 100 percent.

## Palin Strikes Back

Sarah Palin may be dumb, but she's not an idiot. (Watch that debate with Biden again. She *did* exceed expectations.) So within two days after the Fox News report, Sarah spoke up for herself on CNN:

> *No, it's not true, and I do remember havin' a discussion about NAFTA, so . . . if there are allegations based on questions or comments that I made in debate prep about NAFTA—and about the continent versus the country when we talk about Africa there—then those were taken out of context. And that's cruel, it's mean-spirited, it's immature, it's unprofessional and those guys are jerks if they came away with it, taking things out of context and then tried to spread something on national news. It's not fair and not right.*[4]

You'll notice, of course, that this is a classic non-denial denial. She follows the boilerplate "if . . . then" pattern of claiming that "if there are allegations . . . then those were taken out of context." In other words, of course she said what she's accused of saying. She's just shocked that loyal McCain advisers would rat on her. Welcome to the Lower 48, Sarah!

Now that the election itself was over and the transition news hadn't really started yet, the Sunday shows had a heyday with the Palin Africa story. Every network other than Fox fixated on who the unnamed source was for the Fox interview. Was it Steve Schmidt or Rick Davis or Mark Salter distracting attention from their push to pick Palin in the first place? Maybe it was Nicolle Wallace, bitter that Palin had treated her like a glorified maidservant and thrown her under the bus for the Katie Couric interview. Or maybe one of these former Bushies was seeking to cleverly elbow Palin out of the way so another candidate, say Jeb Bush, could be the front-runner in 2012.

But while all my erstwhile colleagues were getting name-checked on every network in the alphabet, rarely did anyone speculate that *I* was the source of the leak. Me, Marty Eisenstadt! Maybe I had flown too far under the radar for anyone to care. Maybe when the campaign books and *Newsweek* special editions were written, my contributions to the McCain efforts would also be forgotten. I feared that in two years' time, when Jeb Bush or Mitt Romney or Bobby Jindal would start their runs for 2012, maybe they too would ignore me.

No. I had just generated the biggest story on the planet, and I'd be damned if someone else got the name recognition for it. I knew there'd be backlash if I outed myself as the source. The Palin wing of the party was already rallying to her defense. *The New York Times* quoted Palin's new BFF Randy Scheunemann as saying, "The people that are spreading these lies . . . obviously have no loyalty to John McCain or to the person John McCain chose to be his vice president." Poor Randy. Just a week before the election, word leaked from the campaign that he'd been "fired" for falling under Sarah's spell.[5] Randy vehemently denied the accusation, and said that just because his e-mail was cut off and his BlackBerry confiscated, that did *not* mean he was fired.[6] The fact that his last paycheck was voided by the campaign probably didn't mean that either.[7]

## Admitting the Africa Leak

Had I learned nothing from this campaign? Like the Paris Hilton story, like the Joe the Plumber leak, like the Iraqi lobbying apology, I had to own the story. I had to make it mine. And on my own terms, before some pesky reporter like Anderson Cooper outed me as Carl's source.

So on Monday morning, I grabbed my trusty ThinkPad, typed up the following, and told Danny to post it right away.

### Eisenstadt the source for Sarah Palin Africa leak . . . and proud of it.

November 10, 2008, by Marty

By now you've all heard the Fox News report last week that "unnamed" former McCain advisers leaked that Sarah Palin was confused about whether Africa was a continent, and which countries were in NAFTA. I was perfectly happy staying under the radar as an anonymous source for Fox News' Carl Cameron, but now that Palin has accused her accusers of being "unprofessional . . . jerks . . . cowards . . ." and begun to cast doubt on the Fox News report, maybe she's right to a certain extent. For those of us on the McCain campaign who thought that she acted like a rogue diva and lost John the election, maybe we DO have a responsibility to come out in public. But Sarah . . . careful what you ask for: some of us may have more to reveal.

So yes, to be clear, last week I was the one who leaked those things to Carl Cameron. Carl's a good guy, and I don't want him to have to worry about protecting his sources (and going through the wringer ala Judith Miller or Matt Cooper) on something like this.

As you know, I was one of the foreign policy advisers on the McCain campaign who worked with Randy Scheunemann to help prep Sarah on her debate with Joe Biden. Did we outright give her a geography quiz when we started the prep? No, of course not. But

*David Shuster*

*Former governor Sarah Palin*
*(Courtesy of Harding Institute/MSNBC)*

yes, in the context of the prep, it slowly became apparent that her grasp of basic geo-political knowledge had major gaps. Could she have passed a multiple choice test about South Africa or NAFTA? Probably. But it was clear that she simply didn't have the ease of knowledge that we come to expect from a major party political candidate.

Within an hour, Danny came running into my office.

"Marty, Marty, I think you need to see this."

"Danny, what?"

"Great news! MSNBC. They just teased a story that they've got breaking news on the Palin Africa thing."

I went into the bullpen, and the staff and I gathered in front of Danny's computer screen. (He's somehow figured out how to get regular cable news on his computer. I'm not sure it's legal, but in times of crisis, I'm glad he's got it.) The report started with the distinctive "swoosh, whoosh" sound effects over the animated graphic "Breaking News." Then cut to the clip of Sarah Palin saying her accusers were "jerks and unprofessional."

With the headline "McCain Campaign Adviser Admits Leaking Palin Information to Media" on the screen, a stern-looking David Shuster intoned: "Jerks? Unprofessional? Out of context? So who did tell Fox News that Palin could not identify the countries involved in NAFTA and that she thought Africa was a country instead of a continent? Turns out it was Martin Eisenstadt, a

McCain policy adviser who has come forward today to identify himself as a source of the leaks."[8]

Shuster then turned to two dial-a-pundits who happened to be sitting across from him in the studio: "Republican strategist" Todd Boulanger and "Democratic strategist" David Goodfriend. Boulanger had the temerity to say, "Well, I mean that's just one person's word against the senior campaign officials who said she was just fine. I mean, like it or not, Sarah Palin's here to stay."

Goodfriend and Boulanger

Look, I've got nothing against Boulanger. Sure, he's got great credentials as Jack Abramoff's former assistant, but not as a "Republican strategist." Todd's main strategy seems to have been picking out the red M&Ms from the MSNBC greenroom. And that strategy was working great until a few weeks after his Shuster appearance when he pled guilty to federal influence-peddling charges, crimes for which he will likely serve eighteen to twenty-four months in prison.[9]

My only beef was that MSNBC had a guy like Boulanger on the air to talk about me instead of *me* talking about me. Have they no standards for their pundits?

"Danny, did Shuster try to reach us for a comment or an appearance?"

"No. Nothing."

"Rats."

"Wait, here we go." Danny was checking his e-mail. "We just got an interview request from them. But they just sent it. *After* the story aired."

"Better late than never, I suppose." I certainly have my issues with NBC, and even Keith Olbermann's used me as a source on several occasions, so at least it was nice that this time they gave me full attribution. "Okay, Danny, get my lapel pin ready. It's punditing time!"

I ducked back into my office, straightened my tie, slicked back my hair, and put on my jacket. "Danny!" I shouted out to the bullpen. "Any more requests come in?"

"You bet, boss: ABC News, CBS *Early Show*, Sky News in England, NHK in Japan, even *Access Hollywood*."

I surveyed my crew like Napoleon did with his troops just before Waterloo. "After all this time, we finally hit the mother lode. See, guys, this is how it pays off!"

Danny danced an inelegant jig. Marwan jabbed his fist in the air in his best Marv Albert "Yes!" Jimmy and Poppy tongued each other like puppies in love.

"Okay, team: Danny, you schedule the interviews. Jimmy, you start monitoring the Internet. Poppy, check the blog for comments. And Marwan, see if the foreign press has picked this up yet. Today's a great day!"

Of course, as soon as the MSNBC story ran, all hell broke loose on the Internet. Jimmy reported that the right-wing blogosphere had started linking to my blog even before the MSNBC story ran (which is how they found out about it, apparently). Poppy saw that my blog post from that day was deluged with comments—mostly angry, vitriolic death threats from the trans-fat wing of the GOP accusing me of being a traitor to Sarah Palin. There were 532 comments in all, even more than we'd gotten on the Jonas Brothers posts.

No matter. I'm a big-time media pundit in Washington. I would soon be appearing on all the major networks. The blogosphere was for losers who live with their mothers and don't wear pants. (To be crystal clear: I live in my *own* basement apartment *under* my mother's house. Not in it. And my pants were on.)

"Danny, when's that first interview?"

Danny had his office phone in one ear and his cell phone in

the other. And his fingers were darting around his keyboard like a Thai masseuse at a WTO convention.

"Marty, I think we have a problem."

"What? Too many interviews? Prioritize, Danny. Stack them according to time zones: *Hardball* and Blitzer first, Larry King tonight, the Japanese and British later, and I'll do the morning shows from their D.C. studios. As for the Sunday shows, we aim for the full Ginsburg. All five, baby. What's the problem?"

"They're starting to cancel."

"Who is?"

"Everyone, Marty, everyone!"

"Why?"

"I dunno," Danny sputtered. "They're giving me the runaround. Saying they don't have slots available, there's other news, they're asking me a lot of questions."

"About what?"

"If you exist."

"You've got to be kidding me!!!"

Jimmy piped in. "Yup, that's the word on the Internet now. People picked up that old story that you don't exist and now they're all making fun of MSNBC and Shuster for falling for a hoax."

## Denying the Rumors

My heart sank. All this work . . . a lifetime spent building up to this one day of massive punditification. And now they wanted to take it away from me. But I wasn't going down without a fight! I pounced on my ThinkPad and blurted out an update to that morning's blog post in which I reminded my readers that every single one of these fallacious Internet rumors could be attributed to a single source—a so-called Mr. Wolfrum, whom we'd previously established is a cyber-stalking, tranny-loving golf blogger living in Brazil. And for those wondering why he would go after me now and try to discredit my views on Sarah Palin, I reminded them that Wolfrum himself used to live in Alaska. Coincidence? Or just plain chance?

The update stemmed the tide a little bit, but the big networks were now too confused to trust their own judgment and too lazy to do their own research. Was Marty Eisenstadt real enough to put on the air? What junior producer or booker was going to put her own career on the line by vouching for my veracity? It was quicker and easier for all the networks to pile on MSNBC and say that they fell for a hoax. Network *schadenfreude*. (There, my winsome editor Mitzi's happy I finally used that highfalutin German word. I'm sure she'd be even happier if I could use *mummenschanz* in a sentence, too, but the book is almost over and I don't see that happening soon.)

What press I did get in the next couple of days—and there was still plenty of it—mostly consisted of regurgitating Wolfrum's old claims that I was nonexistent.

It was infuriating. On the one hand, I was going on the record, willing and happy to do on-camera interviews to prove that I was real and admit that I was the source of the Palin leak. But if that was a lie, then where were the other McCain advisers to speak on the record to deny that I ever worked for McCain? Nowhere! Even Carl Cameron never categorically said I *wasn't* the source for the Palin story, and no one else from the campaign— *to this day!*—has ever stepped forward and admitted they were the source.

## *The New York Times*: From Pundit to Undit

This week was not going as planned. At best, my reputation was just barely treading water, and at worst, people didn't believe I existed at all. Gout be damned. By midweek, I'd cracked open a secret stash of bourbon I kept in my desk drawer. The more I drank, the more my toe hurt. The more it hurt, the more I drank to numb the pain. Historians say it's this vicious cycle of gout

## To E-mail Is to Be

One e-mail exchange I had with a reporter from the blog TVNewser (part of the Mediabistro blog empire) should give you some flavor of how frustrating things were going.

***

Martin

My name is Steve Krakauer and I am the associate editor of TVNewser.com, the leading blog about the TV news industry. I wanted to write about how MSNBC picked up your fake story, but before I make the claim others are making, I wanted to ask you if you can prove that you, and your organization, are not fake. Please call or email. Thanks very much,

Steve

***

Steve

thanks for the email. It's strange for me (and all a bit Hegelian) to get requests to prove that I exist. But I appreciate your journalistic responsibility to do so . . . In the meantime, it is only fitting of me to ask if *you* are, indeed, real? all the best,

Marty

***

Marty

Thanks for your response. And yes, I am also in fact real . . . You'll have to forgive me that I'm still skeptical and think

that ultimately brought down the British Empire. (Take a look at Winston Churchill and Mahatma Gandhi: guess which one had gout.) At least my sore toe served the same function as pinching yourself when you're awake. I ached, therefore I was.

Toward the end of the week, Danny stormed in. "Marty, I've

you've run a very effective and elaborate hoax. Tell me exactly your back-and-forth with Carl Cameron? I've reached out to FNC for comment as well. Thanks,

Steve

---

Steve

You flatter me that I could construct such an elaborate ruse. I suppose if I didn't exist, it would indeed be impressive to have made all this up.

I can appreciate and respect the position you're in. I am curious, though; you say in your article that you've been making calls all day, but other than your correspondence with me, and some basic internet research, you don't actually seem to quote anyone in the piece. Am I wrong?

Don't you find it ironic that the one person who goes on the record is the one who is accused of not existing? Makes you wonder if anyone in Washington exists anymore. best,

Marty

---

Marty

Alright I understand. We'll present both sides, and I guess see what develops.

Steve

got good news and bad news. There's a big story about you in *The New York Times*." He dropped the paper on my desk.

I looked at the headline: "A Senior Fellow at the Institute of Nonexistence." The article started fine, with a recitation of what happened with the Palin Africa leak. Until it got to the part about

MSNBC and the Shuster story: "Trouble is, Martin Eisenstadt doesn't exist. His blog does, but it's a put-on. The think tank where he is a senior fellow—the Harding Institute for Freedom and Democracy—is just a Web site. The TV clips of him on YouTube are fakes."[10]

The story went on to say that I was actually the creation of two "obscure filmmakers"—a Mr. Eitan Gorlin and Mr. Dan Mirvish—who had created me as an elaborate hoax (there's even a picture of one of them wearing a ridiculous hat in a messy office). By the end of the piece, though, it added this nugget: "And then there is William K. Wolfrum, a blogger who has played Javert to Eisenstadt's Valjean, tracking the hoaxster across cyberspace and repeatedly debunking his claims . . . And how can we know that Mr. Wolfrum is real and not part of the hoax? Long pause. 'Yeah, that's a tough one.'"

Yup, this was definitely the bad news. *The New York Times*, as much as we on the right like to belittle it, is still the newspaper of

*(Courtesy of The Yes Men)*

record and the most influential source of news on the planet. For the *Times* to say that I didn't exist was a much bigger deal than one little post on Google. If the *Times* says I'm not real, then maybe I'm not.

"Okay, Danny." I slammed down another Maker's Mark. "Then what's the good news?"

"What you just read isn't from *The New York Times*."

"What?"

"It's not real, it's a fake."

"Danny, you're freaking me out. What the *hell* are you talking about?!"

"It turns out that a group of professional hoaxsters called The Yes Men printed 1.2 million copies of a fake version of *The New York Times* today and handed them out in lower Manhattan. The main headline declared 'Iraq War Ends.' It's all a bunch of left-wing agitprop hooey, but to make their newspapers thicker, they did all kinds of fake articles in there. Including the one about you."[11]

"Well, that's a relief." I put my bottle away. Time to sober up. "But we've still got some serious damage control to do. And Danny, what's the story with these guys Gorlin and Mirvish? Are they even real?"

"Yes. I did some digging on them." Here's what he found.

Gorlin, who admittedly bears a slight resemblance to me, had directed a left-wing Israeli movie a couple of years back called *The Holy Land* about prostitutes, rabbinical students, and suicide bombers that played in fifty U.S. cities and won him some awards. Apparently he was also a key grip on a TV show called *Lez Be Friends*. And Mirvish's last movie was a real-estate musical called *Open House*. By all accounts, the movie, which featured scenes of people having sex in open houses, led to a national trend of people doing what's called "house humping." Some say that's what finally burst the real-estate bubble, leading to the subprime mortgage collapse and the largest economic crisis in world history.

## Create Your Own Neocon!

In the faux *New York Times* article, the point is made that my name is a construct of a Christian first name and Jewish last name, just like all the other neocons of the Bush administration. That's utterly ridiculous! For one thing, my full name is Martin Thomas Eisenstadt. For another, just see how hard it is to come up with credible neocon-sounding names from the two lists below of Saint and Apostle first names, and Arguably Jewish-Sounding Last Names.

- Saints and/or Apostles: Peter, James, John, Andrew, Philip, Bartholomew, Randall, Matthew, Robert, Thomas, James, Thaddeus, Simon, Judas, Douglas, Jonah, Richard, Martin, Paul, William, Charles, Scooter

- Arguably Jewish-Sounding Last Names: Friedman, Peretz, Wolfowitz, Perle, Zoellick, Eisenstadt, Goldberg, Krauthammer, Feith, Krugman, Kristol, Scheunemann, Libby (short for Liebowitz)

"Danny, I'm confused. So are they part of The Yes Men?"

"No, they don't seem bright enough or talented enough to pull off a big newspaper prank. The Yes Men probably just had stock pictures of them and built their story around that."

There was still a rather vexing problem. Apparently when *The New York Times* is itself the victim of a hoax, it is not quick to report that fact in its own pages. Consequently, not too many other people realized the November 12 paper was a fake. Which meant that a *lot* of other media outlets still thought the fake article about me was real.

As a result, the fake *New York Times* story that said I don't exist was picked up by *The Washington Post*, ABC News, CNN, NPR, and the BBC. Once the Associated Press picked up the fake

*Times* piece, it was only a matter of time before it showed up literally in almost every newspaper and TV station in the world. From *The Guardian* in the U.K., to *L'Express* in France, to *Die Zeit* Germany. And that was just Europe! From Taiwan to Argentina, from Norway to Australia, there was not a country on the planet where people weren't reading that the Sarah Palin Africa story was leaked by former McCain adviser Martin Eisenstadt . . . who was a hoax!

My mother tried to console me. "Marty," she e-mailed me, "all press is good press . . . just so long as the words 'unindicted coconspirator' don't precede your name." She's slept with enough of them over the years to know. And also, would it kill her to come to the basement and actually tell me these things in person?

The great irony is that "Martin Eisenstadt" finally became a household name. It took forty-four years, but it's every young pundit's dream come true. I'd finally be able to have the leverage to go to CNN and get a full-time "consulting" gig on Blitzer's *Situation Room*. And if Wolf didn't offer me enough, I'd go down the street to see my pal Chris Matthews at MSNBC or Shepard Smith at Fox. I'd be able to hold my head up high with the Carvilles, the Begalas, the Braziles, and the Buchanans of the world. I'd have enough money to buy *them* drinks after the show. I'd have enough to support my beloved Harding Institute and maybe hire a real ringer for this year's softball team. I could finally move out of my mom's basement and get a swanky loft in Foggy Bottom. *Then* we'll see if Marnie Vander Helsing wants to be seen with me in public. I daresay, she might then have to wait in line!

But.

But, but, but. That name recognition is now universally tied to the belief that I do not exist. People think I'm a nonentity, a never-was, a shadow of my former self, if my self had ever had a shadow. Forget about not being a pundit, you may as well lose the *p* and call me an *un*-dit!

## Kurtz: The Horror

The next few days were a blur. It was chaos at the office. One minute the phone would be ringing off the hook, and the next it was deathly silent. Clifford Harding III called to say that I had sullied the good name of his granduncle, Warren G. Harding. Marketing execs at Coca-Cola called to try to revoke naming rights to our conference room (thankfully, they're bound to a five-year contract).

I remember at one point watching CNN's *Reliable Sources*, hosted by the *Washington Post*'s media critic Howard Kurtz. He introduced the show by saying, "Martin Eisenstadt is a fake, a fraud, a scam artist!"[12]

Kurtz, that hurts.

I've known Howie for years (we worked the ring-toss booth in the late nineties at a District-wide Purim carnival) and he's usually a careful analyst of the media, but ever since he took a foul ball in the noggin at a Nationals game last year (so much for those primo *WashPo* first-base seats), his long-term memory has been a little shaky. But he still has a 300-watt smile and fills his Men's Wearhouse suits well with his washboard abs. As eye candy, he's always been a strong lead-in to Blitzer's Sunday show on CNN and I know Wolf likes having him around. But c'mon, Howie. Inviting to your show the charlatans Gorlin and Mirvish who perpetuated the canard that they had created me? For a couple of patsies used by The Yes Men, they sure seem to be willing opportunists, all too happy to be portrayed as brilliant media satirists.[13]

## Phenomenology of the Jonas Brothers

Winter had come to Washington and the cold, rainy city was abuzz with the upcoming inauguration. I walked backward sometimes, checking to make sure I was making footprints. (I

Kurtz, Mirvish, Gorlin *(Courtesy of Harding Institute/CNN)*

was.) I went to the Lincoln Memorial—the site where my mother named me—and looked for myself in the reflecting pool. (There I was.) If *I* had no lingering doubts about my own existence, then why should so many others?

I flashed back to my old American University class on political theory. Of course I remembered the raven-haired TA with the tight jeans and diaphanous peasant blouses, but I also took solace in the words of such existential masters as Descartes, Sartre, and those early twentieth-century Germans whose names invariably all started with the letter H. The one exception to the H rule was the brilliantly pretentious Theodor Adorno, who once said, "Today self-consciousness no longer means anything but reflection on the ego as embarrassment, as realization of impotence: knowing that one is nothing."[14] I can't for the life of me figure out what that means, but it seems relevant and depressing all at once.

In mulling this over in the halls of the Harding Institute one evening, I was struck by some songs emanating from my young associate Poppy's earbuds as I leaned over to see what she was working on (and pressed my ear ever so gently against hers).

She was in the process of reediting one of the videos Danny had shot of me right after the *New York Times* story broke. Turns out that when Danny edits, we don't get too many hits. So Poppy decided to sneak onto his computer one night and remix in music from the Disney Channel's teenybopper hit cable movie *Camp Rock*, starring the keffiyeh-wearing, terror-loving Jonas Brothers.

It occurred to me, as it apparently had to young Poppy (who by this time had whirled around in her chair, inadvertently bumping into my chin), that the Disney mandate of safe happy songs by postpubescent chastity-vowed teens all contained messages of self-esteem and self-realization. But were these songs so different from the hard-thought philosophical teachings from the halls of academe? I had Poppy put together a little quiz.

## Existential Disney Quiz

**Match the phrase on the left with its source on the right.**

| | |
|---|---|
| 1. This is real, this is me. | a. Immanuel Kant |
| 2. To know oneself, one should assert oneself. | b. *Camp Rock* soundtrack |
| 3. Who will I be, it's up to me. | c. Martin Heidegger |
| 4. Being is what it is! | d. Max Horkheimer |
| 5. Being is not a Being. | e. Albert Camus |
| 6. What can I know? | f. Søren Kierkegaard |
| 7. That's how you know. | g. Friedrich Nietzsche |
| 8. Consciousness is a being, the nature of which is to be conscious of the nothingness of its being! | h. Hannah Montana/Miley Cyrus |
| | i. Martin Buber |
| 9. Raise your hands up in the air and scream! | j. *Enchanted* soundtrack |
| 10. Existence precedes and commands essence! | k. Georg Wilhelm Friedrich Hegel |
| 11. We are not certain, we are never certain! | l. Jean-Paul Sartre |

12. Well-informed cynicism is only another mode of conformity.

13. Hell is other people.

14. Do it or do not do it—you will regret both.

15. I can almost see it. That dream I'm dreaming.

16. The dreams have no dream!

17. We're finding our voice, following our dreams.

18. This is the life, hold on tight.

19. Only one man ever understood me, and he didn't understand me.

20. There is no way you'll be ignored, not anymore, so here I am.

21. Never yet has there been a Superman.

22. I looked upon myself as something of a Superman.

23. Who said I can't be Superman?

24. To like is intrinsically to be conscious.

25. The gates of heaven will open wide, I will be, I will rise.

26. Through the Thou a person becomes I.

m. The Jonas Brothers

n. Edmund Husserl

o. Theodor Adorno

**Answers:** 1-b, 2-e, 3-b, 4-i, 5-c, 6-a, 7-j, 8-l, 9-b, 10-l, 11-e, 12-d, 13-l, 14-f, 15-h, 16-o, 17-b, 18-h, 19-k, 20-b, 21-g, 22-e, 23-h, 24-n, 25-m, 26-i

## All About Sarah

The real rub was that this whole mess had single-handedly rehabilitated Sarah Palin's reputation. Now the prevailing conventional wisdom was that since the source of the Africa leak had been discredited, then the whole story must have been a hoax. As the faux *New York Times* story got regurgitated and translated around the globe, the headline became simplified and reduced to three simple words: "Palin. Africa. Hoax." Palin was now free to raise money and run unfettered for the job that rightfully should have been John McCain's.

I had to wonder: Had that really been the goal of The Yes Men or of Wolfrum—to single-handedly rehabilitate Sarah Palin's image? Or maybe it had just been to destroy my own. At this

*(Courtesy of Danny Sadler/Harding Institute)*

point, it was hard to say. But with a little more time to think, I would eventually solve the mystery.

There were larger issues at play here, and I had to forget about me and my existential crisis. To the extent that I was alive and kicking, I would survive. Martin Eisenstadt always does.

# Conclusion:
# Who Dunnit . . . ?

**A**ND NOW IT WAS CLEAR: every single article or story about me saying I was fake all emanated from the golf blogger in Brazil. Not a single journalist had ever bothered to do any original reporting to the contrary. It's a sad state of media affairs that so many can be so lazy and succumb to being so fooled by so few.

I learned a long time ago from John Ehrlichman that the simplest explanation for a conspiracy is that there is no conspiracy. John learned the hard way that it's too tough to keep a secret in this town. It's always easier to manipulate people than to trust them.

If that's the case, then the real question wasn't who is Wolfrum, who is he working for, or does he exist. No, the simplest explanation is that he is who says he is: a lone blogger working out of Brazil. An expatriate American who longs for the day when he was a real journalist and is willing to believe the canard that bloggers *are* the new journalists. The blogs aspire to be *The Washington Post*, and the bloggers aim to be Woodward and Bernstein. Something else I learned from Ehrlichman: conspiracy theories persist because people—especially those who think

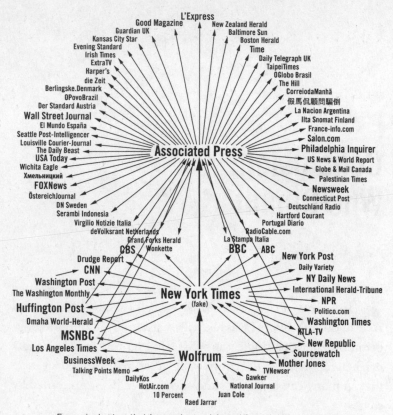

Every single story that I was a hoax originated from the Wolfrum blog.

of themselves as journalists—*want* to believe. They want to give meaning to a meaningless world. Find order where there is chaos. These are the people easiest to manipulate.

The *real* question then is, Who is manipulating Wolfrum? Who's feeding him disinformation? Laying down the bread crumbs, but letting him find his own way; taking advantage of the fact that he's distrustful by nature. As a sometime hoaxster himself, Wolfrum would know to be dubious of any tips, distrustful of any information fed his way. If a dubious source said X, he would print Y. And he would do it proudly and vainly. That was his nature. That was his character.

So who was tipping him off? The one clue Wolfrum gives is that he received an e-mail about the Denny Hastert tranny-lobbyist story from a Kareem Wahiri at "kwahiri@gmail.com." He later tracks down an abbreviated name, "kwah," to blog comments written about the stealth Giuliani ads. Any unsolicited e-mail to him saying, "Hey, I love your blog! Go check out this crazy McCain adviser's site . . . !" would look to the savvy blogger like a ham-fisted sockpuppet, planted by the self-aggrandizing McCain adviser himself.

But stop for a second. Why would a "fake" McCain adviser with such an "elaborate hoax" so torpedo his own efforts by sending such an obvious cry for investigation to the very sort of blogger who would uncover the subterfuge in a matter of days? It makes no sense.

If indeed I was some fake invention—some creation of two "obscure filmmakers," as the fake *New York Times* said—it would have taken years to create a background as rich and fabled as my own. It would have taken dozens of people and millions of dollars to write, produce, act, and edit the Giuliani ads, the Iraqi video, the BBC documentary, and the rebuttal videos. How on earth would this massive two-year operation have been kept quiet? It couldn't be a conspiracy. No, the answer was much simpler. By Ehrlichman's rule, it had to be.

Much more likely was that someone—someone out to get me—had sent the initial e-mails to Wolfrum. Someone who knew that if he (or she, or they, even) phrased the e-mails the right way, that Wolfrum's first instincts would be to hunt down the person who sent them. Hunt down Kareem Wahiri.

So then the real question is, Who is Kareem Wahiri? This couldn't be a real name. That's a given. Okay, then who *was* the master-mind guiding Wolfrum to bring about my inevitable downfall?

Whoever it was, I needed to follow the few clues I had. What about the e-mail handle kwahiri@gmail.com? Anyone who's ever taken an East African studies class, knows that *kwahiri* is Swahili

## Suspects

In my short time on Earth, I've tried to live a good life. Be nice to people, be kind to animals, and not tempt fate with unnecessary acts against nature. But are there people out there who don't see things the way I do? People who might have it in for me for some imperceptible slight they've interpreted as personal, not professional? Someone who even says he's my friend and secretly plots my comeuppance? I wonder aloud who some of these people might be.

- *Jamie and Nabil*—accused me of padding my resume and sabotaging their Green Zone project. It's possible they still think I owe them money.

- *Sarah Palin*—obviously had the most to gain from my downfall, and had the Alaska connection to Wolfrum.

- *Joe the Plumber*—he met me too recently, but if he really was a plant the whole time, anything is possible.

- *Meghan McCain*—she's proven to be quite the resourceful vixen on the Internet, and might just blame me for her father's loss.

- *Lorne Michaels*—still bitter that I outed his contributions to Obama. He's a control freak who probably didn't like me manipulating who would appear on his show.

- *Rudy Giuliani*—could be blaming everyone on his team for his primary loss. Might be concerned that the "Jew-liani" term stuck.

for "goodbye." For that matter, anyone who's ever gone to a party at the Kenyan embassy would know it, too (the lovely consular hostesses always say "*kwahiri*" when you leave). I remember my frequent trips there during the 2003 softball season, when I played on the Committee for the Liberation of Iraq team. So was some-

- *Eliot Spitzer*—probably suspects that I tipped off the feds to his visits with Ashley Dupré.

- *Ashley Dupré*—probably mad that I didn't tip off the feds to Eliot Spitzer's visits with her earlier.

- *Eli Perle*—my slippery old assistant knows enough about me to get me into trouble and might erroneously harbor resentment about the way I treated him.

- *The Jonas Brothers*—they probably didn't like being called out on their poor fashion choices. If they really do have terrorist tendencies, I may have been their first target.

- *Iranian Revolutionary Guards*—upset that I spilled the beans on their doctored missile-test photo. They also suspect that I outed Ahmed Chalabi as a spy.

- ██████ ██████—probably thinks I'm the one in Rehoboth who crapped 360-style in his washing machine. (It was dark. Anyone could have made that mistake!)

- And finally, anyone on the McCain campaign who blames me for the loss: Steve Schmidt, Charlie Black, Randy Scheunemann, Mark Salter, Rick Davis, Nicolle Wallace.

one sending me a message . . . in Swahili? "Marty Eisenstadt— *goodbye*, once and for all!" I don't know.

And then it struck me. Just as I had used the backward name of a town in India for Abrad, maybe I should look at "kwah" spelled backward: h-a-w-k. Oh my God, the CLI softball team! Chalabi had given each of us nicknames, and one of us he called "the Hawk"!

Ironic, I thought, that of all the Semitic faces on that team, the one guy who got that nickname received it not because of his nose but because of his eyes. As the catcher, the Hawk noticed when Norman Ornstein tried to steal second in the American Enterprise Institute game, and threw the ball to Bill Kristol for the tag out. When he was up to bat in the Heritage game, the Hawk's sharp eyes saw the fast pitch to his head and ducked in time for umpire Lanny Davis to take it in the mask. And after each game, at the Kenyan embassy, the Hawk was the one who always spotted when the caterer was bringing fresh trays of semilegal zebra kabobs for the happy hour buffet. So who was the Hawk?

Randy Scheunemann.

Scheunemann? Yes. My old pal Scheunemann. Suddenly it all made sense. Breaking the sweaty Turkish *kisbet* in the back of his Saab. Getting onto the McCain campaign through Lieberman's graces, not his. Telling everyone that his buddy Chalabi was a spy. I never realized it, but he must have hated me.

Now that I think about it, wasn't it Randy who tipped me off to the Hilton family angrily complaining to the campaign? Did he know me so well that he assumed I would spill the beans? He must have, and probably figured I would get fired for it. But what he didn't count on was how my leak actually kept the story alive and marked the turnaround in the campaign.

But how had he done it? How did he have the expertise, the time, and the wherewithal to navigate the technical side of the Internet? I remember now when I first hired Danny last summer. I told Randy I had a geeky new intern from Rutgers who was going to bring me kicking and screaming into the twenty-first century. Randy shot back, "Rutgers, ha! I've got a hotshot kid from MIT. He's on parole from Cumberland, where he did two years for hacking into the DoD computer. That's MY geek squad."

Last May, Randy must have tipped Wolfrum off. He used him as a patsy to spread the word I was a hoax. He knew how powerful that word is on the Internet. It's the modern scarlet letter: H. Giving him the benefit of the doubt, maybe he did it as a joke. Or just a subtle dig to set me back a little with punditing jobs. Maybe he didn't quite realize how persistent and unrelenting Wolfrum would be. Or how sticky his hoaxing references would become on Google.

But by the time the campaign was coming to an end, he must have seen the writing on the wall. He'd been co-opted by Sarah Palin, and the rift between her camp and McCain's was growing every day. He threw his eggs into the Palin basket and paid the price when the rumors flew that he'd been fired. Knowing him, he probably blamed me for that leak, too.

So even before election day, he must have hatched a plan. He knew he needed to find someone on the campaign who could be portrayed in the election postmortems as *more* incompetent, *more* disloyal, and with a bigger target on his back. And for that, I was the biggest patsy of all.

I suspect that when Randy spoke to Fox's Carl Cameron, it went something like this: "Hey, Carl, you want to know what those McCain-i-philes think of Sarah? Then go ahead and ask Eisenstadt—*he'll* spill the beans, for sure." Carl's a good reporter. He knew what to ask me and how many drinks I'd need to answer.

Randy probably loved the fireworks that erupted when Carl's piece aired on Fox. Yikes, Palin must have been furious, but if he

The suave Randy Scheunemann at the 2006 NATO summit in Riga, Latvia. Come to think of it, Randy bears a striking resemblance to Wolfrum— could they be one and the same?
*(Photograph by Madara Zandberga/LATO)*

said anything at all, he must have said, "Sarah, just wait. Ride out the storm for a couple of days, and trust ol' Randy. In the meantime, the best thing you can do is to put pressure on Cameron to name his source."

"Would Carl do that?"

"Of course not."

"Then why even bring it up?"

"The next step is to bait the source. Tell the world he's a crumbum and a knave."

"Randy, I think I'd rather say 'coward and jerk.'"

"Of course, Sarah, that's definitely more you."

"I thought so."

"Trust me, if I know the 'source,' his ego will be big enough, his sense of self-righteousness just inflated enough, that he'll out himself in a matter of days."

"Is it that Eisen-whoey guy? It is, isn't it? He kinda creeped me out the night I was getting spray-tanned at the convention there."

"You'll see, Sarah. But trust me, when all's said and done, your image will be back and ready for 2012."

"Okeydokey, Randy. If you say so . . . Mr. Chief of Staff!"

And sure enough, they were right. My ego *is* that fragile. And I *am* that much of a narcissist that I wouldn't let myself stay cloaked in anonymity forever on one of the biggest stories since the election. They played me for a sucker.

# Afterword

S O  W H A T  T O  D O about Randy? He very cleverly didn't
break any laws, and he covered his tracks well enough so
that he could—and probably will—easily deny every allegation
I've made against him. But if people trifle with Martin Eisenstadt, there are consequences! And try as I might to set the record straight on my blog and on our Harding Institute videos, I
have always known that my ultimate revenge would have to be
won in the court of public opinion.

That's the reason I took my good friend Joe Lieberman's advice, over a boxed kosher lunch in the Senate dining room, to
write a book. No one can argue with a book. Books are filled
with undeniable *facts* and *charts* and *graphs* and *opinions* that say
to the world: "I am more than just a TV pundit. I am an *author*."
It will be my version of events, not Randy's, which will be collected in libraries, pored over by historians, and memorized by
stoned political-science students for centuries to come. And on
a purely practical level, Google searches for "Martin Eisenstadt"
will now glaringly refer people to an Amazon page which verifies
that I exist and that I am somebody to be taken seriously.

Now, sure, I've written books before. But they were mostly
limited-run treatises from the Harding Institute Press and are

now out of print. (All think tanks worth their weight have their own "press," even if the actual printing is done at the corner copy shop.) No, for this book I needed a classy professional publisher so no one could claim that I received any special editorial treatment from the editors at Harding Institute Press (myself and Poppy).

So I called the most prestigious imprint I could find: Farrar, Straus and Giroux (FSG) in New York. They've had twenty-one winners of Nobel Prizes in Literature, and an equal number of Pulitzer Prize winners. If I wanted to get people to take me seriously, then this was the publisher I needed!

I spoke with one of their new editors, Mitzi Angel, a coquettish hotshot straight off the boat from England. Coincidentally, she'd read the *New York Times* article and realized immediately that it was the fake Yes Men edition of the *Times*. The British are very sharp and not easily fooled. We met in New York, and after a couple of drinks, she made an offer on the spot. She told me I'd sell more copies if they publish the book under FSG's hipster Faber and Faber label (named after the college in *Animal House*, I imagine). Okay, I said, so long as she doesn't do anything crass like putting a scantily clad woman on the book spine.

Now if I know one thing about the book world, it's that you need a good agent. A ruthless shark. I checked my wallet and found the card that Joe the Plumber had given me at the *Saturday Night Live* after party. "Patrick Whitesell, Endeavor Talent Agency." It was Rahm Emanuel's brother's firm. If they weren't sharks, I didn't know who would be. I called Patrick and Endeavor signed me on the spot, negotiating the deal with Mitzi within mere days. (I'm told that it was on the strength of signing me that they subsequently merged with tobacco giant William Morris.)

Of course, I've also come to learn that FSG is actually owned by publishing giant Macmillan in New York, which is in turn owned by Verlagsgruppe Georg von Holtzbrinck GmbH of Germany. Altogether, they publish the works of such esteemed authors as Agatha Christie, Jean-Paul Sartre, and Ernest Hemingway. So if my own humble book feels by turns like a whodunit, an existential treatise, or a drunkard's travelogue with macho pretensions, it's probably because some of their pages got shuffled together with mine at the publisher's office. (It could also explain why Mitzi kept insisting that I use the occasional German word in the book.)

I won't lie to you. It's been hard since this whole identity debacle. Phoning people and having them hang up because they think you're a prank caller. Having Facebook ban me from their site because someone (Scheunemann?) ratted me out as a "fake" person. And this after some of the best political/media personalities in Washington signed on as my Facebook "friends"— Senator Chuck Grassley, Ali Velshi, Miles O'Brien—guys, it's me! Don't believe Facebook! Besides, Danny says that Facebook is *so* 2008. And my degenerate friend Stanley Rubin says that Facebook is like MySpace without sixteen-year-olds, thus defeating the purpose.

The good news is that in recent months, my old Sprint contract finally expired and I was able to dump my unreliable clamshell. I made Danny run out and get me a proper BlackBerry, just like everyone else—so that I could send secret messages directly to Barack Obama. It was only when Danny told me he locked me into a spankin' new four-year BlackBerry contract that I realized that all the cool people now had iPhones. Rats.

In theory, at least, with my new BlackBerry I should be able to Twitter now. These days, everyone who's anyone who thinks they're someone has to have Twitter. I'm not entirely sure what it is, but Rick Sanchez at CNN told me it's the hot new thing. He even "tweeted" me to say that his midday news show will now be all Twitter all the time, devoid of any actual news. If Twitter's the new Facebook, then is Rick Sanchez the new Anderson Cooper? If Rick sends me a tweet that he's now shaving his chest, then I'll know the answer's yes.

No bird craps on me in this town and gets away with it.
*(Courtesy of Andrew Perreault/Harding Institute)*

As a matter of fact, after I tweeted from the 2009 White House Correspondents' dinner, *Time* magazine named me one of America's elite "Twitterati," along with Ashton Kutcher, Newt Gingrich, and Meghan McCain.[1]

As for my place in the new Obama-nation, there is still plenty to be done. As the new administration works on redistributing the wealth, an already accredited institute like mine is well positioned to help in that effort. When Obama dives further into the Afghanistan quagmire, a man of my expertise will be called on for expert advice: if not by the administration itself, then most certainly at the behest of the twenty-four-hour cable news channels. And ultimately that is the advantage to being in the loyal opposition in America. As a pundit, I will survive.

And that brings me back to this book itself. My publisher has promised that I will be going on an extensive book tour to promote the book. For astute TV watchers, you'll notice that pundits always get booked more when they have a book to sell (in fact, that's where the TV news expression "booked" comes from). If nothing else, it gives the news directors a nice cutaway shot of the book jackets while the pundit is talking.

As you're reading this book, and as it begins the inevitable march up the *New York Times* bestseller list, I can't help but ponder if the book might inspire some sort of Hollywood adaptation. That's what happens to political books on the bestseller list, right? John Ehrlichman once told me when I visited him in prison: "If *I'd* written *All the President's Men*, it would have been *me* portrayed by Robert Redford, not that little prick Woodward." So Ben Affleck as Marty Eisenstadt—why not? This is why I have the sharks at William Morris Endeavor on my side. And if they let me down, I can always call Eli Perle at his start-up management company, Provocation Entertainment, to set it up. He owes me.

Just between you and me, though, I'm getting a little nervous. If those who have been out to discredit me could have so successfully manipulated the world's news media, how can I be so sure that they won't be able to influence the publication of this book, too? Hmmm, the German über-publisher Verlagsgruppe Georg von Holtzbrinck? Randy *Scheunemann*, of German descent? Hard to say if there's a connection. Come to think of it, if the book printing is outsourced to Brazil (where I insisted that endangered mahogany trees be clear-cut to make these pages), could the Brazilian golf blogger Wolfrum have infiltrated the printing presses? I wouldn't put it past him.

So look carefully at the copyright page and the cover of the book. Those are the last things that go to press—long after I've had my final pass on the edit. After Mitzi does her pass. Even after the lawyers do their redactions.

My name is still there, right? It hasn't been replaced with those opportunistic filmmaker patsies Dan Mirvish and Eitan Gorlin, has it? Oh God, I hope not. And the title, it should say very clearly, *I Am Martin Eisenstadt: One Man's Adventures with the Last Republicans*. They didn't scribble anything else in there, did they? That's all I need. All this work, all this writing, for nothing! If Denny Hastert still takes my calls, I will hire Dickstein Shapiro! We will sue people! Lots of people! The name of Martin Eisenstadt will not be besmirched! I *am* Martin Eisenstadt.

## Postscript: July 22, 2009

As this book goes to press, Sarah Palin just resigned as governor of Alaska (something about "point guards" and "dead fish" and "hiking the Appalachian Trail"). I've heard one reason is that she was afraid of what was in these pages. Sarah needed the spare time to work on her own memoir, in which she will undoubtedly write false denials and spurious allegations about me. Meanwhile, the likes of Meghan, Joe, Steve, and Randy continue to squabble in the media. The election may have ended in 2008, but it appears the campaign has, and will, linger far into the future.

# Legal Disclaimers

## Legal Disclaimer #1

I'd like to apologize to you, my loyal reader. I'm sure that by now you've just finished my book with a satisfying sense of closure. You're still in your Stickley leather armchair, enjoying a fine Napoleon Cognac and thinking about how many superlatives you can write in an Amazon review without appearing to be one of my so-called sockpuppets. So I'm very sorry to break your mood, but please, this is important.

I'm starting to suspect that my beguiling British editor, Mitzi, at Faber and Faber may not actually have my best literary interests at heart. It seems the economy is tough and she's desperately afraid of the publishing company getting sued. Rightly so, I suppose. So Mitzi's referred my entire manuscript to the veteran publishing attorney ████ ████, Esq., who may have subsequently redacted portions of this book, possibly including her own name. Given the nature of my contract with Faber, the aptly named Ms. ████ gets the chilly last word—right before the book goes to the printer. My associate Danny did some digging on Ms. ████, and apparently she attended ████ in the early seventies. In that case, it wouldn't surprise me if she's redacted a few chapters from her own life, too. Nevertheless, and with all due respect to Mitzi and ████, if there was any ambiguity or interruption in the narrative flow of the book owing to these redactions, I would like to apologize.

## Legal Disclaimer #2

My attorneys at Dickstein Shapiro LLC have advised me that to avoid any accusations of libel that could arise from this book, I should try not to defame anyone other than myself. The safest way they said to do that was to restrict myself to saying only nice things about everyone. (You may have noticed that I frequently referred to people as "handsome," "pretty," or "well-endowed" during the course of the book.) Since you can be sued only on the grounds of "*de*famation" and not actual "famation," I should be safe.

## Legal Disclaimer #3

The attorneys at Robbins, Russell, Englert, Orseck, Untereiner & Sauber LLP in Washington have taken umbrage at any possible confusion between myself and Mr. M████ █. Eisenstadt. Please note that I address this issue in depth in Chapter 5, but for now, let me just say that M████ is a fine and honorable fellow, and I'm quite sure that Robbins, Russell, Orseck, Untereiner & Sauber are as well (Englert? Perhaps the less said, the better). So to be clear, the M████ Eisenstadt they represent who lives in suburban Washington, D.C. (as opposed to the *other* M████ Eisenstadt, M████ M. Eisenstadt, who also lives in suburban Washington, D.C.) is a good-looking, clean-shaven policy wonk. I, on the other hand, am a good-looking, bearded pundit with a thick head of hair. Also, our first and middle names are different.

## Legal Disclaimer #4

The powerhouse legal and lobbying firm of Covington & Burling LLP in Washington has expressed their concern to my attorneys at Dickstein Shapiro about the similarities between my name and that of their partner Stuart Eizenstat. For the record, I am *not* the same person as Stuart Eizenstat, who served honorably in the Carter and Clinton administrations before joining Covington & Burling. Nor, in fact, do I even spell my name the same way. Ambassador Eizenstat (as he likes to be called) is a recipient of the French Legion of Honor and has been named "the Leading Lawyer in International Trade" in Washington, D.C., by *Legal Times.* Like many wonks, he is balding and clean shaven, but still exquisitely handsome for a man of his distinction.

## Legal Disclaimer #5

My attorneys at Dickstein Shapiro LLP have advised me not to keep referring to them as "my attorneys," as it might give people the wrong idea about the kinds of clients they represent. Apparently they were not pleased to read about themselves so much in early galleys of the book and they fear that any mention of them might portray them in a negative light. On the contrary, I said. I would be sure to tell everyone that they are a fine and honorable law firm, they have a winning softball team in the DC Legal League, and they hire some of the most attractive receptionists of any firm in the District. Nonetheless, they think it best if I just stop talking about them so much, since people are now starting to think that *they* don't exist. I can assure you, nothing could be further from the truth.

## Legal Disclaimer #6

The law firm of Paul, Hastings, Janofsky & Walker LLP, with offices around the world, including Washington, D.C., has advised me that one of their own attorneys is named Michael Eisenstadt. Though based in their Atlanta office and bearing even less resemblance to me than certain other Eisenstadts I've just mentioned, from what I understand, this Eisenstadt fellow is also handsome and adept at his job. Again, though, his name is Michael and not Martin.

## Legal Disclaimer #7

The attorney Martin A. Eisenstadt of Southfield, Michigan, has not yet contacted me, but I expect that he soon will. So to save him the trouble, let me just say that I am in no way the same person as Martin A. Eisenstadt of Southfield, Michigan, who I'm sure is a strikingly handsome man and an excellent lawyer.

## Legal Disclaimer #8

Same goes for Martin L. Eisenstadt.

## Legal Disclaimer #9

I have also been contacted by the strikingly tall and handsome attorney John Sloss, of Sloss Law Office LLP in Manhattan, representing Ms. Debra Eisenstadt of New York. Ms. Eisenstadt would like it known that she is in no way related to me, nor indeed to my side of the Eisenstadt family. In particular, she should in no way be construed as my "ex-wife," to whom I occasionally refer in this book. Despite taking umbrage with her claim that I have "sullied the Eisenstadt name for generations to come," I understand that Ms. Eisenstadt is a very talented film director, writer, and actress and, from the pictures I've seen on the Internet, is very good-looking indeed. Furthermore, Ms. Eisenstadt is apparently also the mother of three young children, and she claims that none of them are mine. (DNA tests are pending.)

# Notes

## 2: The Life of Marty

1. www.jimmycarterlibrary.org/documents/diary/1979/d092279t.pdf
2. www.highbeam.com/doc/1P2-3836020.html
3. en.wikipedia.org/wiki/Mika_Brzezinski
4. www.andiquote.co.za/authors/Jacob_Zuma.html

## 3: The Mysterious Giuliani Stealth Campaign

1. myrightword.blogspot.com/2007/07/wonkette-threatens-me-with-legal-action.html
2. blogs.abcnews.com/theblotter/2007/07/dirty-tricks-do.html
3. www.time.com/time/nation/article/0,8599,1635929,00.html
4. politicalblogs.startribune.com/bigquestionblog/?cat=45

## 4: The Annapolis Peace Conference

1. www.vanityfair.com/politics/features/2005/09/edmonds200509?currentPage=6
2. www.trutv.com/library/crime/terrorists_spies/assassins/warren_harding/6.html

## 6: What's in a Name?

1. www.openleft.com/showDiary.do?diaryId=6059
2. www.eisenstadtgroup.com/2008/05/30/shame-on-dennis-hastert/
3. www.feministe.us/blog/archives/2008/05/30/i-guess-there-was-a-point-to-that-stupid-lgbt-acronym-after-all/
4. www.nctequality.org/contact.html
5. www.feministe.us/blog/archives/2008/05/30/i-guess-there-was-a-point-to-that-stupid-lgbt-acronym-after-all/
6. www.politico.com/blogs/anneschroeder/0508/While_its_jeans_and_puppies_week_on_the_Hill.html
7. www.toledoblade.com/apps/pbcs.dll/article?AID=/20080907/ART16/809070280
8. en.wikipedia.org/wiki/Donna_Brazile
9. hotair.com/archives/2008/05/30/video-oreilly-flips-out-over-nbc-msnbc-russert-pretty-much-everyone/
10. www.eisenstadtgroup.com/2008/05/31/boycott-nbc-and-its-tranny-sympathizers
11. thecaucus.blogs.nytimes.com/2008/05/31/the-dnc-deliberates/?hp
12. shakespearessister.blogspot.com/2008/06/m-thomas-eisenstadt-is-john-mccains-new.html
13. crooksandliars.com/2008/05/22/cls-late-nite-music-club-with-blondie/#comment-682790
14. shakespearessister.blogspot.com/2008/06/m-thomas-eisenstadt-is-john-mccains-new.html
15. shakespearessister.blogspot.com/2008/06/michael-eisenstadt-denies-being-m.html
16. shakespearessister.blogspot.com/2008/06/conservative-blogger-m-thomas.html
17. www.williamkwolfrum.com/about/
18. www.worldgolf.com/blogs/william.wolfrum
19. booksiloved.com/23/
20. www.saddoboxing.com/author/william-wolfrum/
21. shakespearessister.blogspot.com/2004/10/inside-jokes-faqs-wev.html#click3
22. shakespearessister.blogspot.com/2008/03/benjamin-h-grumbles.html
23. www.eisenstadtgroup.com/2008/06/11/rebuttal-to-the-internet-police/
24. shakespearessister.blogspot.com/2008/06/sourcewatch-places-hoax-warning-on-m.html

25. americanpublichousereview.com/2008.02/Whitehorse_NYC/
26. www.eisenstadtgroup.com/2008/06/17/whats-in-a-name/

## 7: The Jonas Brothers Are (Probably) Not Terrorists

1. en.wikipedia.org/wiki/Thomas_Paine
2. atlasshrugs2000.typepad.com/atlas_shrugs/2008/05/rachel-ray-dunk
   .html
3. www.debbieschlussel.com/archives/2008/05/dunkin_donuts_r.html
4. www.eisenstadtgroup.com/2008/05/29/debbie-schlussel-leave-
   mccains-family-alone/
5. www.eisenstadtgroup.com/2008/07/15/jonas-brothers-terrorists-the-
   keffiyeh-conspiracy/
6. www.topnews.in/obama-s-daughters-are-huge-jonas-brothers-
   fans-223051
7. www.eisenstadtgroup.com/2008/07/17/obamas-daughters-huge-
   jonas-brothers-fans-coincidence/
8. tpmcafe.talkingpointsmemo.com/talk/2008/07/mccain-adviser-
   thinks-obamas-d.php
9. www.eisenstadtgroup.com/2008/07/23/response-to-last-post-was-
   overwhelming/
10. www.eisenstadtgroup.com/2008/08/04/jonas-brothers-losing-their-
    religion-becoming-barack-obama/
11. latimesblogs.latimes.com/thedishrag/2009/01/sasha-malias-su.html

## 8: The Art of the Apology: My Inglorious Moment on YouTube

1. mccainsource.com/corruption?id=0006
2. www.judicialwatch.org/blog/2008/may/mccain-fires-campaign-s-
   fifth-lobbyist
3. blogs.abcnews.com/politicalpunch/2008/02/lobbying-on-the.html
4. firedoglake.com/2008/02/21/mccains-cronies-rick-davis-uber-
   lobbyist-at-the-helm/
5. www.juancole.com/2008/06/casino-on-tigris.html
6. tenpercent.wordpress.com/2008/06/26/the-rape-of-iraq-casinos-
   whores/
7. raedinthemiddle.blogspot.com/2008/06/yes-democracy-is-alive.html
8. www.youtube.com/watch?v=L27uHysoQP0
9. www.nicovideo.jp/watch/sm3632265
10. www.onthemedia.org/yore/transcripts/transcripts_011405_pundit
    .html

11. gatewaypundit.blogspot.com/2007/09/first-las-vegas-style-casino-opens-in.html
12. shakespearessister.blogspot.com/2008/07/wolfrum-shakesville-are-hoaxers.html
13. www.eisenstadtgroup.com/2008/07/11/im-no-rocket-scientist-but-let-the-hoax-handwringing-begin
14. www.nytimes.com/2008/02/21/us/politics/21mccain.html?pagewanted=1&_r=2&hp
15. www.washingtonpost.com/wp-dyn/content/article/2008/02/20/AR2008022002898.html?nav=rss_politics
16. www.washingtonpost.com/wp-dyn/content/article/2008/02/21/AR2008022101131_pf.html
17. money.cnn.com/2008/06/20/magazines/fortune/Evolution_McCain_Whitford.fortune/index.htm?postversion=2008062314
18. www.washingtonpost.com/wp-dyn/content/article/2008/06/23/AR2008062301979.html
19. www.asiaone.com/News/AsiaOne%2BNews/World/Story/A1Story20080624-72509.html
20. www.nypost.com/seven/03062009/news/regionalnews/weiners_naughty_hottie_158268.htm
21. www.politico.com/blogs/jonathanmartin/0708/Schmidt_takes_control_of_daytoday_operation.html
22. www.huffingtonpost.com/richard-valeriani/july-7-2008-news-update_b_111332.html
23. www.motherjones.com/mojoblog/archives/2008/07/8918_mccain_adviser_1.html?welcome=true
24. timesofindia.indiatimes.com/articleshow/3216132.cms
25. www.huffingtonpost.com/2008/04/28/emnew-york-timesem-circul_n_98991.html; timesofindia.indiatimes.com/articleshow/1152489.cms

## 9: When Think Tanks Play Softball . . .

1. www.westwingwriters.com/team/orzulak.html

## 10: Paris Hilton and Beyond

1. www.eisenstadtgroup.com/2008/03/07/mccain-is-right-for-our-times/
2. www.eisenstadtgroup.com/2008/07/31/paris-hiltons-family-fuming-at-mccain-campaign/
3. latimesblogs.latimes.com/washington/2008/07/paris-hilton-mc.html

4. www.huffingtonpost.com/kathy-hilton/mccains-celebrity-ad-friv_b_116593.html
5. www.nytimes.com/2008/04/06/magazine/06wwln-essay-t.html

## 11: The Sarah Palin Choice

1. www.huffingtonpost.com/2008/10/17/report-mccain-using-same_n_135699.html
2. www.theatlantic.com/doc/200810u/palin-clothes
3. www.fec.gov/finance/disclosure/efile_search.shtml
4. thecaucus.blogs.nytimes.com/2008/10/24/pains-makeup-stylist-fetches-highest-salary-in-2-week-period/
5. www.eisenstadtgroup.com/2008/09/25/mccain-knows-what-hes-doing/

## 12: Joe. The. Plumber.

1. www.newsweek.com/id/167950/page/5
2. www.newsweek.com/id/167950/output/print
3. query.nytimes.com/gst/fullpage.html?res=9D0CE3DC143EF933A25751C1A967958260
4. www.cbsnews.com/stories/2008/10/17/usnews/whispers/main4527926.shtml
5. michellemalkin.com/2008/10/16/is-joe-wurzelbacher-related-to-charles-keating-and-does-it-matter/
6. www.youtube.com/watch?v=5ruXEh8S12E
7. www.williamkwolfrum.com/2008/10/17/why-is-it-so-hard-to-google-the-name-martin-eisenstadt-before-going-on-a-plumber-joe-freakfest/
8. www.weeklystandard.com/weblogs/TWSFP/2008/10/obamas_november_surprise_anoth.asp; extratv.warnerbros.com/2008/10/barack_going_back_to_snl.php
9. www.eisenstadtgroup.com/2008/11/01/mccain-to-appear-on-snlbecause-of-my-blog-ges-contributions-to-gop/
10. www.politico.com/news/stories/1007/6427.html

## 13: If Africa Doesn't Exist, Do I?

1. joetrippi.com/blog/?page_id=1374
2. www.politico.com/blogs/bensmith/1008/Harsh_GOP_robocall_hits_Ayers.html?showall

3. www.pportals.com/jcw/Miscellaneous/Recordings.htm

4. www.youtube.com/watch?v=oJv0q5xk-Uc&feature=related

5. www.nytimes.com/2008/11/08/us/politics/08palin.html?_r=2&bl&ex
   =1226293200&en=13ba3abeed17e92e&ei=5087%0A&oref=slogin

6. politicalticker.blogs.cnn.com/2008/11/06/mccain-adviser-disputes-
   campaign-i-was-not-fired/

7. query.nictusa.com/pdf/664/29932242664/29932242664.pdf#
   navpanes=0

8. www.youtube.com/watch?v=ucfA86t7sH4

9. www.sourcewatch.org/index.php?title=Todd_A._Boulanger and www
   .time.com/time/nation/article/0,8599,1876091,00.html

10. www.nytimes.com/2008/11/13/arts/television/13hoax.html?ref=arts

11. www.reuters.com/article/marketsNews/idUSN1229433020081112

12. www.youtube.com/watch?v=fvIOtPD7_08

13. www.huffingtonpost.com/2008/11/30/filmmakers-behind-fake-
    mc_n_147216.html

14. www.brainyquote.com

## Afterword

1. www.time.com/time/nation/article/0,8599,1897138-1,00.html

# Acknowledgments

Thanks to Rachel, Rebecca, Jonathan, Miriam, Greg, Karine, Kenny, Des, Kutch, Jacques, Sue, Lynda, Sidney, Dov, Dani, Leora, Alan, Bill, Oren, Chris, Carolle-Shelley, Andrew, Paul, Karin, Adrian, Darryl, Ric, Doran, Alison, Eli, Danny, Jimmy, Poppy, Marwan, Mitzi, Chantal, James, Rami, Mike, Michal, Ari, Steven, Dahlia, Denny, Connie, Izzy, Stanley, Clifford, Daniele, Jules, Levi, Peter, and Kevin.

# Index

Please note: If you are mentioned in this book, you will likely find yourself in this handy index. For any of you who are considering suing me, this should save you and your lawyers considerable time and trouble. On the other hand, if I've neglected to mention you, please bring this book to my next book signing, and I will happily insert your name here: _____.

## Members of Congress Mentioned in the Book

For all you interns, junior staffers, receptionists, legislative correspondents, and personal assistants who were sent on an errand to B. Dalton at Union Station to see if your congressional boss is included in this book, you can now safely say that he or she is! You've done your job. And you did it well. You know your boss won't actually be reading this book. It'll sit in the oak bookshelf behind his/her desk and look very important as a backdrop for meetings and interviews. So, please, do us both a favor and buy the book. While you're at it, ask for a Snickers bar and tell the clerk to put it on the same expense account. You deserve it! (And if your boss has you tied to a desk and makes you shop online, just try Amazon's fancy "Look Inside" feature and search for your boss's name. Yup, it's still here!)

HOUSE:

Neil Abercrombie, Gary Ackerman, Robert Aderholt, John Adler, Todd Akin, Rodney Alexander, Jason Altmire, Michele Bachmann, Spencer Bachus, Brian Baird, Tammy Baldwin, J. Gresham Barrett, John Barrow, Roscoe Bartlett, Joe Barton, Melissa Bean, Xavier Becerra, Shelley Berkley, Howard Berman, Marion Berry, Judy Biggert, Brian Bilbray, Gus Bilirakis, Rob Bishop, Sanford Bishop Jr., Tim Bishop, Marsha Blackburn, Earl Blumenauer, Roy Blunt, John Boccieri, John Boehner, Jo Bonner, Mary Bono Mack, John Boozman, Madeleine Bordallo, Dan Boren, Leonard Boswell, Rick Boucher, Charles Boustany Jr., Allen Boyd, Kevin Brady, Robert Brady, Bruce Braley, Bobby Bright, Paul Broun, Corrine Brown, Henry Brown Jr., Ginny Brown-Waite, Vern Buchanan, Michael Burgess, Dan Burton, G.K. Butterfield, Steve Buyer, Ken Calvert, Dave Camp, John Campbell, Eric Cantor, Joseph Cao, Shelley Moore Capito, Lois Capps, Michael Capuano, Dennis Cardoza, Russ Carnahan, Christopher Carney, André Carson, John Carter, Bill Cassidy, Mike Castle, Kathy Castor, Jason Chaffetz, Ben Chandler, Travis Childers, Donna Christensen, Judy Chu, Yvette Clarke, William Lacy Clay, Emanuel Cleaver, James Clyburn, Howard Coble, Mike Coffman, Steve Cohen, Tom Cole, Mike Conaway, Gerald Connolly, John Conyers Jr., Jim Cooper, Jim Costa, Jerry Costello, Joe Courtney, Ander Crenshaw, Joseph Crowley, Henry Cuellar, John Culberson, Elijah Cummings, Kathy Dahlkemper, Artur Davis, Danny Davis, Geoff Davis, Lincoln Davis, Susan Davis, Nathan Deal, Peter DeFazio, Diana DeGette, Bill Delahunt, Rosa DeLauro, Charlie Dent, Lincoln Diaz-Balart, Mario Diaz-Balart, Norm Dicks, John Dingell, Lloyd Doggett, Joe Donnelly, Mike Doyle, David Dreier, Steve Driehaus, John Duncan Jr., Chet Edwards, Donna Edwards, Vern Ehlers, Keith Ellison, Brad Ellsworth, Jo Ann Emerson, Eliot Engel, Anna Eshoo, Bob Etheridge, Eni Faleomavaega, Mary Fallin, Sam Farr, Chaka Fattah, Bob Filner, Jeff Flake, John Fleming, J. Randy Forbes, Jeff Fortenberry, Bill Foster, Virginia Foxx, Barney Frank, Trent Franks, Rodney Frelinghuysen, Marcia Fudge, Elton Gallegly, Scott Garrett, Jim Gerlach, Gabrielle Giffords, Phil Gingrey, Louie Gohmert, Charles Gonzalez, Bob Goodlatte, Bart Gordon, Kay Granger, Sam Graves, Alan Grayson, Al Green, Gene Green, Parker Griffith, Raúl Grijalva, Brett Guthrie, Luis Gutierrez, John Hall, Ralph Hall, Debbie Halvorson, Phil Hare, Jane Harman, Gregg Harper, Alcee Hastings, Doc Hastings, Martin Heinrich, Dean Heller, Jeb Hensarling, Wally Herger, Stephanie Herseth Sandlin, Brian Higgins, Baron Hill, Jim Himes, Maurice Hinchey, Rubén Hinojosa, Mazie Hirono, Paul Hodes, Pete Hoekstra, Tim Holden, Rush Holt, Mike Honda, Steny Hoyer, Duncan Hunter, Bob Inglis, Jay Inslee, Steve Israel, Darrell Issa, Jesse Jackson Jr., Sheila Jackson Lee, Lynn Jenkins, Eddie Bernice Johnson, Hank Johnson, Sam Johnson, Timothy Johnson, Walter Jones, Jim Jordan, Steve Kagen, Paul Kanjorski, Marcy Kaptur, Patrick Kennedy, Dale Kildee, Carolyn Cheeks Kilpatrick, Mary Jo Kilroy, Ron Kind, Pete King, Steve King, Jack Kingston, Mark Kirk, Ann Kirkpatrick, Larry Kissell, Ron Klein, John Kline, Suzanne Kosmas, Frank Kratovil Jr., Dennis Kucinich, Doug Lamborn, Leonard Lance, Jim Langevin, Rick Larsen, John Larson, Tom Latham, Steven LaTourette, Bob Latta, Barbara Lee, Chris Lee, Sandy Levin, Jerry Lewis, John Lewis, John Linder, Daniel Lipinski, Frank LoBiondo, David Loebsack, Zoe Lofgren, Nita Lowey, Frank Lucas, Blaine Luetkemeyer, Ben Lujan, Cynthia Lummis, Dan Lungren, Stephen Lynch, Connie Mack, Dan Maffei, Carolyn Maloney, Don Manzullo, Kenny Marchant, Betsy Markey, Ed Markey, Jim Marshall, Eric Massa, Jim Matheson, Doris Matsui, Carolyn McCarthy, Kevin McCarthy, Michael McCaul, Tom McClintock, Betty McCollum, Thaddeus McCotter, Jim McDermott, Jim McGovern, Patrick McHenry, John McHugh, Mike McIntyre, Buck McKeon, Michael McMahon, Cathy McMorris Rodgers, Jerry McNerney, Kendrick Meek, Gregory Meeks, Charlie Melancon, John Mica, Mike Michaud, Brad Miller, Candice Miller, Gary Miller, George Miller, Jeff Miller, Walt Minnick, Harry Mitchell, Alan Mollohan, Dennis Moore, Gwen Moore, Jerry Moran, Jim Moran, Chris Murphy, Patrick Murphy, Scott Murphy, Tim Murphy, John Murtha, Sue Myrick, Jerrold Nadler, Grace Napolitano, Richard Neal, Randy Neugebauer, Eleanor Holmes Norton, Devin Nunes, Glenn Nye, Jim Oberstar, Dave Obey, Pete Olson, John Olver, Solomon Ortiz, Frank Pallone Jr., Bill Pascrell, Ed Pastor, Ron Paul, Erik Paulsen, Donald Payne, Nancy Pelosi, Mike Pence, Ed Perlmutter, Tom Perriello, Gary Peters, Collin Peterson, Tom Petri, Pedro Pierluisi, Chellie Pingree, Joe Pitts, Todd Russell Platts, Ted Poe, Jared Polis, Earl Pomeroy, Bill Posey, David Price, Tom Price, Adam Putnam, Mike Quigley, George Radanovich, Nick Rahall, Charles Rangel, Denny Rehberg, Dave Reichert, Silvestre Reyes, Laura Richardson, Ciro Rodriguez, Phil Roe, Hal Rogers, Mike Rogers, Mike Rogers, Dana Rohrabacher, Thomas Rooney, Peter Roskam, Ileana Ros-Lehtinen, Mike Ross, Steve Rothman, Lucille Roybal-Allard, Ed Royce, C. A. Dutch Ruppersberger, Bobby Rush, Paul Ryan, Tim Ryan, Gregorio Kilili Camacho Sablan, John Salazar, Linda Sanchez, Loretta Sanchez, John Sarbanes, Steve Scalise, Jan Schakowsky, Mark Schauer, Adam Schiff, Jean Schmidt, Aaron Schock, Kurt Schrader, Allyson Schwartz, Bobby Scott, David Scott, F. James Sensenbrenner Jr., José Serrano, Pete Sessions, Joe Sestak, John Shadegg, Carol Shea-Porter, Brad Sherman, John Shimkus, Heath Shuler, Bill Shuster, Mike Simpson, Albio Sires, Ike Skelton, Louise Slaughter, Adam Smith, Adrian Smith, Chris Smith, Lamar Smith, Vic Snyder, Mark Souder, Zack Space, Jackie Speier, John Spratt, Pete Stark, Cliff Stearns, Bart Stupak, John Sullivan, Betty Sutton, John Tanner, Gene Taylor, Harry Teague, Lee Terry, Bennie Thompson, Glenn Thompson, Mike Thompson, Mac Thornberry, Todd Tiahrt, Patrick Tiberi, John Tierney, Dina Titus, Paul Tonko, Edolphus Towns, Niki Tsongas, Michael Turner, Fred Upton, Chris Van Hollen, Nydia Velázquez, Pete Visclosky, Greg Walden, Tim Walz, Zach Wamp, Debbie Wasserman Schultz, Maxine Waters, Diane Watson, Mel Watt, Henry Waxman, Anthony Weiner, Peter Welch, Lynn Westmoreland, Robert Wexler, Ed Whitfield, Charlie Wilson, Joe Wilson, Rob Wittman, Frank Wolf, Lynn Woolsey, David Wu, John Yarmuth, C. W. Bill Young, Don Young

SENATE:

Daniel Kahikina Akaka, Lamar Alexander, John Barrasso, Max Baucus, Evan Bayh, Mark Begich, Michael Bennet, Bob Bennett, Jeff Bingaman, Kit Bond, Barbara Boxer, Sherrod Brown, Sam Brownback, Jim Bunning, Richard Burr, Roland Burris, Robert Byrd, Maria Cantwell, Benjamin Cardin, Tom Carper, Robert Casey Jr., Saxby Chambliss, Tom Coburn, Thad Cochran, Susan Collins, Kent Conrad, Bob Corker, John Cornyn, Mike Crapo, Jim DeMint, Chris Dodd, Byron Dorgan, Dick Durbin, John Ensign, Mike Enzi, Russ Feingold, Dianne Feinstein, Al Franken, Kirsten Gillibrand, Lindsey Graham, Chuck Grassley, Judd Gregg, Kay Hagan, Tom Harkin, Orrin Hatch, Kay Bailey Hutchison, James Inhofe, Dan Inouye, Johnny Isakson, Mike Johanns, Tim Johnson, Ted Kaufman, Edward Kennedy, John Kerry, Amy Klobuchar, Herb Kohl, Jon Kyl, Mary Landrieu, Frank Lautenberg, Patrick Leahy, Carl Levin, Joe Lieberman, Blanche Lincoln, Richard Lugar, Mel Martinez, John McCain, Claire McCaskill, Mitch McConnell, Robert Menendez, Jeff Merkley, Barbara Mikulski, Lisa Murkowski, Patty Murray, Ben Nelson, Bill Nelson, Mark Pryor, Jack Reed, Harry Reid, James Risch, Pat Roberts, Jay Rockefeller, Bernie Sanders, Charles Schumer, Jeff Sessions, Jeanne Shaheen, Richard Shelby, Olympia Snowe, Arlen Specter, Debbie Stabenow, Jon Tester, John Thune, Mark Udall, Tom Udall, David Vitter, George Voinovich, Mark Warner, Jim Webb, Sheldon Whitehouse, Roger Wicker, Ron Wyden